The View from Above in American Literature

There is no reality that precedes the literary image.
Gaston Bachelard, *Air and Dreams*

The View from Above in American Literature

Aerial Description, the Imaginary and the Form of Environment

David Rodriguez

EDINBURGH
University Press

Edinburgh University Press is one of the leading university presses in the UK. We publish academic books and journals in our selected subject areas across the humanities and social sciences, combining cutting-edge scholarship with high editorial and production values to produce academic works of lasting importance. For more information visit our website: edinburghuniversitypress.com

© David Rodriguez 2024, 2025

Edinburgh University Press Ltd
13 Infirmary Street
Edinburgh EH1 1LT

First published in hardback by Edinburgh University Press 2024

Typeset in 11/13 Adobe Sabon by
IDSUK (DataConnection) Ltd

A CIP record for this book is available from the British Library

ISBN 978 1 3995 2292 2 (hardback)
ISBN 978 1 3995 2293 9 (paperback)
ISBN 978 1 3995 2294 6 (webready PDF)
ISBN 978 1 3995 2295 3 (epub)

The right of David Rodriguez to be identified as the author of this work has been asserted in accordance with the Copyright, Designs and Patents Act 1988, and the Copyright and Related Rights Regulations 2003 (SI No. 2498).

Contents

List of Figures	vi
Acknowledgements	vii
Introduction: Flights Without Wings	1
1. Foundations for the View from Above in Literary Fiction: Description, Form and Indeterminacy	16
2. Extent, Built Form and Willa Cather's Landscapes	50
3. Verticality and Empty Thematics in Paul Bowles's Novels	91
4. 'Only Scenery': Scale, Whole-Earth Images and Don DeLillo's 'Human Moments in World War III'	123
Conclusion: On Drone and Satellite Images	163
Bibliography	180
Index	190

Figures

Figure 1.1 James Wallace Black, 'Boston, As the Eagle and the Wild Goose See It' — 19

Figure 1.2 Photograph from pigeon-mounted camera by Julius Neubronner — 19

Figure 2.1 *National Geographic*, July 1924, 'The Non-stop Flight Across America' — 56

Figure 4.1 Original NASA photo AS08-14-2383 — 133

Figure 4.2 NASA photo AS08-14-2383 reproduced as *Earthrise* — 133

Figure 4.3 Original NASA photo AS17-148-22727 — 134

Figure 4.4 NASA photo AS17-148-22727 reproduced as *Blue Marble* — 134

Figure 4.5 Robert Rauschenberg, *Stoned Moon Book*, Page 10 — 138

Acknowledgements

I would like to thank the English Department at Stony Brook University for cultivating such a rich and rewarding atmosphere in difficult institutional circumstances. My time in the doctoral programme there where this project was born was filled with so many original thinkers and thoughtful listeners, not to mention bold interdisciplinary experimenters. E. Ann Kaplan ran a full-steam environmental humanities program at the Humanities Institute, while Jeffery Santa Ana, Justin Johnson and Michael Tondre all contributed to generate a real sense of urgency and excitement about the field in our department. Eric Haralson and Stacey Olster were the best guides into American literature I could have asked for. Celia Marshik, Patricia Dunn and Drew Newman all provided valuable guidance and mentorship in academic life.

This book could not have come to be without the careful guidance of John Lutterbie, who is my friend, mentor and prime model for a freethinking and clear-communicating academic. Brook Belisle contributed immensely to the extra-literary parts of this project from the beginning and provided valuable feedback. Mike Rubenstein guided my dissertation carefully but not obtrusively, and this project has better origins for it. I am grateful for his friendship and our long conversations.

Scott Zukowski is somewhere in the background of this book, in ideas shared in a tiny interior office that also housed a mainsail, bicycles and camping supplies. J. Caity Swanson took the show on the road with me and we talked all the way from Brooklyn to Detroit and back when we cycled to the ASLE conference in 2017. Those long miles and canal-side campsites changed my life immeasurably. Dan Irving and I made a deserted island of the weird at Stony Brook, and now we've taken it to unexpected places.

I would especially like to thank Erin James for her incredible energy and cool intensity since the very beginning. And Marco Caracciolo, who has been an inspiration, a fruitful collaborator and a loyal friend.

The Roger Brown Study Collection granted rights for the beautifully fitting cover of this book. The Robert Rauschenberg Foundation gave permission for the rare reproduction of a page from the unpublished *Stoned Moon Book* in Chapter 4. De Gruter granted permission to use some paragraphs in Chapters 2 and 3 from my article in *Frontiers of Narrative Studies* vol. 4.2. Special thanks to the librarians of the Frank Melville, Jr. Memorial Library at Stony Brook and Axinn Library at Hofstra for their guidance and patience. At Edinburgh University Press, Michelle Houston, Susannah Butler Emily Sharp and Fiona Conn have smoothly and professionally guided me through this publishing experience.

Karyn Valerious and the English Department at Hofstra University have continued to float me along and provide institutional support during this project. And during the COVID-19 pandemic, Bernardo, Brent, Keith, Maya, Mer, Patrick and Rashad at Baltimore Bicycle Works taught me how to run a business in the most unexpected of circumstances. Their friendship and generosity helped me persevere during those strange years.

Finally I would like to thank Marlene Marcussen, with whom I could spend the rest of my career describing description. And those others who have been invaluable teachers, collaborators and listeners during my career: Julie Steward, Karin Kukkonen, Lieven Ameel, Anna Ovaska, Kaisa Kortekallio and Amy Cook.

Laura Oulanne is there with Alma and I thank them, yes.

Introduction: Flights Without Wings

Harry Mathews's very short story 'Franz Kafka in Riga' from *The American Experience* (1991) presents a compact example of the complexity of aerial images in fiction. The narrator recalls a time when he 'decided to climb these steps in order to enjoy the view to which I imagined they would bring me'.[1] The first paragraph of the story briefly describes the castles in Riga, then, in the second paragraph, the first-person narrator describes the tricky (and embarrassing) process of ascending to the top of a tower:

> I finished my ascent more or less on my hands and knees, or rather my *hand* and knees, with my other hand clapped on top of my head – a posture that provoked derisive laughter from my companions below, although I scarcely heard them through the shudders of dizziness that had by now begun to afflict me. When at last I reached the vantage point so laboriously striven for, I beheld, instead of Riga and the waters of the Baltic, only unbroken fog, as dingy as an old newspaper under the clouded sky.[2]

The next paragraph transitions to sometime after the trip, when the narrator has learned that Kafka once took this same trip to Riga and describes it in his notebooks. The fourth paragraph is Kafka's quoted description, a nearly word-for-word reproduction of the second paragraph; Kafka has already written down the experience of the narrator. The narrator concludes: 'I was angry that Kafka had rendered this experience with such unaccountable inaccuracy.'[3] This is a punchline, but notably the only difference in the two passages is in the first sentence. Kafka's written account omits 'I imagined': 'I decided to climb these steps in order to enjoy the view to which they would bring me.' He does not imagine beforehand the view that would be afforded by the climb.

The narrator attempts to create an image of the clear view from the tower before climbing and is disappointed. Kafka's image is deferred until after he climbs and cannot see the city, and so he creates an image of the newspaper-fog in his notebooks. The narrator's imagination is destabilised because the fog was not included in his initial concept of the view from above, so when the Kafka description does not have an allusion to his imaginative expectations, the narrator questions the motivation for Kafka to climb the tower in the first place. The subtle difference hints that Kafka values the foggy image as much as the imagined clear view of Riga and the bay, and the narrator cannot comprehend the lack of disappointment in what the climb afforded. Kafka reserved the imaginary for the simile of the newspaper-fog in his description, which in his account is not toned with disappointment, as in the narrator's, but instead is a positive image of the environment as it appeared to him, which so happens to be the same way the environment appeared to the narrator.

There are traces here of how description functions in literary narrative generally. The way that the human figure relates to what is 'unseen' – something that is either not perceived or positively imagined – drives this minimal narrative, eventually disrupting its progression. In three different instances – the narrator's account, Kafka's notebook and the story itself – the unavailability of a conventional view from above to describe puts an end to the storytelling. Narratives do not often resolve the frustrations of description in this way, as most integrate lyrical descriptions into the plot (as is the dominant popular mode of the contemporary novel, critiqued by Zadie Smith as 'lyrical realism'[4]) or the text thematises the impossibility of accurate or clear description – the legacy of modernism. In this book, I read beyond these narrative-focused and anthropocentric theorisations of the ways that description functions in fiction. I add a third piece into this pair of description and narration: the nonhuman environment enters narrative discourse through description, and it initiates a clash between the form of environment and the form of the text. In this way I present a slant take on ecocritical approaches to literature by building a nonanthropocentric theory of literary images through analysis of the view from above in twentieth-century American fiction.

In the Mathews story, the chiasmus of reality and fiction is left bare by the use of this postmodern doubling, shuttling between both representations as temporally earlier and so ontologically primary. The reader can empathise with the narrator's frustration that his experience is mediated by text, but the reader can also engage with the materiality of the images as articulations of the form of environment, afforded by the experience of the newspaper-fog. The realism of the other texts I study in this book bury, though cannot neutralise, the function of description revealed by Mathews's story: the literary image comes before experience, and the form of environment it articulates is made available after encountering the description. The reader has the opportunity to encounter the environment as imaginary through fictional literature in a way not available to everyday perception. The way that the fog and the city structure the encounter in this story is the first example of the 'form of environment', the primary term I develop throughout this book.[5] This is defined as an analogue to the more familiar use of form as it pertains to the literary text. Though the environment is not a text, as such, it has a form independent of its perception that affords articulation in literary images and so clashes with the anthropocentric constraints of human narrative.

The Primacy of Description and Imagination

The parameters of realistic space as experienced in daily life are usually projected into literary art through representations of perception. The specific affordances of language simultaneously reveal this as unstable, unreliable or unrecognisable, questioning the primacy of word or world. In this way, the realistic text functions through rearrangements of perspective that allow behaviour as well as objects to be experienced or interpreted in novel ways. The disruption of perspective and perspective-taking through the spatial process of rearrangement is a primary discovery of the Russian Formalists. More recently, Timothy Morton has coded this as 'medial writing' or, specific to depictions of the environment, 'ecomimesis', where contact with the environment is foregrounded over the content of the environment itself.[6] In this book, I identify the negation of familiar, everyday ways of communicating distance, perception and spatial relationships between subjects and objects as the basic function of form – both the form of the text and the form of environment. Rethinking these categories of perspective, space and environment is an urgent task of the critic in the present, to 'generate alternative descriptions' of our world, as Bruno Latour argues.[7]

There is a paradox here: how are we able to identify reality or, rather, realistic descriptions in literature when this is precisely the material being destabilised and rearranged? Pierre Ouellet offers a clear statement of this problem: 'Asking questions about the relationships between the world and fiction always comes back to the same thing: acting as though we do not know what fiction is and, inversely, assuming to know fully well what the world is.'[8] The concept of the real world as stable, knowable and the primary referent of fictional utterances is an essential problem of studying a concept such as the view from above, which seems to necessitate a 'real' and 'stable' point from which to define the subjective act of perspective-taking and objective reality, figured as below.

Literary and cultural interpretations of the view from above often take for granted the perceptual reality of perspective, assume literature can function as a simulation of perception, and critique subjects who inherit the power of seeing and claim possession over what is seen. For example, Mary Louise Pratt labels this figure the 'monarch-of-all-I-survey'. This standard critique requires the metaphorical distanced observation of the critic and so often falls into the same power dynamics of surveying texts to draw parallels with historical patterns, assuming the actual world is stable and interpretable in order to define and critique its fictional analogue in possible worlds.

But is the view from above and the figure surveying the environment the source and symbol of dominance and power, or is this just one amongst many functional interpretations of this point of view? Consider the primary term of Pratt's formulation – 'survey'. 'I am the monarch of all I survey' is the opening line of William Cowper's poem 'The Solitude of Alexander Selkirk'. Pratt notes this, but does not note an earlier appropriation of the phrase. In *Walden*, Henry David Thoreau quotes this Cowper line after a short passage describing how he bought and immediately returned a farm for the same price after the owner changed his mind. Doing so changes the definition of 'survey'. Thoreau is the 'monarch' of this land by negation, by the very act of not possessing: 'imagination carried me so far that I even had the refusal of several farms – the refusal was all I wanted – but I never got my fingers burned by actual possession'.[9] Imagination and the negation of possession brings value to the land for Thoreau, and he surveys not exclusively with a view from above but through direct encounter on the ground by way of his work as a professional surveyor.

Edward S. Casey similarly redefines what it means to encounter the environment via survey:

> As the word 'sur-vey' implies, the view is typically from above, from an elevated point of view. But the point of view is not itself a 'point,' that is, a fixed position in space. The viewer is suspended in

an indefinite viewing area that lacks determinate location. Nevertheless, the viewing itself is felt to take place at a considerable distance, though a distance that represents a privileged access to the scene surveyed below. The privileged access stems from the basic sense that the viewer, however distantly situated, nevertheless belongs to the surveyed space.[10]

He notes that the immediate associations that follow from concepts like 'point', 'distance', 'privilege' and belonging are tied together not only as conceptual metaphors structured by an above-below hierarchy, but also through their inherent contradictions: a point in space is not always concrete or fixed; distance is frequently indeterminate; privilege is not the antithesis of belonging. This book highlights the simultaneity of both far-out distance and close-up dwelling given by the affordances of the view from above, foregrounding the imaginary, indeterminacy and an investigation of the various forms of encounter between a subject and their environment. The superficiality of height in the view from above in literature is an essential space of close encounter with the environment.

From Ouellet's formulation given above, an experiment begs to be conducted. What if we considered the fictional world as the stable ground from which to define the 'real world'? For, surely, the articulation of the world in aesthetic objects is a part of the world, one that demands attention if the 'world' as such is to be defined. Michel Butor offers up something like this in his essay 'The Novel as Research', in which he claims that 'though veracious narrative always has the support, the last resort, of external evidence, the novel must suffice to create what it tells us. That is why it is the phenomenological realm par excellence, the best possible place to study how reality appears to us, or might appear.'[11] In this way, I develop an approach that analyses the way that the 'real world' might appear in descriptions of the view from above in the literary work of art.

A corollary to this experimental focus on a 'stable' fictional world as opposed to a 'stable' real world is a turn to the primacy of imagination rather than perception. Literary images of the view from above have an imaginary ecology, one that spatialises images in a network of encounter between reader, text and environment. 'Distance' between subject and object in the description of an environment down below does not have an objective geometry measurable as in aerial photography or mappable like geographical space. Nor is this apparent distance necessarily symbolic, inheriting the dominance of top-down hierarchies or the supposed objectivity of panoramic sight. Rather, the signs or suggestions of distance given in aerial description are a means to confront the reader with the radical closeness or entanglement of the reader in the environment. The paradox of represented distance and experiential closeness is essential to interpreting references to the environment in fiction.

In addition, the environment has a form. The apparent contradiction between entanglement in the environment and the distance implied by a subject describing what is far below and spread around is resolved by the way the experience of the literary image brings near the form of environment perceived as an inaccessible ideal. The aspects of this form that are identified in subsequent chapters – extent in Chapter 2, verticality in Chapter 3 and scale in Chapter 4 – are applicable to other environments, or at least the method of encountering the actual environment in fictional texts is the same. This book primarily presents a portable method or model to be applied to other texts and other environments. As such, in my conclusion, I suggest how this method can be applied to the contemporary literary use of images from unmanned aerial vehicles and satellites.

Nineteenth-Century Aerial Description

In this book, I give a theoretical and analytical account of aerial description in twentieth-century US American fiction and literary criticism. The diachronic structure of the chapters as well as the commentary on technology suggests a historical account in addition to my literary theoretical arguments about environment and imagination. The history of flight, aerial photography and its reception is well documented.[12] The literary history of these images – specifically in the United States – has not been explored as thoroughly.[13] Though this is not the primary goal of this book, I hope that my theoretical focus can also suggest a way to analyse the historical development of these images in fiction. Here in the introduction, I want to further this suggestion by presenting a few examples of nineteenth-century aerial description in American fiction as a preamble to the period of my primary study that coincides with the proliferation of static, technological forms of aerial perception with the development of flight in the United States. (In my conclusion, I will also extend this historical account into the twenty-first century.) These stories present three prototypes of narrative and description of environment: 1) Description – what is seen – structures the literary text more than (representations of) the act of seeing. 2) Description emphasises difference rather than precision by introducing paradoxical frames of reference. 3) Description stages a clash between the material environment and conceptualisations of the environment. Throughout this book, I explore these attributes by challenging anthropocentric readings of the texts I analyse.

A paradigmatic example of the nineteenth-century panoramic sketch is Nathaniel Hawthorne's 'Sights from a Steeple' (1831). Hawthorne experiments with a static narrator and a fixed perspective split into four quadrants of what the narrator describes as the 'visible circle'. The narrative affordances of this view from the church steeple are few: the only recognisable story is based on the minimal romantic tensions when a haggard young man is caught mingling with the daughters of a wealthy merchant when a storm drives them all home out of the rain. The narrator makes clear that this sight is conventional and not worth dwelling on: 'All this is easy to be understood.'[14]

He is also aware of other potential narratives embedded in this scene, though, curiously, he feels blocked from any speculation beyond what is seen. He knows, generally, what goes on in a town such as this – 'How various are the situations of the people covered by the roofs beneath me, and how diversified are the events at this moment befalling them!' – but he does not develop any sustained meditation upon them: 'There are broad thoughts struggling in my mind, and, were I able to give them distinctness, they would make their way in eloquence. Lo! The raindrops are descending!'[15] This is a kind of parody of the serious powers of the extradiegetic narrator and the similar position adopted by viewers of popular panoramas, but the reflexivity about the difficulties of narration is undercut by the imposition of changes in the environment. Rather than continue the brief self-deprecation about his inability to invent narratives about the people below him, he is compelled to describe. The descriptions of the storm go beyond parody and introduce a pattern in which the nonhuman environment consistently disrupts the narrator's faint interest in human activity.

The narrator becomes frustrated at the narrative limitations of his own method: 'I love not my station here aloft, in the midst of the tumult which I am powerless to direct or quell, [. . .] I will descend.'[16] The narrator has ascended to test his powers as an observer of human behaviour – and to tell the story of what he has seen – but his height affords more information than is possible to order into an interesting story, so he instead focuses on the concrete particulars of what he is able to see. Naturally, the shift to the ways things influence his ability to see foregrounds the environment. Here, descriptions of the environment introduce tension between what is seen and the act of seeing. While the normal focus of literary criticism is in how these acts are organised into narrative, foregrounding description considers how prioritising the act of seeing in criticism undercuts the primacy of description in literary fiction. In this case, because of both the physical limitation of the roofs and the psychological inability to narrativise what could possibly be going on under the roofs, the narrator cannot capitalise on the reader's natural interest in the dynamics of the act of seeing and instead describes the nonhuman environment, the weather and the geometric structure of the town.

'Sights from a Steeple' exploits a cliché of readerly habit put well by Gaston Bachelard: 'Readers "skip the descriptions" because no one has taught them to appreciate "literary imagination."'[17] In Hawthorne's sketch, trying to read for plot leads to an essentially blank reading experience. Many narratologists have made the mistake of interpreting this supposed readerly habit into the structure of the literary work, assuming that it is perception and perspective-taking that is at stake, not imagination. But this denies the 'literary imagination' that Bachelard defends. Instead, it relies on perceptual model of space that infers that the same (or analogous) process is either present or not present in literary descriptions of space and attendant perspective. I discuss these narratological issues at length in Chapter 3.

Another story that presents a clash of description and narration is Edgar Allan Poe's 'Descent into the Maelström' (1841). The story presents a paradox of literary description: multiple corroborations do not lead to a fuller, more precise picture of a given thing, but put into question the authority of the describer and defers the authority to the reader, who has access to multiple descriptions. The story centres on a Norwegian sailor's account of escaping from the mythic vortex through quick deduction as his ship is being sucked down. It is framed by an unnamed, presumably American, narrator whom the sailor has taken to the brink of a cliff to witness the maelstrom from the story for himself.

The narrator has read about the whirlpool before, and also describes it in detail as they watch the storm develop from choppy waves, to a series of small whirlpools, to their combination into a massive vortex that is the maelstrom. He is stricken with terror, not just at what he has seen, but in how it differs from what he expected. All before the sailor tells his story, the narrator describes the maelstrom that he sees down below, presents transcriptions of two scientific descriptions of the maelstrom, and reproduces part of the *Encyclopædia Brittanica* entry for the maelstrom. The sailor then tells his story of shipwreck and escape, uninterrupted, and the short story ends without comment by the narrator; the frame remains open. The sailor frequently defers to the impossibility to describe the intensity of the storm on that day, emphasising that this is the reason why he has taken the narrator to the top of the cliff to see for himself.

That the frame is left open complicates the structure of the story. Does the narrator believe the story now that he has seen the storm from above in the present, or are all of these descriptions in addition to the narrative presented to the reader through the kind of metaphorical 'view from above' associated with omniscience? The prototype of description that this story foregrounds is description as a juxtaposition of frames, specifically the way that corroborated descriptions do not lead to an increased sense of their reality. As multiple descriptions of the storm layer on top of one another, a certain form begins to emerge from the variations in the descriptions.

Normally, frames are considered as narrative devices that layer stories within further contexts related to one another in time (that is, the situation of natural narrative in which one story is paused in order to tell another). What Poe's story does by layering descriptions is emphasise that narrative is ultimately framed in space by the form of environment in which the story is implaced. The proliferation of descriptions in this story puts into question the fidelity of the narrator's story itself, and leads to the sailor's conclusion: '"I told them my story – they did not believe it. I now tell it to you – and I can scarcely expect you to put more faith in it than did the merry fisherman of Lofoden."'[18] The sailor has now told his story in a new context – where his audience can see the storm for himself – but rather than make his story more plausible, the repeated descriptions of the maelstrom become more interesting than the story that the sailor attempts to tell about it. That the frame is left open also keeps the reader implaced at this nested level of the story, able to forget that the story is framed by a witness and student of the maelstrom itself. The reader, then, relies on the image and the form of environment more than the form of the text to answer the sailor's call to believe.

The silent child in Sarah Orne Jewett's 'A White Heron' (1886) also becomes overwhelmed in the indeterminate space afforded by the view from above, and she attempts to end a story by concealing what she learns from this perspective. Unlike the sudden ending of Poe's story, here the extradiegetic narrator breaks in to make the story tellable through its own descriptive dynamic. The story opens with Sylvia, who lives with her grandmother in the Maine woods, looking for their cow in the darkening forest. A hunter from the city interrupts Sylvia's playful search and announces he would like to stay at the house so he can continue to look for a white heron in the morning. Sylvia is scared, and the man is described as an aggressive enemy until later that night, at home, when he describes the white heron.

The name of the bird means nothing to Sylvia, but, with the description, she imagines a variety of relative spatial descriptors of a memorable instance in which she had encountered the heron. She has an embodied memory of the 'open place' associated with the bird's presence, but it is not clear if she knows how to lead the stranger there, or if she trusts her memory. Before sunrise the next morning, Sylvia locates a famous pine for being the tallest and oldest in a second-growth forest nearby. She climbs it to try to find the bird mentioned the night before. Notably, this view is not romanticised; it is presented with a tinge of the picturesque, but the scene is strangely animated by the narrator's forceful imposition of perspective:

> Now look down again, Sylvia, where the green marsh is set among the shining birches and dark hemlocks; there where you saw the white heron once you will see him again; look, look! a white spot of him like a single floating feather comes up from the dead hemlock and grows larger, and rises, and comes close at last, and goes by the landmark pine with steady sweep of wing and outstretched slender neck and crested head. And wait! wait! do not move a foot or a finger, little girl, do not send an arrow of light and consciousness from your two eager eyes, for the heron has perched on a pine bough not far beyond yours, and cries back to his mate on the nest and plumes his feathers for the new day![19]

The text moves from Sylvia's concrete perspective to the narrator's intrusion that sets a distinct frame for where both Sylvia's perception and the reader's imagination are focused. Sylvia becomes excited and seemingly wants to share what she has seen. Though she may desire to tell when she is up in the tree, it is unclear if she is really entertaining this, or if she is feeling a conventional excitement at the kind of information the aerial perspective affords, enforced by the narrator's intrusion. This is the same experience as the speaker from 'Sights from a Steeple', who feels the potential in the 'broad thoughts', but when it comes down to telling, he cannot do anything but describe.

When she arrives home, Sylvia refuses to tell the hunter the location of the bird. The extradiegetic narrator similarly interjects here as the interdiegetic narrator in the Hawthorne story: 'No, she must keep silence! What is it that suddenly forbids her and makes her dumb? Has she been nine years growing and now, when the great world for the first time puts out a hand to her, must she thrust it aside for a bird's sake?'[20] This ambivalent address is a mix of wonder, fear, admiration and, eventually, exasperation when Sylvia decides not to tell the stranger or her grandmother what she had seen. In the end, the narrator is equally left out of the imaginative experience that Sylvia conceals; the narrator only has access to perception.

In these three cases, description of the environment backgrounds the experience of the human figure, destabilises the human figure's sense of reality, and emphasises the ways preconceptions determine and preclude encounter with the environment. They are each an example of frustrated, unstable or aborted storytelling situations that reach their terminus once description of the environment has spaced out beyond the limited perspective of the narrator. These stories are particularly unique in that they do not attempt to recuperate this frustration through narrative, but instead demonstrate the limits of narrativisation in accessing the nonhuman world. In this book, I show how foregrounding description – even in texts that do not formally foreground description – affords consideration of how literary texts are primarily structured by their relationship to the physical environment. I also show how the aesthetic experience of reading is structured by the changing relationship between art, technology and the environment.

These changes involve the rapid naturalisation of technological processes in concepts of experience. These three nineteenth-century stories are influenced by landscape painting and panorama, but retain the primacy of imagination because of their material context. In the present, these stories can be read from ecocritical points of view focusing on weather, climate, catastrophe or extinction, motivated by contemporary climate change science, fuelled by view-from-above models of the world via satellite and mapped data visualisation. This is one of the reasons why the aerial view is a fascinating case study for thinking about description and environment, as the relatively recent technological reality of flight takes precedence over the historically and prehistorically predominant imaginary role of flight.

Bachelard writes that our dreams of flight are natural; if we recall a dream and describe the wings we used to fly, we have introduced a rationalisation. The sensation of flight from dreams gives us the experience of the dynamic imagination, before rational image-making. For Bachelard, dream flight is an experience of lightness and heaviness, not the tools that we believe make flying possible – 'static forms' like wings betray the ways material imagination is dynamic, centred on movement, 'vectorial'.[21] The materiality of images in fiction literature also presents this vector, and because the essence of the literary image I am studying is our shared environment we have the chance to understand the form of environment in addition to Bachelard's insights into the elemental imagination. The clearest place to study these images is lyric poetry (as Bachelard does), because the mode presents the image before or in place of narrative. But studying descriptive images in narrative fiction allows the reader the pleasures of inverting normalised anthropocentric, plot-based reading habits to tease out the suppressed and buried work description as a mode and the materiality of literary images have for the existence of the literary work of art and our experiences of it.

Book Summary

I use instances of the view from above – which I term 'aerial description' – to present a model applicable for all descriptions of environment. I spend considerable space developing the functional theoretical background for why aerial description is a particularly important case for a nonanthropocentric study of literature and outline its theoretical relevance for literary narrative. In doing so, I detach from the predominant critical narrative that Caren Kaplan argues is reliant on the assumptions of a 'unified technodeterminism of aerial perception'.[22]

Indeterminacy becomes the key term for organising the relationship between literary form and the form of environment given by aerial views, in opposition to the determinate products of technology and the apparent determinacies of perception. I adapt the concept from Roman Ingarden and Wolfgang Iser by supplementing what is absent in their theories, that is, consideration of nonhuman elements in the literary work.

In Chapter 1, I develop my theory of indeterminacy in literature through critique of prior studies of the view from above. My understanding of form and the definition of the form of environment stems from Caroline Levine's recent work and what has been labelled as New Formalism. I discuss how her work informs my theories of description and how it applies to my analyses in the subsequent chapters. In these analyses, I discuss the ways that this renewed, ecological definition of form challenges the anthropocentrism of narratological models of fictional texts. By foregrounding description within narratology, I apply the tools of narrative theory to determine not the form of certain texts, but rather, the form of environment.

In this way, my book is a thoroughly literary study, and though I utilise relevant contemporary studies of the view from above (of which there are many) and rehearse the ever-present keystone of these studies, the 'whole Earth' from the US Apollo mission photographs in Chapter 4, this study has different goals than these visual histories and cultural theories. The imposition of visual and perceptual models onto literary representation is challenged by my theorisation of views from above by using studies that focus on literary imagination, and it stands beside recent attempts to reinterpret the view from above in the current context of climate change.

In the subsequent chapters I present a diachronic study of aerial description in three key figures of American modernism and postmodernism to illustrate the interaction between technological progress in perceiving the environment from above and changing literary technics for imagining the aerial view. To do so, I identify three aspects present in aerial description: extent, verticality and scale. These three forms are present in the aesthetics of literary description as the articulation of the same forms in the actual environment encountered from above. In addition, each of the three literary case studies are read directly beside a relatively contemporary philosopher in order to emphasise the alternative ways of reading that are present but need to be further foregrounded. I look at George Santayana, Gaston Bachelard and Timothy Clark to define, contextualise and complicate the concepts of extent, verticality and scale as it pertains to aerial description.

Chapter 2 analyses 'extent' in aerial description in *O Pioneers!* (1913) and *Death Comes for the Archbishop* (1927) by Willa Cather. As aerial photography became popularised, there is a growing clash between perceiving the extended environments of the American West in relation to human progress and imagining how extent cannot be contained by narratives of expansion. Cather's fiction interacts with other spatial images that organise American space, in particular Santayana's image of America as defined by the point of view offered by the skyscraper in opposition to the colonial mansion. Aerial description in these two novels emphasises the extended form of environment as imagined from above by situating the patterned repetition of both the farmland in the Midwest and the desert landscape in the Southwest as articulations of the nonhuman organisation of space on the verge of elimination.

Chapter 3 develops 'verticality' as the second aspect of aerial description in *The Sheltering Sky* (1949), *Let It Come Down* (1952) and *The Spider's House* (1955) by Paul Bowles. These novels present another twentieth-century 'frontier', as their American characters travel North Africa. But they are not depicted as mere existential outsiders, with the associated Eurocentric, 'horizontal' implications of a journey out into the colonial unknown. Rather, Bowles's novels emphasise a constant desire to retreat into vertical space as an opportunity to encounter the environment through its integration into imagination. I develop the concept of verticality and imagination through a reading of Bachelard's work on air and space.

Chapter 4 analyses 'scale' in 'Human Moments in World War III' (1983) by Don DeLillo. Aerial description is implaced within a third frontier as I consider literary images of the 'whole Earth' after the Apollo missions. The newly perceived image of the 'whole Earth' presents a limit case for large-scale aerial descriptions, particularly the difficulty of integrating description of this environment into cohesive narrative. I outline the material and rhetorical history of the 'whole-Earth' images and how these assumptions pervade general theoretical discussions about scale as well as criticism of the DeLillo story. I show how the story opens up the 'whole Earth' specifically and aerial description in general as an indeterminate image because it remains unnarrated in the story. I use Timothy Clark's concept of 'scale effects' to show the difficulty of escaping scalar logic when dealing with such apparently outsized figures such as the 'whole Earth', as well as the environment as a concept.

In conclusion, I analyse aerial descriptions after twenty-first-century technological developments such as unmanned aerial vehicles and the daily presence of satellite imagery. This includes the interesting absence of drone perspectives in literary fiction and the incorporation in autofiction of commercialised surveillance and tracking technologies in navigation applications. These examples finally show how the ways that my analysis of extent, verticality and scale can apply to other descriptions of environment, and I suggest a kind of smooth zoom form afforded by aerial description in contemporary fiction.

Notes

1. Harry Mathews, *The Human Country*, 111.
2. Ibid., 112.
3. Ibid., 113. The final lines continue: 'In saying this, I am not referring to his hat, which had nothing to do with my feelings; or, at least, nothing particular.' This is an allusion to Richard Brautigan's comically bleak poem 'Kafka's Hat'.

4. See Zadie Smith, *Changing My Mind*, 72.
5. I recognise 'form of environment' (vs 'form of *the* environment') is not a grammatical omission of the article. I have created this term to emphasise form and evoke a concept of 'total environment'. James J. Gibson uses this term in order to redefine the environment's affordances: 'The total environment is too vast for description even by the ecologist, and we should select those features of it that are perceptible to animals like ourselves.' In this way, I show how the part of the total environment that is available to readers is its imaginary form. See Gibson, *The Ecological Approach to Visual Perception*, 36.
6. Timothy Morton, *Dark Ecology*, 57.
7. Bruno Latour, *Down to Earth*, 94.
8. Pierre Ouellet, 'The Perception of Fictional Worlds', 80.
9. Henry David Thoreau, *Walden*, 67.
10. Edward S. Casey, *Representing Place*, 161.
11. Michel Butor, *Inventory*, 27.
12. See William L. Fox, *Aeriality*; Jeanne Haffner, *The View from Above*; Patrick Ellis, *Aeroscopics*.
13. For an interesting study of flight, generally, in literature, see Lawrence Goldstein, *The Flying Machine and Modern Literature*; relevant to American literature, see Goldstein, 'The Airplane and American Literature'.
14. Nathaniel Hawthorne, *Tales and Sketches*, 47.
15. Ibid., 46.
16. Ibid., 47.
17. Gaston Bachelard, *Air and Dreams*, 27.
18. Edgar Allen Poe, *Poetry and Tales*, 448.
19. Sarah Orne Jewett, *Novels and Stories*, 678.
20. Ibid., 679.
21. Bachelard, *Air and Dreams*, 27.
22. Caren Kaplan *Aerial Aftermaths*, 11.

Chapter 1

Foundations for the View from Above in Literary Fiction: Description, Form and Indeterminacy

The view from above has a strange, unavoidable attraction for pinpointing the essence of epistemological and ontological relationships between humans and the world. There are three terms in the phenomenology of the view from above: the subject that sees, the object that is seen and the context that structures this encounter. It is easy to imagine the subject as human, though, materially, it is often an animal or a machine. The object can be any kind of 'view', from a natural feature to a human settlement. The context of this experience can be a meditation during a mountain hike, a terrified stare in flight, a bored glance from a tall building or a camera pointed vertically down at a shoreline, obliquely across a desert or moving automatically to track a target. In daily experience, the object is primary; I look down from the top of this peak and wonder at how the trees are reflected off a lake to show the scene twice. But in analysis, the context or the subject is considered primary: who sees, why and how?

In this book, I will maintain the object as the main term in my study of the view from above. But there is a twist, because I am considering the objectivity of fictional descriptions of the view from above. To do so, I am constructing a different third term: the form of environment mediated by literary images in description.

In literary and cultural criticism, the context is almost always taken for granted to be as real as the first two terms, and it is usually considered to be the ideology of dominant, globalising reflection. Only recently have critics begun to challenge this third term by developing other, nonanthropogenic definitions: Caren Kaplan in *Aerial Aftermaths* considers the materiality of war and Heather

Houser in *Infowhelm* thinks about climate change. Unlike Patrick Ellis's valuable recent book *Aeroscopics* that details the forgotten archival responses to the popular amusements of pre-aeroplane aerial images and experiences such as balloon rides and panoramic paintings, I focus on the ways that the reading experience and the literary work of art as an object affords its own, specifically imaginary structure of the view from above and the environment implaced in it. In this chapter, I develop a model of environment, imagination and indeterminacy by focusing on description, and I show how prior critiques structure the view from above while still hinting that something remains beyond the grasp of their anthropocentric theories.

Edward S. Casey traces the development from pre-modern landscape art to maps and calls these representational practices creative 're-implacements' of the environment. He provokes:

> Does not the vast implacable river below me speak for itself? Is this not enough already? Why move to representation when the experience of landscape is dense enough, and frequently pleasing enough, in its own way? Why seek *other* ways, particularly representational ones that appear to signify a secondary status and that only complicate matters further? Why re-present what is already presented so effectively and thoroughly in ordinary direct experience?[1]

Casey splits 're-present' to supplement the static, mimetic suggestions of representation with the idea that aesthetic engagements with the environment create effects of 're-implacement', where a place is re-formed as it appears with the aesthetic object.[2] This re-implacement not only sets a place down into a new context, but stages representation itself, making representation of representation a primary aesthetic experience in description of the environment: 'The world-as-picture is a world that has become a totality of objects that solicit us to remake them – which is to say, to represent them in their very representedness – by our own descriptive and depictive actions.'[3] While he refers to visual media – maps and landscape painting – this also applies to literary images in the act of describing the environment.

The form of any narrative is afforded by the environment in which it is in the process of re-implacing, an experience readers follow as they encounter the form of environment represented in literary description. In this sense, narrative form is dependent on the affordances of the spatial form of landscape. My definition of narrative form asserts that the form of environment affords the eventual aesthetic forms given in descriptions embedded in narrative texts, as opposed to other studies of 'space in narrative' in which places are narrativised in ways not integrated into aesthetic experience.[4] The term 'affordance' will be used throughout this book in its original definition by James J. Gibson. Caroline Levine has recently brought the term from design into literary theory by foregrounding a general meaning related to 'possible use'. But Gibson provides a stronger definition of 'affordance' to analyse the 'complementarity of the animal and the environment' and denote what the environment 'offers' or 'furnishes' for the subject.[5]

A phenomenological account that focuses on the affordances of a reflexive representation of representation is missing from prior studies of the view from above. As seen in Harry Mathews's short story 'Franz Kafka in Riga' discussed in my introduction, reflexivity builds the backbone of all description of environment in literature, though it is concealed by realistic literary technique. On the other hand, Denis Cosgrove's influential book *Apollo's Eye* presents the conventional interpretation of the features of the view from above: it is the position that most clearly unites objectivity, power, control, perception, and technological and historical progress. While there is no denying that the impact of more accessible, higher-resolution and more definitive images of landscape or even the 'whole Earth' from above are a major part of the contemporary development of concepts like freedom and objectivity – as well as the ability to deploy these images to assert dominance over the environment – such direct causality impedes alternative interpretations of these images. Interpretations with wider temporal scales beyond modernity or alternate spatial scales beyond the human appear irrelevant to analysis that takes for granted that the view from above is a human's view from above, even when technologically mediated.

An interchangeable concept, 'bird's-eye view', immediately reveals this anthropocentrism. No eagle or goose sees Boston as it is so composed in James Wallace Black's famous, original photograph of the city from a manned balloon (*Figure 1.1*), while an 'actual' bird's-eye view in Julius Neubronner's pigeon-mounted cameras (*Figure 1.2*) is more notable for its inhuman, uncomposed qualities and the intrusion of the bird's wings, which foregrounds the bird much more than the view. In the recent counter-narratives of legibility of the view from above, these types of early photographs become exemplary for how they reveal the discomposure afforded by the view from above.[6] But these images have an even more complex texture than just the disoriented affect they can cause: progressive attempts to utilise technologies of perception to 'see more' empower the viewer to *imagine* more than what can be represented.

Foundations for the View from Above in Literary Fiction   19

Figure 1.1 James Wallace Black, 'Boston, As the Eagle and the Wild Goose See It' (1860). The Metropolitan Museum of Art, New York, Gilman Collection, Purchase, Ann Tenenbaum and Thomas H. Lee Gift, 2005. https://www.metmuseum.org/art/collection/search/

Figure 1.2 Photograph from pigeon-mounted camera by Julius Neubronner (c. 1903). Image Courtesy Stadtarchiv Kronberg im Taunus.

Focusing on the environment rather than the human, as in this book, is not mutually exclusive of former research on the view from above, but rather it offers a complementary study of aeriality from a poetic perspective. Aerial images do not just have a life in perception, but also hold a potential imaginary life. Literary descriptions are a primary space to encounter what is not seen in the view from above.

This differs in part from two foundational accounts of aeriality from Roland Barthes and Michel de Certeau, who link aesthetic experience and the view from above in a unidirectional, linear sequence of perception and discovery.

Barthes and de Certeau both find modern architecture – the Eiffel Tower for Barthes and the World Trade Center for de Certeau – to be a concretisation of the relationship between human and environment. The tower becomes a symbol, the foregrounded object of description, in their accounts. Barthes affectionately calls the Eiffel Tower 'an utterly useless monument':

> for the world ordinarily produces either purely functional organisms (camera or eye) intended to see things but which then afford nothing to sight, what *sees* being mythically linked to what remains *hidden* (this is the theme of the voyeur), or else spectacles which themselves are blind and are left in the pure passivity of the visible. The Tower (and this is one of its mythic powers) transgresses this separation, this habitual divorce between *seeing* and *being seen*; it achieves a sovereign circulation between the two functions; it is a complete object which has, if one may say so, both sexes of sight.[7]

The observer in its belvedere is able to briefly participate in the Tower's sight, which transcends both perception and representation through its uselessness. The subject becomes caught up in the Tower's disruptive presence, and the view offered 'makes the city into a kind of Nature' because the subject is habituated, as a tourist, to look out over a landscape taken for granted as natural: 'the city joins up with the great natural themes which are offered to the curiosity of men: the ocean, the storm, the mountains, the snow, the rivers'.[8] The form of environment itself is primary, blurring the concepts 'nature' and 'culture'. In this perceptual act, 'every visitor to the Tower makes structuralism without knowing it'.[9]

De Certeau figures the World Trade Center differently and more conventionally, though with a similar interest in the work that the subject does when confronted with the view:

> His elevation transfigures him into a voyeur. It puts him at a distance. It transforms the bewitching world by which one was 'possessed' into a text that lies before one's eyes. It allows one to read it, to be a solar Eye, looking down like a god. The exaltation of a scopic and gnostic drive: the fiction of knowledge is related to this lust to be a viewpoint and nothing more.[10]

De Certeau also describes a kind of 'structuralism' that the view affords when the subject is lifted up above a city. But both Barthes and de Certeau remain anchored in a visual and perceptual paradigm for interpreting the view from above, and so interpret what I call the 'form of environment' as a structure or a text, transforming the environment into linguistic media in order for it to be interpreted semiotically.

Their focus is on new knowledge afforded by unprecedented towers, where the human figure now has more valid opportunities to confirm the imaginations of the past. For Barthes, 'the Tower materialises an imagination which has seen its first expression in literature',[11] and de Certeau recognises, 'the desire to see the city preceded the means of satisfying it. Medieval or Renaissance painters represented the city as seen in a perspective that no eye had yet enjoyed.'[12] But while literature or painting were an original resource for encountering the environment from above, their value is stripped once the point of view is actualised: for Barthes, an actual aerial view 'gives us the world to *read* and not only to perceive',[13] and for de Certeau 'the 1370 foot high tower that serves as a prow for Manhattan continues to construct the fiction that creates readers, makes the complexity of the city readable, and immobilizes its opaque mobility in a transparent text'.[14]

Despite a similar opposition between perception and 'reading' as is held in my definition of the reading experience and the imaginary, 'reading' is formulated for Barthes and de Certeau as quantitatively increased perceptual access to environment, rather than a qualitatively alternate form of access. For this reason, de Certeau's view from above is a text that becomes 'transparent' and, for Barthes, 'a panorama can never be consumed as a work of art'.[15] The impulse to associate the aerial view with aesthetic, and particularly literary, imagination is correct, but their accounts end up locked within the technodeterminism that subordinates imagination to perception.

In this chapter, I will outline the three concepts that animate my theory of the view from above in literary images. First is my concept of 'aerial description', which is the unique function of the view from above in literature. Second is 'form of environment', which is a portable model that draws from theories of aesthetic response and formalism. Third is 'indeterminacy', which is primary in aerial description as literature clashes with the determinacy of perceptual views from above.

Aerial Description

Aerial description is my term for instances of the view from above in literary fiction. I foreground description rather than 'view' to argue that it is primarily description (as opposed to a perceptual 'view') that is most valuable about the environment embedded in fictional narrative. These aerial views do not function in the same way as the images analysed by prior studies, such as Barthes's Eiffel Tower as the mythic realisation of the desire to define structures, Mary Louise Pratt's 'verbal painting' that is an instance of colonial aesthetics, or Cosgrove's 'whole Earth' symbolised by 'Apollo's Eye'. As I will show in the next three chapters, aerial description presents the opportunity to defy official perception of the environment in Willa Cather, it disrupts and critiques conventional narrative progression in Paul Bowles, and it reveals the anthropocentrism of narrative form in Don DeLillo.

Aerial Views and Top-Down Power

The relative lack of literary theoretical analyses of the view from above is surprising given the attention it has received in other fields. Cosgrove offers a definitive account of what he calls 'Apollo's eye' from ancient to modern history, a genealogy of the drive to rise above and claim objectivity. His method is geographical, but he pulls from literary and cultural history, media studies and anthropology to develop a through-line from Greek myth to Google Earth. Cosgrove shows how Western globalisation is directly tied to the project to hide its own contradictions, specifically 'the paradox of a universality that is necessarily proclaimed for a positioned location', that is, the West.[16] He directly ties 'the West' with an image of the globe that has developed throughout history through an escalation of its assumed power. Apollo becomes the figure that recurs in all attempts to concretise ideology into a communicable image, usually a representation of the 'whole Earth'.

For Cosgrove, the view from above is always symbolic, which allows him to retrospectively fill in its meaning. The texts (or even the environments) he is looking at are rarely foregrounded. In this way, he emphasises the perceptual realities that come to dominate images of the Earth from above, implying that these images are always functionalised into and appropriated by the dominant system, that is, in his geopolitical study, globalisation. This is particularly evident in an essay in which he applies this method specifically to the United States. In 'The Measures of America', he unites the conceptual foundations of America with the initial imagination and then eventually the instantiation of the view from above:

> The rectangular grid is the perfect spatial expression of the republic's democratic imperative. [. . .] It is the landscape measure of America's

commitment to life, liberty, and the pursuit of happiness, distributing power equally across space. And the vastness of this conception, corresponding in its universality to the Enlightenment belief in a single, rational order in nature, is a fundamental determinant of America as landscape rather than landscapes.[17]

The singular landscape of America is thus a product of a top-down drive to actualise ideal democratic society, in opposition to Old World Europe. This also informs Cosgrove's assumption that geometric regularity should be recognised as 'human insensitivity to nature', as if patterned and rhythmic forms are necessarily 'unnatural'.[18] He points out how the current concept of landscape as well as the actual environment was originally structured by Enlightenment ideals – which resulted in resoundingly irrational treatment of the environment and its original human and nonhuman inhabitants – but he retains the determinist idea that this original relationship to the environment has continued to dominate into the present.

Because the American landscape is structured by this view from above, Cosgrove sees it as a privileged place from which to critique Enlightenment objectivity:

> Nowhere have these two themes – of space annihilated by time [through air flight] and of an ecological unity of nature and human life threatened by our own hubris [in the 1972 'whole Earth' photograph] – played themselves out more vocally than in the United States, in part because of the pivotal economic, political, and cultural role the country has played in the twentieth century.[19]

He figures the United States at the nexus of a variety of global issues, which all seem to be determined and structured by the overt power the view from above has had over American society and environment. But by privileging the US American environment – claiming that 'American landscape makes sense from the air. This is not so true for elusive European landscapes, which level with the observer more slowly, only as we enter into them'[20] – Cosgrove becomes implicated in reproducing the discourse of objectivity and exceptionalism that he later critiques as the function of globalisation in *Apollo's Eye*.

Cosgrove claims that it is the abstract ideas about democracy that led to the supposed legibility of America from above, but he effaces the materiality of the American environment and its role in the dynamics of the aerial views that he studies. This is apparent when we consider another, more recent, critique that makes virtually the same claims but with respect to the European continent. In

Down to Earth, Bruno Latour asserts Europe as the location that is privileged to see the consequences and solutions to globalisation and its image of the 'whole Earth', as it is the original locus of the globalisation project.[21] He has pointed out that criticism that is centred around globalisation often runs into the problem of not specifying precisely what the term 'global' could mean. Indeed, Cosgrove builds his account of 'globalisation' without clearly defining to what the reference 'global' points. Latour differentiates the double movement of globalisation and shows how both the ideology and its critique inevitably pull toward the same attractor: an assumption that the global is constituted by human actions alone.[22]

That the God's-eye view 'proclaim[s] disinterested and rationally objective consideration across its surface' in its use by Western culture is undeniable.[23] The maps constructed for exploration, government and decoration by colonial nations throughout history structure the perceptual habits of both expert map-users and connoisseur aesthetes, as Cosgrove shows. While there can be debate about how the total view from above functions ideologically, there is no doubt that these material artefacts played a major part in restructuring how 'the global' was conceptualised, however vaguely. The more open question pertains to the subject of aerial views that became more and more accessible via direct experience – not the 'whole Earth' or the mythical conception of Apollo, but one's own view of a concrete space.

The relationship between landscape painting, nationalism and aesthetics in art history offers a more nuanced debate as pertains this question of the accessibility of the view from above. In particular, nineteenth-century landscape painting in the United States is a productive starting point for thinking about the view from above in literature, as it also presents a clash of the depiction of landscape with cultural narratives. The most common interpretation of traditional landscape painting, and indeed most nineteenth-century landscape depiction, is its function as a concretisation of the Burkean sublime.[24] This is associated with massive mountain vistas, large-scale perspective and the act of perception implied by a diminutive human figure in the foreground.[25] This aesthetic structure has been functionalised as anthropocentric, imperialist and Romantic. For example, Angela Miller critiques representations of the environment in mid-nineteenth-century painting and literature because 'gazing at such images was a soul-expanding ritual of national self-affirmation'.[26] Miller foregrounds how these cultural objects work specifically as composites of real environments that ultimately erase the violent realities – Western expansion, native displacement, slavery – of the landscapes they depict.

Elisa New argues that the very tradition of criticising these images relies on its own version of 'Romantic vision' that is projected onto the works. New responds to this presentism by showing how Miller is falling into a problem of her own making. She argues that by tying an 'objective' and elevated point of view directly to imperialism, Miller ignores the more pressing, formal issue of the clash between perception and imagination of the environment that is staged in the artistic work. New shows instead how the depictions of the environment in mid-nineteenth-century literature and art are open to what she calls 'a shared, essentially pragmatic belief that the experience of nature is itself part of nature',[27] an investigation of the environment and not just its direct exploitation. Rather than the view from above deterministically implying objectivity and even nationalism, as Miller claims, these types of encounters became opportunities to explore the environment in its imaginary form.

The affordances of form are not causal or historical, but are dependent on the indeterminate context of the encounter with the aesthetic work. Of course, the ways these aesthetic affordances led to their functionalisation in imperial projects has much support, but New's counterpoint is a window into an alternate functionalisation of aerial images that attempts not to read a causal effect into an indeterminate aesthetic work. This encounter often does take place in contexts controlled by the ideologies of colonialism and imperialism, but it is important to highlight that reading these images otherwise is part of the project to resist these hierarchical contexts.[28] Both interpretations stand side by side, but once technology is brought into the foreground with the movement from landscape painting to aerial photography, these determinist arguments become even more prevalent. The study of aerial photography has largely followed the ideology of the God's-eye view of myth and exploration as outlined by Cosgrove.

Photography, mapping, urban planning and other ways of representing the landscape from above seemed to have reached the apotheosis of their usefulness just after World War II, before Marxist thinkers like Henri Lefebvre began to criticise these methods as an analogue and tool of top-down control and oppression. In general, critique such as Lefebvre's has continued to the present, despite further developments in technology for aerial vision and novel applications. Hannah Arendt, at the very outset of the Apollo missions in 1963, follows a similar line when considering the totalising ambitions of the US space program: 'the journey into space and to the Archimedean point with respect to the earth is far from being a harmless or unequivocally triumphant enterprise [. . .] the new world view that may conceivably grow out of it is likely to be once more geocentric and anthropomorphic'.[29] By the 1970s, the aerial view was not only criticised for being representative of spectacle taking over meaning in everyday life or state control of society, but was seen as an affront to even the concepts of possibility, resistance and change.[30] As such, critique of the aerial view in culture has followed a trajectory of deepening pessimism caused by officially 'improved' technologies of sight.

Caren Kaplan, on the other hand, challenges this critical trajectory. For Kaplan, cultural critics and philosophers too quickly accept the popular hegemony of the visual image, and simply adopt one hierarchy (above–below) to critique another (subjugator–subjugated or coloniser–colonised). If technologies of aerial vision and violence-from-above are identified as the main problem, and their representation of the environment are the main subject of analysis, Kaplan wonders at the elision of other technologies that enable aerial images to exist – thus materially equally important – and specific behaviours associated with the images. How would analysis change, for example, if critique was centred not on the image itself but instead on the fax machines or now computer networks that transmit aerial images or the latency between image-capture, transmission and interpretation? In the context of war, she notes: 'The "God's-eye" through line can create a highly selective, mystified narrative of modern war. [. . .] the visual is only one part of the apparatuses and practices at work in warfare.'[31] While Kaplan's focus is on warfare and aerial imagery, the shift away from perception can be applied to refocus the critical history of aerial imagery in literature.

Like the material elements of war, considerations of climate change expand the ways the view from above can be interpreted. Heather Houser argues:

> the aerial does not only serve Eurowestern military and imperial ambitions for domination. It may also serve spiritual purposes or be a medium for subjective, embodied experience of place. Yet, as we see from this critical conversation, an influential narrative in the humanistic study of aerial vision tags it as a technology of imperialism and militarism that instantiates Enlightenment values.[32]

She focuses on environmental art and the ways aerial views are repurposed to subvert the everyday assumptions about objectivity and the view from above outlined in this chapter. But Houser, like other recent studies of the aerial view, remains only thematically interested in mobilising a new interpretation of aerial perspective, focused on how the texts seem to utilise the aerial view for fictive-psychological processes. By contrast, my study is interested in the affordances of aerial description and how this involves, primarily, the reader's experience, literary form, the affordances of description and the form of environment.

Imperial Perceptions

Literary description is the primary, most accessible medium that highlights the non-visual, non-perceptual aspects of the view from above that Kaplan and Houser foreground. But the lack of sophisticated analysis of the aerial view in literary theory has meant that literary criticism has taken up where prior studies of the aerial view in culture and visual media have left off. This is the track that is followed by the most important – and only – extended study of the view from above specific to literature, Mary Louise Pratt's *Imperial Eyes*.

Interpretations of point of view and perspective are central to the literary theoretical organisation of many other narrative strategies. The clearest example is the ideological interpretation of the view from above as necessarily dominating, imperial and masculine. Pratt presents this argument about the specific instances of travel writing by Europeans in South America during the late seventeenth and early eighteenth centuries. Her argument and careful theorisation of the 'seeing-man' is a useful figure for postcolonial criticism, with well-delineated tendencies. These techniques are the motor behind the process of meaning-making, in which 'the verbal painter must render momentously significant what is, especially from a narrative point of view, practically a non-event'.[33] In the historical context that Pratt analyses, indeed, this staged, colonial 'discovery' is a non-event, as it is more so the narrativisation of appropriation and conquer rather than genuine discovery. Pratt notes this is concretised in the ironic figure of the native guide in travel narratives, who not only is not having the experience of discovery but has no influence over the seeing-man's much-belated 'verbal painting' when he is home writing his description of the 'new' landscape.[34]

As such, the 'seeing-man' or 'monarch-of-all-I-survey' is predicated on a 'rhetoric of presence'.[35] Presence, in Pratt's case, depends on an emphasis on perception. This account of travel writing and post/colonialism is especially important because it points out authorial perspective's strange self-confidence that functions to balance and create suspense or fear in the reader when the 'seeing-man' sometimes fails to see. Pratt presents a symmetrical account of seeing and being seen that follows colonialism and post-colonialism. As such, description turns from the heroic authorial 'discoveries' of landscape through aestheticised descriptions to a readerly sense of exhaustion (representative of the exhausted landscape) that requires the similarly aestheticised gaze of the other.[36]

The figure of the 'seeing-man', though developed in the context of non-fictional travel writing, has been widely applied to fictional 'seeing-men'. This converts Pratt's useful historical critique into a diminution of fictional perspective, which does not rely on the perceptual, perspective-taking techniques of travel writing. The 'reality' of descriptions of foreign landscapes – despite the techniques of the 'seeing-man' – primarily rely on their authorisation; their aestheticisation is secondary. On the other hand, in the fictional text, the formal arrangements of space and perspective are foregrounded and the authorisation is secondary. The perspective of the 'seeing-man' in the fictional text instantiates the form of environment rather than its historical reality.

The use of this trope, in fiction, is often made complex by the representation of real places and foregrounds the representation of representation, or the reflexive use of the 'view from above' to invoke the reader's recognition of a place (real or imagined) and a mode (objective sight) in order to subvert it.[37] My interest in building off of Pratt comes from similar criticism by Erin James, who recognises that Pratt accurately and powerfully describes generic truths when it applies to travel writing, but through close reading it appears that the 'seeing-man', and so what is seen, is not always determinate and a signal of a unified, imperial project.[38] Accounting for imagination in addition to these framed perceptions can even strengthen Pratt's critique, while giving us more tools to extend her analysis. This challenges determinate associations with imagined height to actual height that do not account for the form of environment being described, instead focusing on the existence of the human figure as a symbol for power, rather than a figure located in the more indeterminate space of 'height' as strangely unfixed from distance where belonging can be modelled through this experience of the environment in its imaginary form, from above.

Another View from Above

The former accounts of aeriality and the view from above reduce the image to a single, historicised meaning. This is a valid and functional interpretation, but one that sentimentalises and exaggerates the function of aerial images through what Kaplan calls critics' unjustified presumption of the 'unified technodeterminism of aerial perception'.[39] Kaplan offers a singular critique of this sentimental narrative: it reduces the apparent dominance of the visual in modernity to a causal relationship with technological progress associated with speed, height and travel, which 'recur with a regularity that borders on scholarly obsession'.[40] Kaplan points out that this is a contradiction, as these critiques rely on a 'totalized vision that requires a single world, always already legible'; she argues that, on the other hand, what is most vital about aerial views and their representation is 'the possible presence of the unseen or unsensed'.[41] By shifting the binary from seer and seen – high and low – to the systems of imagination and affect that embody the viewer when encountering a view from above or its representation, Kaplan opens up a space of interpretation that foregrounds ambiguity rather than determinate systems of power symbolised by towers, aerial photography or mountain heights.

Another mode of access to the form of environment, as I have been suggesting, is the imaginary. This is a unique mode of access because it does not foreground actualities – as identified by Cosgrove as a part of history, as described by Pratt as constitutive of travel writing, by Barthes as constitutive of cultural structures, and by de Certeau as definitive of sight – but potentialities. The main difference is that perception is about how things (in this case the environment) appear; the imaginary involves cases of how they *might appear*. In addition, imaginary objects necessarily do not fit into these other organisational models; their existence does not cohere with rational laws or perceptual reality. Nonetheless, the imaginary is related to the environment as a negation of these modes of access. As Sartre terms it, the imaginary is the *world-negated*. In this way, it is a mode of access to the form of the actual environment in its imaginary valence. The imaginary object that is the subject of this book is literature, specifically literary description, and very specifically, descriptions of the environment from above. Indeed, Sartre writes not just that the image is the *world-negated*, but that it is specifically '*the world negated from a certain point of view*'.[42]

The organisation of urban space and the attendant systems for interpreting its meaning also play off the opposition between the view from above and the view from below. For Lefebvre, creating this 'readable' – or what he calls 'legible' – space is the work of the engineer or urban planner (as opposed to the architect), who use a top-down perspective to organise space. This type of work not only excludes the bottom-up perspective but, more importantly, it also discourages a synthesis of the two perspectives in a more productive construction of liveable space. Lefebvre, in opposition to Barthes and de Certeau, argues that this readability or legibility is in fact the antithesis of a valuable text:

> Visual legibility is even more treacherous and better ensnared (more precisely, ensnaring) than graphic legibility, that is, writing. Every legibility stems from a paucity: from redundance. The fullness of text and space never go together with legibility. No poetry or art obeys this simple criterion. At best legibility is blank, the poorest of texts![43]

The view from above is not intrinsically valuable because it affords access to readable structures (as it is for Barthes) nor dangerously 'fictional' (as it is for de Certeau) but as the signal toward a synthesis of perspectives that complement one another and balance legibility with openness – reality and fictionality.

Literary aerial imagination is not subject to the determinacy of perception or technological mediations of perception. Rather than icons of objectivity and progress, the literary image of the aerial view and the environmental forms it articulates are indeterminate spaces. Edward Soja follows Lefebvre and calls this blended view from above and view from below an example of his concept of 'thirdspace', which is a reaction to 'a tacit, if not exclusive, preference for the "view from below"' in critical theory.[44] The hierarchy privileging the view from below by blaming the view from above as part of the 'masculinist hegemony of the visible'[45] is not tenable for Soja for the same reason that Kaplan more recently identifies: it requires the belief in a singular, real world, shared by all who perceive, with all perspectives legible, available and totalisable in a singular interpretative system, epitomised in the view from above. Even privileging the 'view from below' in its actual or metaphorical forms reinforces a hierarchy that grants the view from above undue power. As Soja concludes: 'There is always an-Other view.'[46]

The view from above in fictional narrative, or what I call 'aerial description', affords consistent access to 'another view'. But my definition of aerial description differs in two ways from what I think Soja suggests: 'an-Other' is not necessarily a human subject, and the view can be imaginary rather than perceptual. This book uses literary aerial views as the material for its theorisation of the view from above rather than views from above in everyday life, urban planning, photography or cultural geography, as in previous analyses.

Literature is particularly valuable as it necessarily backgrounds the critical assumptions from these prior studies that the view from above is primarily visual and perceptual.

Form of Environment

The form of environment is the imaginary articulation of the environment in literary fiction. Through encounter with description of the environment in literature, the actual environment enters and influences literary form through its own specific set of affordances. The environmental/literary forms specific to aerial description studied in the next three chapters are extent, verticality and scale. In this section, I will show how my definition of form develops from the structural theories of Roman Ingarden as well as contemporary formalists.

The Spatial Form of Aesthetic Experience

The literary work of art affords a unique opportunity to encounter the environment by foregrounding its spatial form. Reading's spatial form has been backgrounded by attempts to plot temporality. Despite its continued reference as a classic study, Joseph Frank's essay 'Spatial Form in Modern Literature' did not launch a critical or philosophical legacy that can rival that of another fundamental text, Paul Ricœur's *Time and Narrative*. Roman Ingarden offers a curious argument about the essential spatiality of the literary text that subverts Ricœur's reader-oriented focus: 'Usually one says that the literary and the musical work are both works of "temporal" art and means by that they are temporally extended. As plausible as this may appear at first, it is false, and arises from the confusion of the literary work itself with its concretisations, which are constituted when the work is read.'[47] The theoretical division between the work and its concretisations is an important starting point for analysing how the work is related to the environment it references, which, like the environment, stands apart from our 'concretisations', or experiences, of it.

Consider a metaphor that Ingarden provides for the onset of aesthetic experience:

> To take an example: how often when walking a mountain path – occupied with paying attention to the details of the way, which is not always safe – we are involuntarily 'struck' with the so-called

beauty of the landscape. Then we stop automatically. The details of the bends of the path we had climbed up to the summit have turned uninteresting; we have no time for them, something else is 'attracting' us now.[48]

This is an illustration of what Ingarden terms the 'primary aesthetic emotion' that sets off the encounter with the literary work of art. It is a *'change of attitude* from a practical one, assumed in everyday life, or from an investigating one, to an aesthetic attitude', in which something 'strikes' us, 'imposes itself on us', and brings about 'astonishment that it is "such a one".'[49] This is the movement toward the *'secluded whole'* of the work of art, where the reader is afforded the possibility to carry the momentum of the preliminary emotion into this autonomous stream.[50] The error of the passive consumer of art is to praise the work as beautiful in itself, imposing our own 'improvements' upon it by interpreting this emotion as part of the object.[51] The effort to encounter the aesthetic object driven by the preliminary emotion should be to think about these new, 'attractive' qualities not as part of what qualifies the object as *real* (really beautiful), but as a prompt to explore the object 'with a view to finding in it such qualities as would give with the initial quality a *harmony of qualities*'.[52] This is the act of processing the work of art into a personal arrangement, or concretisation, communicable as an interpretation that is a necessarily selective but simultaneously complete encounter with the work of art.

Engagement with the literary work of art is active and generates a complex ontology of reference and referent. 'Truth in literature', for Ingarden, flows from 'quasi-judgments' that 'progress beyond the world' to create the literary world.[53] Importantly, quasi-judgment does not imply quasi-reality or even quasi-form and some kind of lack, but that the referents are concretised and brought into the work of art from experience, as a 'blend'.[54] Ingarden's hiking metaphor is not as simple as it seems: the image evokes, without directly describing, the view from above. The path is effaced – though Ingarden minimally describes that it is 'not always safe', with bends and a summit – and the landscape overwhelms. But the turn toward the aerial view is not the primary move away from 'everyday life', as the climb itself is set apart; the aerial image is a doubly secluded whole.

Applied distinctly to the literary work of art, and fiction in particular, this metaphor tracks most accessibly onto the typical conceptualisation of temporal narrative progression, where every element refers back to narrativity: the plot advances by new events that perturb the system and so momentarily invite a pause to 'widen' the view and invite further avenues of progress – continuing his metaphor – along a different path, across the valley, to 'set up camp' or advance down the mountain. In this conceptualisation, descriptive 'pauses' that open up to the view from above are merely, as Alexander Gelley puts it, 'analyzed as micro-narratives which need to be assimilated to a larger narrative pattern'.[55]

But an alternative, spatial interpretation of this metaphor also applies: narrative is the path and description instantiates visionary 'pauses' that are part of the pattern – or form – of environment, not just the narrative. The former interpretation provides the dominant model for narrative in the literary work of art. The most robust paradigm is David Herman's conceptualisation of 'story logic', which is event-based, or James Phelan's often-quoted rhetorical definition of narrative as 'Someone telling somebody else on some occasion and for some purpose(s) that something happened.'[56] Foregrounding description may rephrase this to represent the reading experience more accurately: 'Someone *describing something while* telling somebody else on some occasion and for some purpose(s) that something happened.'

Present in Ingarden's image is not only the metaphorical hike up a mountain, but also the form of an actual mountain that affords its recognition in this minimal description. Through lived experience, the reader knows what it is like to put forth an effort and climb to a height and see; equally (or maybe exclusively) he or she has experienced the reverie associated with imagining the view from a height. The literary work of art is the third space on the indeterminate edge of these different intentional relationships to environment: fictional descriptions of the view from above are structured through reference to the recognisable features of the real environment seen from above, but the 'climb' to the imaginary height of this 'secluded whole' follows the subjectivity of the individual's aesthetic attitude.

New Formalism and Narrative

Literary description – particularly aerial description – is one of the most effective forces in undoing the supposed determinacies of perception. By bringing the formal arrangement of the nonhuman world into literary and cultural criticism, ecocriticism's interdisciplinary reach has been, in some sense, fulfilling the inclusive version of formalism evident in Ingarden, which is not about rejecting 'content' as such, but about foregrounding formal relations between the superficially very separate worlds of subjects and objects – humans and nonhumans. Another early structuralist, Jan Mukařovský, highlights this approach:

> The analysis of 'form' must not be narrowed to a mere formal analysis. On the other hand, however, it must be made clear that only the *entire* construction of the work, and not just the part called 'content,' enters into an active relation with the system of life values which govern human affairs.[57]

The dominant strain in all waves of ecocriticism has been an analysis of content-level interactions with the environment and associated concepts.[58] Recently, critics influenced by narrative theory have begun to consider how what Mukařovský's calls 'the *entire* construction of the work' functions in the context of the 'formal' knowledge of the environmental sciences.[59]

Ecocriticism not only benefits from a rereading of space and indeterminacy in the structuralists, as outlined above, but it also benefits from contemporary criticism that has renewed attention to form. Caroline Levine has recognised the effectiveness of formalist approaches in developing a method for functionalising literary art as a part of a New Formalism, which seems to look a lot like the 'old' formalism of Mukařovský and others that has been backgrounded for some time. She describes the reading experience as an encounter with latent potential, or affordances: 'Rather than asking what artists intend or even what forms *do*, we can ask instead what potentialities lie latent – though not always obvious – in aesthetic and social arrangements.'[60] Because literary critics are adept at recognising and interpreting literary forms, she sees a similar ground for study in social forms, such as wholes, rhythms, hierarchies and networks, which she analyses in and out of literature in her book, *Forms*. The main concern here is not in the activist claims Levine makes for a New Formalism, but in her willingness to draw direct lines between literary form and social form.

These lines can also be drawn between literary form and the form of environment, or the ways that literary images articulate the environment. The form of literary description holds the latent potential to disrupt what is normally perceived as real in other mediations of the environment. This latent potential is evident in the tension between readability and illegibility in Barthes and de Certeau as described above, as well as determinacy and indeterminacy in the reading experience in Ingarden. These are accounts of perception and general aesthetic experience, respectively, so my analysis of the forms of literary description and their specific affordances for articulating the form of environment picks up on a related, third mode, literary narrative.

Though it is not her primary subject, Levine develops a unique definition of narrative and its function:

> The form that best captures the experience of colliding forms is narrative. [. . .] What narrative form affords is a careful attention to the ways in which forms come together, and what happens when and after they meet.[61]

> I have not understood literary texts in this book as reflections or expressions of prior social forms, but rather as sites, like social situations, where multiple forms move surprisingly easy across social and literary contexts, and narratives are among the very best forms for identifying and tracking the unfolding of relations among different forms.[62]

Levine is interested in what happens after a narrative's end, in how the forms that clash within the novel continue to perturb everyday concepts. In this way, she sees political power extend directly from the existence of the literary work of art.

There is also an internal clash in the text that splits her homogeneous definition of 'narrative' into a clash between elements within the text: part of what produces the lasting, futural effects of the literary text is the collision between the temporality of narrative and the spatiality of description. This collision is amplified when it is not just the human, social forms at play in narrative, as Levine considers in *Forms*, but the nonhuman form of environment that disrupts narrative through its introduction in description.

De-forming Description

Gaston Bachelard writes that imagination 'deforms what we perceive'.[63] I want to use this idea to mobilise the ways that description uses the affordances of language for an encounter with the images of the form of environment (and I will elaborate further on deformation in Chapter 3). The novel – in addition to being a site for social forms to collide, as Levine argues – stages the collision inherent in the very attempt to integrate these nonhuman forms into human discourse, which can be seen in the clash between description and narration, and more specifically, as I am arguing here, description and environment. Philippe Hamon presents a provocative version of this argument: 'description is the point where the narrative comes to a temporary halt, while continuing to organize itself: [. . .] it can thus be seen that the fundamental characteristic of realist discourse is to deny, to make impossible, the narrative, any narrative'.[64] For Hamon, description is not the primary vessel of the 'reality effect' in narrative, but it has a more radical possible function: it jams narrativity.

I am differentiating the *form* of environment from just *the* environment or 'form of *the environment*' because it is useful to denaturalise the way we think about the interrelation between figure and ground, in this case human and environment. Thinking about the forms of each allows us to consider how their organisational principles creatively collide with each other and disrupt a coherent, non-contradictory conceptualisation of either term. In the case of literature, the novel as a mode stages this collision of the form of description and the form of environment; when the environment is described the affordances of both the particular environment and the affordances of descriptive language limit and alter each other.

Naturalised reading practice treats human figures as nodes to which all discursive technique connects. My goal is to avoid reading this experience into our formal typologies for narrative – which revolves around the rational coherence between the way the ground is described and the status of the figure – and to read descriptions of the environment from above as formal articulations of the environment, how the environment itself is the node which gathers and determines narrative discourse.

My use of the term 'form of environment' follows this emphasis on imagination and indeterminacy and links with the methods of New Formalism: the form of environment is part of the essential structure of the 'total environment' that can be accessed only through encounter with the imaginary.[65] The environment can be seen via perception in daily life, its perception can be mediated by visual art and artefacts, or its encounter can be structured by architecture. But the literary text – specifically fictional narrative – functions to subvert these varyingly determinate modes by suspending, or negating, the primacy of perception. As Bachelard puts it in the epigraph for this book: 'There is no reality that precedes the literary image.'[66] The 'real' environment is not available in the encounter with the descriptive image because the literary text cannot reproduce the frame of reference of the real system, but instead utilises the affordances of literary form to articulate the form of environment that is recognisable to the reader. This also works in reverse:

as the form of the text 'overlaps' with the form of environment in description, then the 'reality' that may later appear to the reader in perception is influenced by this imaginary structure.

The function of description in the overall experience of the literary work becomes a key question. Does it also have the lasting, futural thrust as Levine sees in narrative? Levine is not alone in privileging narrative as the dominant paradigm for defining the form of a literary work. Hamon has challenged this hegemony by criticising prior theories for only dealing with forms that are the most recognisable because they function as positive constructions rather than disruptive forms: 'description might be that place in the text where the generative power of language might show itself most clearly and as quite unmanageable'.[67]

Narrative theory has put a lot of energy in 'managing' descriptive language at the expense of a less anthropocentric idea of literature that places the environment as the organising feature rather than human discourse strategies related to speech, oral storytelling or perceptual experientiality. For example, Gérard Genette views description, though somewhat ambivalently, as necessarily subordinate:

> description could be conceivable independent of narration, but one never actually finds it in a free state. Narration cannot exist without description, but this dependence does not stop it from always playing the first role. The description is naturally *ancilla narratienis* [the handmaiden of the narration], the slave always necessary, always submissive, never emancipated. Narrative genres like the epic, the short story, the novella, the novel, do exist where description can occupy a very large place, indeed the largest, without ceasing to be, by vocation, a simple auxiliary of narrative. However, purely descriptive genres never exist, and we can hardly imagine a work where the narrative acts as auxiliary to the description, outside of the didactic domain or semididactic fiction like that of Jules Verne.[68]

Genette's slavery metaphor picks up interestingly on Hamon's comments about 'unmanageability'. Though Genette sees real, subversive and independent power in description, it is necessarily put into check and controlled by the dominant, normative (and we could say naturalised) experience of narrativity. Again, like with the ideological interpretations of description of the environment from above, I do not want to deny that the experience of even the most unconventional narrative texts often fit under the category of narrativity. But the role of description in these texts becomes even more important when foregrounding the role of the form of environment encountered in these texts.

Throughout narratology, description orbits around narrativity. David Herman elides description's particular role in articulating the environment and instead claims that it is narrativity that gives us access to certain aspects of the world: 'narrative does not merely reflect spatial categorizations of experience but furthermore is one of the chief means by which people go about building spatial representations of a world that they could not otherwise begin to experience at all'.[69] For Herman, narrative is a primary mode of access to the world, particularly spatially, and he makes further claims about how narrative necessarily integrates description to build these representations of the world. There is no metaphorical imagery of narrative as the master over description the slave; Herman's arguments claim scientific authority through cognitive science. Description is a component of cognitive mapping for Herman – hence the representational language surrounding 'narrative domains' and 'mental models' – and this process, when in the context of narrative discourse, is integrated ('managed'), and so the spatial supplement to narrative temporality.

The poetic image – particularly aerial views – exists independently of a perceiving agent, and literary descriptions of the environment offer us consistent access to the object as independent of a perceiver, because the arbitrary organisation is, indeed, 'natural': it follows the affordances of the actual environment. Casey's deconstruction of the term 'description' makes this clear: 'Not only do [topographic maps] furnish the perimeters that are the stock-in-trade of a purely cartographic representation of a land mass; they also de-scribe – literally, "draw a line around" – the local features that make a place that *particular* place and no other.'[70] Casey's definition of description in early mapmaking is 'to draw a line around'. Through the use of a general form – lines – topographic maps foreground particularity. He is talking about a different kind of description with mapmaking, which makes geographical truth claims, but at the same time both reading maps and reading texts are about a reader's relationship to a particular environment. In this case, Casey's definition makes sense even applied to description embedded in fictional texts: the environments themselves are not 'fictional' just because they are embedded in fictional narrative, nor do they necessarily carry the 'signposts of fictionality'. Rather, they carry the signposts of reality – the form of environment – description as 'drawing an imaginary line around' what can possibly be seen to make its form available to the reader.

Indeterminacy

Finally, my third central concept, indeterminacy, is the primary value of encounter with the form of environment in aerial description. Literary fiction undermines attempts to define the function of the environment in daily life. Thus, indeterminacy in literature presents a 'sustainable model' for feeding back into and subverting the perception of the environment.[71]

Imaginary Spaces and Real Environments

To continue with Ingarden's hiking image quoted above, the shift of attention from difficult path to surprising panorama is possible because of the specific form of environment one encounters when hiking up a mountain. It involves a conventional, perceptual relationship between human figure and environment that is patterned by wayfinding navigation. The 'expected expectation' of this system of hiker, path and mountain is the insignificance of the hazardous path as defined by a safe and sublime endpoint (or waypoint) from which to begin a return or plan the next summit. But in the fictional literary text, this *perceptual* 'expected expectation' is subverted by the foregrounding of the *imaginary* spatial form of environment.

Wolfgang Iser extends Ingarden's theory of 'truth in fiction' through an explanation of systems and their limits. For Iser, the literary work, by nature of its limitations and inability to reproduce a real frame of reference, always exists just beyond the edge of reality. In this way, 'As a medium, [literature] can only show all determinacy to be illusory.'[72] The origin of this illusory determinacy is to be found in the model of reality to which the text refers, which Iser terms the 'repertoire'. This is the set of social norms and conventions that define behaviour and setting in a way recognisable to the reader, who is thus situated at a point of a 'stabilization of certain expectations'.[73] What is valuable about literary fiction's interaction with the repertoire is that it thrusts the reader into an open space (Iser calls it an 'open event') in which expectations are constantly revealed to be radically uncertain and indeterminate rather than a basic and stable method for prediction:

> The literary text, however, interferes with this structure, for generally it takes the prevalent thought system or social system as its context, but does not reproduce the frame of reference which stabilizes these systems. Consequently, it cannot produce those 'expected expectations'

which are provided by the system. What it can and does do is set up a parallel frame within which meaningful patterns are to form. [. . .] Instead of reproducing the system to which it refers, it almost invariably tends to take as its dominant 'meaning' those possibilities that have been neutralized or negated by that system. If the basic reference of the text is to the penumbra of excluded possibilities, one might say that the borderlines of existing systems are the starting point for the literary text. It begins to activate that which the system has left inactive.[74]

In addition to 'thought' and 'social' systems, the environment can be considered a system in Iser's sense as a node for organising the perceptual and imaginary frames of reference from which human figures encounter their surroundings.

Ingarden and Iser are both referring to systems of cultural meaning and social behaviour as regards human interpersonal systems. Iser's examples are all about apparently novel behaviour that is integrated into an acceptable and functional system of human relationships in the literary work. Aerial description presents a different case where a human figure encounters the nonhuman environment, in which case the negated, inactive mode of interaction is not new, revolutionary or unrecognisable behaviour, but the imaginary form of environment that is dominated by the perception of the environment prevalent in daily life. This is the function of Pratt's trope of the 'seeing-man', discussed above: it possibly exists in daily life and shapes actual systems of oppression instantiated in imperialism and globalisation, but its use in fiction negates this normal function in order to present alternate, imaginary affordances of the aerial view.

While the perceptual system relating human figure and environment changes rapidly with the advancement of technology, literary description affords the possibility to encounter the negated experiences of environment that are the consequences of technological progress. Consider the different methods of achieving an aerial view of the environment: hiking up an established path for recreation, wayfaring and discovering a path, viewing a painted landscape, a printed photograph from a balloon or kite, riding in an aeroplane, viewing photographs from an aeroplane, looking down from low-Earth orbit, viewing satellite images, seeing the Earth from the moon. Each presents a new phenomenological relationship between human and environment. Each establishes sets of 'expected expectations' that determine what is perceived: a beautiful view, a new area, a landscape, a panorama, a geographical space, a territory, the 'whole Earth'. Literature subverts these expected expectations by destabilising perceptual systems of reference to the environment, instead presenting an encounter with the environment's imaginary form. The above instances of aerial viewing are shifted from their contexts of determinate and objective points of view by subverting expectations through foregrounding the environment's form and not the content of what is seen.

That is, through the view from above the subject encounters the environment in a way that has the potential to suspend these perceptions and foreground the imaginary. Iser puts it succinctly: 'frame of reference is imaginary and not real, and it initiates a process of communication through transformation of positions, as opposed to pinpointing of information and grouping of data'.[75] The conflation of the perceptual realities of the aerial view and the imaginary work of literary description is the main issue with previous studies of the view from above. The assumption of these studies is that the literary text groups data about perception, however chaotically, whereas, from this perspective, the literary text can only complicate data, not represent it.

As such, literature's challenge to the determinacies of the actual is foregrounded in the act of fictionalisation, which draws together real and imaginary: '[Fictionalising] leads the real to the imaginary and the imaginary to the real, and it thus conditions the extent to which a given world is to be transcoded, a nongiven world is to be conceived, and the reshuffled worlds are to be made accessible to the reader's experience.'[76] Here Iser more precisely identifies the elements that make up what Ingarden calls the 'harmony of qualities' of the literary work of art: while these qualities may be reducible to literary figures, their impact is notable because of the way they reshuffle the significance of our familiar, given world and a novel, nongiven world of the text. This is most evident in the description of the environment. While the fidelity or determinacy of a historical human figure in a fictional work can be debated (albeit naively), these same issues are not present when comparing 'given' and 'nongiven' elements of an environmental figure in a fictional work. This is because literary form has the unique ability to harmonise with other, nonhuman environmental forms, an effect being recognised as literary criticism moves toward a more pervasive concern with the environment.

Redefining Indeterminacy

Indeterminacy has become an important concept for thinking about the contemporary environment, destabilising anthropocentric perspectives in ways also useful to revising the conventions of reading and the literary work of art in the Ingarden-Iser tradition. In particular, Kathryn Yusoff is interested in the 'indetermining forces' of ecological relations, Anahid Nersessian has developed the idea of 'nescience' as regards the role of literature in history, and Christine Marran has developed a model of 'obligate storytelling' that emerges from the traumas of the nonhuman world.[77]

Ingarden's strict ontological division between the intentional objects of the literary work of art and the objects as they exist in actual life is a valuable interpretation of 'truth in literature', but its implications do not exclude the value of its opposite. From Ingarden's phenomenologically precise, anthropocentric point of view, both the fictional and the actual worlds require different modes of intention to access their objects. New Materialist philosophy attempts to reverse this intentionality. Jane Bennet argues that 'human intentions [are] always in competition and confederation with many other strivings [. . .]: it vibrates and merges with other currents, to affect and be affected. This understanding of agency does not deny the existence of that thrust called intentionality, but it does see it as less definitive of outcomes.'[78] In the case of literary description of the environment, as a space of indeterminacy, the nonhuman form of environment (or, as Bennett would term it, the environment's 'agency') merges with the human intentionality that is the use of literary form, indeterminately affecting the outcome.

From the perspective of the object – for example, a river valley – existing apart from the arrow of human intentionality, it can be articulated in the products of two types of intentionality, perceptual or imaginary. If the ontological status of the judgments or quasi-judgments of the human subject changes in, say, the utterance in news reportage or a fictional novel, so can the river valley appear in its 'real form' as articulated in either mode. Given a literary fictional form, the actual environment finds its imaginary form articulated through its embeddedness – a re-implacement – in a new context. The river valley is still formed by its extent (the body of water stretches out into space), its verticality (it exists as a function of tiered spatial relationships between bed and cliff) and its scale (its existence is dependent on its size relative to a creek or the ocean). This form, recognisable in literary description, affords its articulation in the literary image. At the same time, the referent of the description – to follow Ingarden – could never be the Rio Grande as such: 'if such objects are to appear in literature at all and if the reader's attention is to be drawn to them rather than to real objects, the sentences that describe them must not be judgments. Otherwise, the intention would be aimed directly at real objects, while the created purely intentional ones would escape the reader's attention altogether.'[79] But, as a continuous presentation of literary and environmental forms, the described environment in its indeterminate relation to the actual environment becomes included – positively added to – both an image of the river valley in general and also whatever 'Rio Grande' means to the reader. The form of environment is made available by literary description and is indeterminately related to both the fictional and the actual.

The upshot of this redefinition of quasi-judgments as they relate to descriptions of environment is the potential for literature to intervene in the 'environmental imagination' associated with a particular landscape. Such an assumption is already the foundation of Lawrence Buell's project to define the 'environmental imagination', as it relates to the nineteenth-century United States and the milieu of the transcendentalists. But the theoretical foundations of imagination in this concept of the environmental imagination have not been articulated, and accounting for how the reader can read or think 'ecologically' without naïve errors as pertains judgments of the literary work of art is necessary for moving forward a mature study of environment in literature.

Indeterminacy is a concept rooted decisively in the present and rethinking its relevance to modes of reading in general is an important step to thinking about the role of speculation and, more specifically, fiction in society. Ingarden's indeterminacy has drifted, indirectly, from literary theory into cultural theory. For example, Yusoff speculates about the changes that foregrounding indeterminacy over determinacy would have in our daily relationship with the world, in a sense, treating our economic relationships as ecological. Indeterminate relations are utilised differently in both systems: in capitalism, the relatively indeterminate world of nonhuman subjects is exploited (her example is the use of oil dispersants to make toxic effects non-local and thus difficult to prove, much less detect), while in nature indeterminate relations between all kinds of subjects lead to an open, flexible and adaptive system. She argues:

> If the planetary gifts of capitalism cannot be subject to restitution and exchange (you can exchange carbon, but not climate change; you can exchange ecosystem services, but not extinction), then there is a 'missing economy' of indeterminacy at play that is intrinsic to, and subtends, the possibility for exchange in the logics of capitalism.[80]

As I have defined indeterminacy in its relation to fictional environments above, I am proposing that literature is part of this '"missing economy" of indeterminacy'. This 'missing part of the economy of environmental relations'[81] is to be found past the edge of the real systems Yusoff describes; it is the space of fiction. The fictive system that includes the environment embedded in a literary narrative is another manifestation of the essential indeterminacy that Yusoff identifies as active both when capitalism exploits the indeterminate origins and effects of its toxic by-products and as an alternative economy utilises the indeterminate effects of gifts within this system. Aerial descriptions embody the 'missing economy' of indeterminacy by confronting the reader with the collision of forms between the real affordances of a familiar landscape and the fictional affordance of its formation in the literary context.

Conclusion

The position outlined above treads the line of valuing what Val Plumwood calls the 'sado-dispassionate' mode of distanced observation. She resoundingly critiques normalisations of disengagement justified as rational and objective analysis (she is aiming at scientific reason, but the same would apply to formalist literary criticism), which claim to obtain 'the passive and "neutral" reception of raw, "pure" observational data by presocial individuals'.[82] This position may look similar to my definition of the form of environment as directly articulated in literary description, in which I have indeed not mentioned the author – the ur-describer – and so have implicitly constructed this figure as 'presocial'. This is the basic, familiar attack of all critiques of formalism. I will briefly respond to this type of critique here, but as the subsequent chapters make clear, backgrounding the concept of the actual or implied author does not compromise an engaged contextual criticism, which I am approaching here by bringing form into the realm of ecocriticism, specifically.

It does not exclude the work of postcolonial scholars who have written on the view from above, such as Pratt, but builds on their work through negation, particularly by redefining 'presocial' to mean 'nonhuman' and experimentally considering the literary work of art as independent of human perception. As Ingarden puts it:

> With reference to the work itself, however, it is evident that, once it has come to exist, it exists *simultaneously* in *all* of its parts and that none of these parts is 'earlier' or 'later' in a temporal sense. Thus the work itself is not a formation that develops and is extended temporally on the axis of its 'beginning' and 'end.'[83]

Ingarden argues that when we call literature a temporal medium (as opposed to the concrete spatiality of painting), we confuse our experience of it – certainly extended in time – with its existence, in space. From this perspective, the literary work or any of its parts is not considered 'presocial' in Plumwood's sense, as it exists simultaneously in relation to other objects, some of which happen to be 'natural' and are included within the work itself – the ontological twist that gives literature its primary originality and authority. Jennifer Wenzel presents a similar criticism as Plumwood, with a bit more leniency. She sees how 'the *autonomy* of the text in the New Criticism might be analogous to the *alterity* of nature or the planet in contemporary environmental thought'.[84] Though she acknowledges the problems in which the critic attempts to efface him- or herself by asserting this autonomy, putting it in relation to the consistently ignored environment demonstrates an important function of the literary text to challenge not just the 'dispassionate' critic, but his or her anthropocentric bias.

The main issue that Plumwood finds in 'sado-dispassionate' reasoning is the construction of subject/object dualism as well as affective disengagement. On the other hand, the present theory of aerial description evokes a kind of object/object dualism, with the environment and the literary text in correspondence with one another. My interpretation is that the evocation of spatial distance in the view from above stages the conventional subject/object split, but the indeterminacy of literary description most frequently subverts this anthropocentric position by directly entangling the reader in an encounter with the form of environment. Unlike in photographic views from above, the moment is not stilled in either time or perceptual space but demands the reader to confront the dynamism of concrete spatiality presented in a linguistic medium. That is, the literary work of art as a spatial object is complete and open to encounter in a variety of ways. As Anežka Kuzmičová has pointed out in experimental studies of reading, imagination is a bodily engaged activity. The embodied aspects of reading are not directly addressed here, but the evidence of both kinaesthetic engagement and enactive construction of storyworlds asserts that what is conventionally thought of as 'disengagement' with reality – that is, foregrounding imagination – is not to be opposed to 'engagement' that explicitly foregrounds affect, bodily situatedness and subjectivity.[85]

As the title of Plumwood's book argues, she is interested in reasserting 'recognition' to help solve 'the ecological crisis of reason'. My book offers the encounter with the environment in literary description as one way of recognising the ways nonhuman forms influence what is thought of as the exclusively 'human' space of imagination. Rather than privileging the view, the act of viewing, or the subject that performs the viewing, I primarily isolate these instances as an example of how 'environment' is uncritically co-defined in previous studies of aerial imagery, and how foregrounding nonhuman forms challenges the norms of literary criticism.

Latour in particular is interested in redefining a new 'attractor' for political and social action in the present. He calls this 'the terrestrial' – his attempt at redefining the 'environment' as inclusive of human and nonhuman actors.[86] Similarly, my approach recognises the form of environment as 'another world' that finds its articulation by colliding with and shaping the human forms of narrative. In the chapters that follow, I open this analysis up to three articulations of this other world, specifically as humans like to formulate them as 'frontiers': the Great Plains in Chapter 2, postcolonial North Africa in Chapter 3 and the 'final frontier' of the cosmic in Chapter 4.

Notes

1. Edward S. Casey, *Representing Place*, xiii; emphasis in original.
2. Ibid., 30. Throughout this book, I will retain Casey's specific spelling of 'implacement' rather than 'emplacement' to signal the adaptation of his concept for aerial description.
3. Ibid., 236.
4. See Marie-Laure Ryan et al., *Narrating Space / Spatializing Narrative*, for study of actual place names in literary texts.
5. James J. Gibson, *The Ecological Approach to Visual Perception*, 127.
6. See Patrick Ellis, *Aeroscopics*.
7. Roland Barthes, *A Barthes Reader*, 238; emphasis in original.
8. Ibid., 241–42.
9. Ibid., 243. This follows Claude Lévi-Strauss, who also saw the readability of the aerial view opening up to ideal societal structures. See Jeanne Hafner, *The View from Above*, 74–75.
10. Michel de Certeau, *The Practice of Everyday Life*, 92.
11. Barthes, *A Barthes Reader*, 242.
12. de Certeau, *The Practice of Everyday Life*, 92.
13. Barthes, *A Barthes Reader*, 242.
14. de Certeau, *The Practice of Everyday Life*, 92.
15. Barthes, *A Barthes Reader*, 244.
16. Denis Cosgrove, *Apollo's Eye*, x.
17. Cosgrove, 'The Measures of America', 8.

18. Ibid., 8.
19. Ibid., 4–5.
20. Ibid., 3.
21. See Bruno Latour, *Down to Earth*, 100–06.
22. For Latour's redefinition of the terms of globalisation, see *Down to Earth*, 82–90.
23. Cosgrove, *Apollo's Eye*, x.
24. See Rochelle Johnson, *Passions for Nature*, and specifically as it relates to literature and painting, Michaela Keck, *Walking in the Wilderness*; Michelle Kohler, *Miles of Stare*.
25. See James Krasner, *The Entangled Eye*; John Conron, *American Picturesque*.
26. Angela Miller, 'Everywhere and Nowhere', 213.
27. Elisa New, 'Beyond the Romance Theory of American Vision', 384.
28. An excellent example of this is Anne McClintock's exploration of the military-enforced media ban that blocked aerial coverage of the Deepwater Horizon event in the Gulf Coast in 2010. In her case, it was achieving the view from above that provides the opportunity to resist the official project of oil extraction and its imperial, militarised origins.
29. Hannah Arendt, 'Man's Conquest of Space', 539.
30. See Hafner, *The View from Above*, 106.
31. Caren Kaplan, *Aerial Aftermaths*, 209.
32. Heather Houser, *Infowhelm*, 180.
33. Mary Louise Pratt, *Imperial Eyes*, 202.
34. Ibid., 202.
35. Ibid., 205.
36. Ibid., 220.
37. See also Anne Baker, *Heartless Immensity*, 87 for an example of how Pratt's thesis fails to obtain in Herman Melville's novel *Typee*.
38. Erin James, *The Storyworld Accord*, 130.
39. Kaplan, 11.
40. Ibid., 9.
41. Ibid., 3.
42. See Jean-Paul Sartre, *The Psychology of Imagination*, 265–70; emphasis in original.
43. Henri Lefebvre, *Writings on Cities*, 312.
44. Edward W. Soja, *Thirdspace*, 313.
45. Ibid., 313.
46. Ibid., 314.
47. Roman Ingarden, *The Literary Work of Art*, 305.
48. Ingarden, 'Aesthetic Experience and Aesthetic Object', 297. See also Ingarden, *The Cognition of the Literary Work of Art*, §24, for an expanded version of the quoted passages from this earlier article.
49. Ibid., 296; emphasis in original.
50. Ibid., 298; emphasis in original.

51. Ibid., 302.
52. Ibid., 304; emphasis in original.
53. Ingarden, 'On So-Called Truth in Literature', 137.
54. Ibid., 161–62; See also Ingarden, *The Literary Work of Art*, 68.
55. Alexander Gelley, 'Premises for a Theory of Description', 77.
56. James Phelan, *Living to Tell About It*, 18.
57. Jan Mukařovský, *Aesthetic Function, Norm, and Value as Social Facts*, 89; emphasis in original.
58. See Lawrence Buell, *The Future of Environmental Criticism*, 31–40 for an analysis of 'first-wave' and revisionist ecocriticism's 'preoccupation with questions of factical accuracy of environmental representation'.
59. See, for example, Erin James, *The Storyworld Accord*; Alexa Weik von Mossner, *Affective Ecologies*; Marco Caracciolo, *Narrating the Mesh*.
60. Caroline Levine, *Forms*, 6–7.
61. Ibid., 19.
62. Ibid., 122.
63. Gaston Bachelard, *Air and Dreams*, 1.
64. Philippe Hamon, 'What is a Description?', 332.
64. In narrative theory, the concept of 'total space' recurs in early theories of spatiality and narrative; see Gabriel Zoran, 'Towards a Theory of Space in Narrative'; Ruth Ronen, 'Space in Fiction'. As such, this idea that the narrative work itself makes up the totality of the space that affects its existence has recurred throughout recent narrative theory; see also David Herman, 'Spatial Reference in Narrative Domains'. Gerald Prince has recently challenged this bias in an approach to which this dissertation is sympathetic: he calls for less study of 'space in narrative' and instead to focus on 'narrative in space'. See David Rodriguez, 'Description in Space'.
66. Gaston Bachelard, *Air and Dreams*, 249
67. Hamon, 'Rhetorical Status of the Descriptive', 25.
68. Gérard Genette, 'Boundaries of Narrative', 6.
69. Herman, *Story Logic*, 298.
70. Casey, *Representing Place*, 156; emphasis in original.
71. The term 'sustainable model' comes from Levine, 'Three Unresolved Debates', 1243: 'I am working to understand how we might use formalist methods to design and enact effective political and aesthetic strategies and how we might successfully build social forms that afford better, fairer, more sustainable models of collective life than those that organize us now.'
72. Wolfgang Iser, *The Fictive and the Imaginary*, xi.
73. Iser, *The Act of Reading*, 69.
74. Ibid., 70.
75. Ibid., 99.
76. Iser, *The Fictive and the Imaginary*, 4.
77. See Anahid Nersessian, 'Two Gardens'; Christine L. Marran, *Ecology Without Culture*.

78. Jane Bennett, *Vibrant Matter*, 21.
79. Ingarden, 'On So-Called Truth in Literature', 161.
80. Kathryn Yusoff, 'Indeterminate Subjects, Irreducible Worlds', 91.
81. Ibid., 99.
82. Val Plumwood, *Environmental Culture*, 43.
83. Ingarden, *The Literary Work of Art*, 306; emphasis in original.
84. Jennifer Wenzel, 'Planet vs Globe', 24; emphasis in original.
85. See Anežka Kuzmičová, 'Presence in the Reading of Literary Narrative: A Case for Motor Enactment'; for a comprehensive overview, see Marco Caracciolo and Karin Kukkonen, *With Bodies: Narrative Theory and Embodied Cognition*.
86. See Latour, *Down to Earth*, 67.

Chapter 2

Extent, Built Form and Willa Cather's Landscapes

In 1936, Willa Cather briefly introduced her essay collection *Not Under Forty* with a famous proclamation: 'The world broke in two in 1922 or thereabouts.' While this ambiguous break has been argued to refer to her personal life, literary history, American culture or as a key to her experiments with narrative form,[1] I will offer a material account for this sense of rupture. Specifically, the early 1920s mark a change in how the environment was depicted and described in both image and language. Cather's fiction is a site in which the form of environment, aerial photography and the poetic image clash, disrupting realist narrative form and acting as the catalyst for her development as an experimental modernist. She described her work *Death Comes for the Archbishop* (1927) as a 'narrative' rather than a novel,[2] which has cued critics to draw contrasts between the narrative structures of her earlier novels and the work after her 1923 Pulitzer Prize-winning World War I novel *One of Ours*.[3] But flagging 'narrative' as the crucial hinge in her work over-emphasises its role as the break between her early and late works. This has resulted in a strengthening of the binary in literary criticism between narrative and description, and backgrounds descriptive technique, particularly for presenting the environment, throughout her work. In this chapter I will compare her late novel *Death Comes for the Archbishop* with her second novel *O Pioneers!* as representative of her work before *One of Ours*.

While not wanting to overemphasise the definitiveness of Cather's statement, I will use the early 1920s as a point from which to track the different ways the form of environment appears in her work. The shift in her descriptions of the environment – in this case the Great Plains and the Southwest – can be tracked alongside material progress in other modes of descriptive technique: specifically, the relationship between flight, aerial photography and transportation during the rapid commercialisation and popularisation of aviation in the 1920s. But rather than construct a direct, mimetic relationship between literary representation and photography, the goal here is to tease out the basic shifts in environmental imagination that are afforded by the collision between foregrounded literary description of the environment and the form of environment it expresses. As such, the focus turns away from what Lawrence Buell identifies as ecocriticism's 'continued interest in the matching, or non-matching, of wordscape and worldscape that takes quite varied forms'[4] toward the way aesthetic form (such as aerial description) and the form of environment (such as its extent) are encountered in the reading experience. This is a specific application of Caroline Levine's reformulation of narrative as an open space rather than a fixed closure, put succinctly in her claim that 'The form that best captures the experience of colliding forms is narrative.'[5] As Cather emphasised, her later works are collections of 'narratives' and so not stories enclosed within the mode of the novel; her novels are the site of collision between the forms of realistic description and the actual environment described.

Cather was not alone in making sweeping proclamations about ruptures driven by modernity; Virginia Woolf made a similar claim for 1910. And in his 1911 essay, 'The Genteel Tradition in American Philosophy', George Santayana identifies not a distinctively split world but a pervasive division in the spirit of the United States:

> The truth is that one-half of the American mind, that not occupied intensely in practical affairs, has remained, I will not say high-and-dry, but slightly becalmed; it has floated gently in the back-water, while, alongside, in invention and industry and social organization, the other half of the mind was leaping down a sort of Niagara Rapids. This division may be found symbolized in American architecture: a neat reproduction of the colonial mansion – with some modern comforts introduced surreptitiously – stands beside the skyscraper. The American Will inhabits the sky-scraper; the American Intellect inhabits the colonial mansion.[6]

Santayana's use of a poetic image (the skyscraper and the mansion as built forms that concretise and determine his identification of 'Will' and 'Intellect') is also what I will track in Cather's fiction – literary description as a built form that articulates the material environment. To do so, I will develop my first element of aerial description, extent, which is a term drawn from Santayana. I will define Santayana's identification of extent as a basic aesthetic principle and elaborate on its relevance to the development of his own architectural image of a cultural split, and then move on to analyse how literature and environment are presented in Cather criticism, in which architectural aesthetics also play a large part. This conceptualisation of extent provides a comparative ground to think about the imagination of the environment that shifted rapidly as the air becomes a perspective from which to see, a zone for possible political control, and a material challenge for description of the environment both visually and in literature.

Technology and Modernity in 1920s Aerial Photography

Technological modernity affects the technics of the novel, specifically by using what has become known through modern science to look back at and describe the past. In an essay on Thomas Mann's *Joseph and His Brothers*, Cather praises the aesthetic quality of 'dreamy indefiniteness' he internalises in the novel's form.[7] For her, this means that the novel does not look back from the present as if the past contains a mystery to be revealed and solved, but that his novel enters the past and looks out at a world that is unsolvably mysterious. Her essay becomes a suggestive critique of a technological modernity that continually attempts to solve indeterminacy, which she sees as working against literature's main function to maintain it. She repeatedly alludes to the 'blinding speed and shattering sound' of 'the relentless mechanical gear which directs every moment of modern life toward accuracy' – technologies, along with new psychological 'sciences' such as behaviourism, that attempt to keep 'the physical machine running smoothly'.[8] She is interested in Mann's four-volume novel about the ancient Israelites because it does the opposite, following 'the movement of grazing sheep' and multiplying indeterminacy for the reader to encounter 'the right kind of development – continual circling and digression'.[9]

Indeterminacy is the core of Cather's method for exploring the meaning of the past in fiction. Her late novels, though, after 1922, begin to stage this search for meaning much more reflexively, releasing herself from the novel as a mode and exploring more indirect forms of episodic narratives that give the reader room to explore the indefinite gaps between what is represented. Foregrounding perspective and maintaining such indefiniteness extends to Cather's treatment of the environment. Cather's value of indeterminacy is curiously reinforced by the severe language against, especially, technology, in her will, forbidding any adaptation of her work: her instructions are 'not to release, license or otherwise dispose of my literary properties for any dramatization whether for the purposes of the spoken stage or otherwise, motion picture, radio broadcasting, television (or any other) mechanical reproduction whether by means now in existence or which may hereafter be discovered or perfected'.[10]

When 'the world broke in two', the environmental imagination was also split between this unreflective drive toward 'accuracy' (embodied in aerial photography) and dreamy indefiniteness (literary description). Description of the environment becomes the ground in which the primacy of fictionality is asserted against this desire for accuracy, speed and control. One type of landscape becomes the central point of contention: extended environments imagined or seen from above. The break in the world Cather sees has much to do with the predominance of aerial imagery entering the popular imagination, part of this shift of interest from the mysteries of the past to the realities of the present. Needless to say, the aeroplane is the primary figure of this progress, and its absence in Cather's work (except in her World War I novel, *One of Ours*) further signals her interest in the force of the imaginary, not just bare technological realities, in changing humanity.

In *Barnstorming the Prairies*, art historian Jason Weems triangulates government photography, aestheticised landscapes in painting and photography, and Midwestern architecture. His historical account emphasises how official government control during the New Deal became the dominant factor for environmental imagination in the Midwest, catalysed by aerial photography: 'The idea of the Midwest became a site of negotiation where different groups of people, from government technocrats and capitalists to local inhabitants and artists, vied with one another in the creation of a new functional and symbolic image for the region.'[11] He reconceptualises the Midwesterner into an active agent in modernity, rather than the prototype of the conservative, passive spectator of change, left behind by modernisation and therefore too stuck in the past to appreciate modernist aesthetics;[12] the Great Plains are 'a dynamic space where people worked to harmonize the core traditions of America's agrarian identity with the more abstract forms of modernity'.[13] The balance between maintaining this authentic 'agrarian identity' became a challenge once aerial photography became the official way to perceive the land:

> Yet by encouraging viewers to imagine order in instances that were in fact indeterminate, the photographs had the potential to exaggerate the regularity of life on the land. The tracks in the snow, for example, took form organically as part of the subjective and even idiosyncratic choices that farmers and livestock made as part of their everyday movement within the landscape. Yet as viewers traced these trails and drew analogies between them and the broader and more intentional geometric patterns that marked the landscape, it was tempting to imagine that all human activities represented in the photograph were directly determined by the rational form and ideology of the grid.[14]

Weems emphasises that fighting this ideology is a challenge to which the Midwestern imagination had trouble adapting: 'As one national journalist had prophesied in 1908, "Aerial transportation put[s] a greater strain upon the average imagination than any other kind ever undertaken." This "strain" soon contributed to a significant reshaping of the form and meaning of the prairie landscape.'[15] Though he concludes that the history of aerial photography 'did allow for important moments of dialectical ingenuity' where 'people on the ground engaged, interpreted, and adapted to their own needs the visions that came to them from on high',[16] in the end his account reinforces the power of perception over imagination.

There is no denying that 'aerial vision', as the subtitle of Weems's book suggests, 'shaped the Midwest'. But this causal relationship does not exclude its opposite – a nonanthropocentric track this book is exploring – that the Midwest shaped aerial vision. For example, the first major, popular utilisation of aerial photography comes from the July 1924 issue of *National Geographic* containing reproductions of over 100 aerial photographs and three long articles: 'The Non-stop Flight Across America', 'Our Country Through the Airman's Camera' and 'Man's Progress in Conquering the Air'.[17] The centrepiece is the first article, written by one of the pilots who completed the first nonstop coast-to-coast flight. The article contains eighty photographs, mostly oblique shots rather than vertical surveys, that originate from a different flight, over an entirely different route (as the photographic equipment would have been impossibly heavy for the nonstop flight). The photographs complement the pilot's general, formal descriptions of the environment from above:

I remember the immense fields and plains of Kansas passing underneath in the ghostly moonlight, with occasionally the twinkle of lights of towns and settlements in the distance, like little groups of stars, the meteors and shooting stars occasionally speeding across the great dome of the heavens, and then the ghostly pallor just preceding the dawn. [. . .] The fields of Kansas merged into the grotesque buttes, little flat-topped plateaus, and eroded topography of New Mexico, with its pastel shades intensified in the eerie light of early dawn.[18]

As this account shows, the pilots continually reconceptualised their point of view and its meaning, as they were apparently concerned with being the first to perceive and so describe such prolonged experience of an aerial view.

One metaphor particularly stands out as a progression from Emerson's transparent eyeball to Santayana's skyscraper: 'we may well imagine we are in another Eiffel Tower, with the advantage that we can carry the tower wherever we will'.[19] This is a comically blunt comparison, as it attempts to functionalise not the point of view of the industrious and meaningful skyscraper as Santayana did, but the 'useless', though beautiful, Eiffel Tower.[20] It reminds the pilots of an aesthetic experience of the view from above, but in its feeling of importance and progress, the transcontinental flight is figured as an improvement over the point of view offered by the Eiffel Tower, because they have control over it.

The captions of the photographs, taken from the pilot's notes, also present early attempts at interpreting the aerial view: 'The airman's camera shows squares, rectangles, and parallelograms scattered higgledy-piggledy over the landscape. Down on earth these geometric figures resolve into farms and cultivated fields, reclaimed from the desert through the magic of irrigation at Idaho Falls, Idaho' (*Figure 2.1*).[21] This is a prime example of early popular description of the view from above. The two airmen primarily have navigational and occasionally aesthetic interest in the aerial views; in this context, the environment is presented in a bare, utilitarian, progressive attempt to 'see all' and present the entire country as visible and contained in one issue of *National Geographic*.

Weems spends more time analysing the use of aerial photography in later 1930s issues of *Life*. Doing so highlights how the naïve descriptions of this earlier *National Geographic* account are part of a progressive de-romanticisation of the agrarian American Midwest. Significantly, later on, *Life* 'made a concerted effort to compose a new image of the Midwestern landscape by constructing pictorial and

THE AIRMAN'S CAMERA SHOWS SQUARES, TRIANGLES, RECTANGLES, AND PARALLELOGRAMS SCATTERED HIGGLEDY-PIGGLEDY OVER THE LANDSCAPE
Down on earth these geometric figures resolve into farms and cultivated fields, reclaimed from the desert through the magic of irrigation at Idaho Falls, Idaho.

Figure 2.1 *National Geographic*, July 1924, 'The Non-stop Flight Across America'

textual narratives that highlighted the modern, business-oriented nature of contemporary agriculture'.[22] This is a vision of the instrumentalised future only suggested in the 1924 *National Geographic* issue. The quaint image of the flying Eiffel Tower stands beside later aerial photography where the 'grid form precipitates the landscape to a mechanistic and rational order not unlike that of a factory, thereby analogising agricultural production to other forms of industrial output'.[23] Whereas attempts at integrating these official images into an empathetic, humanising account replace the myth of expansion with the myth of pastoralism to stabilise the image of the environment in the Midwest, the lack of sophisticated presentation in this earlier *National Geographic* issue aestheticises the images, paradoxically making them more indeterminate despite the goal to present a coherent national mosaic of aerial photographs. Their description and the *National Geographic* issue as a whole are attempts to render aerial description in its experiential force. Weems mentions how 'the popular fascination with the *experience* of flight encouraged other more imaginative estimations of the land',[24] but mostly in the context of painting and architecture. Literary description foregrounds the indeterminacy of this experience and, in Cather's case, its potential for presenting the form of environment before its ideological reconstruction.

Defining Extent – George Santayana and Materiality

An image that recurs in Cather's fiction is series of patterned fields. The extent of this Midwestern US environment is given by experience of vast repetition organised in space. Extent, here, is an imaginary rather than a perceptual form, as it approaches aesthetic experience without an immediate conception of concrete size. In *The Sense of Beauty* (1896) Santayana remarks about the beauty of 'multiplicity in uniformity', that is, the sense of material 'numberlessness and continuity' that makes up the potentially aesthetic experience of extent.[25] One example he gives is the repetition and depth of a vast, starry sky, as well as a curtain, a wall of stone or other similarly smooth surfaces. This is a simple material basis for aesthetic beauty: patterned figuration often affords a seemingly disproportionately great pleasure to its lack of complexity. Notably, Santayana is interested in establishing extent as 'an original sensation' and the most basic way of perceiving form.[26] This is different to perceiving size, which is relative and involves inference rather than the immediate sense of an extended form in which size is irrelevant to the sensation of limitless continuity.

The key to the beauty of extent is foregrounded materiality and spatiality. For 'extension is the simplest and most allied to the material; it gives the latter only just enough form to make it real and perceptible'.[27] The experience of this form is primarily spatial:

> Now the sense of space is a feeling of this kind; the essence of it is the realization of a variety of directions and of possible motions, by which the relation of point to point is vaguely but inevitably given. The perception of extension is therefore a perception of form, although of the most rudimentary kind.[28]

The presentation is simultaneously of the immediate essence of the material (made accessible by the simplicity of extent) and of the affordances of the material (a spatial sense of how the material is unified). In this way, extent is a sensation of the material world through a direct experience of form.

Santayana's examples are in the plastic arts and design, but extent is also relevant as a literary form. The immediate question is whether Santayana's decidedly perceptual experience also applies to the imagination of extent, as in literary descriptions. The answer depends on what one sees as the material ground of literature, on whether the reader sees description as presenting the possibility of autonomous images of environment or if description is primarily a way of framing perception as an expression of abstractions such as ideology.

The latter connection between perception and ideology in literary description of the environment, especially in realism, can be seen in two very different examples in literary theory. In Raymond Williams's classic juxtaposition of 'the country and the city', for example, literary images – such as descriptions of vast countryside – are subordinated as setting or evidence and integrated as part of a metanarrative, in particular a Marxist historical structure: 'The effects of [colonialism] on the English imagination have gone deeper than can easily be traced. [. . .] But from at least the mid-nineteenth century [. . .] there was this larger context within which every idea and every image was consciously and unconsciously affected.'[29] Even if a literary description of environment is interpreted as being a part of a more general, geographical structure, presumably more attuned to the materiality evoked by a number of corroborated descriptions, a strong anthropocentric concept of narrative can get in the way. Such is the case with the work of Franco Moretti, where, in *The Atlas of the European Novel*, there is the possibility to examine the aggregated passages from literary texts for their relationship to the affordances of the actual things or places they describe, but instead his method is to replace the local narrative context of the novel with another container, or a geographical overlay, such as abstract 'fields of power'.[30]

But if the literary image given by description in a narrative text is thought, first and foremost, to be related to the form of environment (rather than the narrative form of history or geography that 'encloses' the description), then we can see how the imagination of extent offers a unique mode of access to formal qualities of the real environment. This is not to deny that literary descriptions of the environment also reveal something valuable about the ideology of the describers, in the case of Williams, or geopolitics, as in Moretti; these instances afford the possibility to reflect on the conceptualisation of place in human history. But literary description also affords access to alternatives to these anthropocentric forms, such as how the material environment is organised, imagined as separate from human perception. Qualities of Santayana's extent, such as the perception of 'numberlessness and continuity' and the attendant foregrounded materiality are thus accessible in literature as part of the form of environment in its imaginary valence.

In Santayana's skyscraper/colonial mansion image, there is a link between his aesthetic theorisation of extent and the material conditions that make extent possible. In *Environmental Evasion*, Willis claims that modernity is marked by an 'environmental schizophrenia' that forced a dangerous binary onto the image of the environment in both American politics and literature.[31] This is seen in the way that 'the nation was seriously confronting the fact that its nature was neither unlimited, nor virginal, nor indestructible' and a new, progressive plan was needed to save the environment from destruction.[32] For Willis, both Santayana and Cather offer a serious threat to real political action in regards to the environment because their work seems to evade political engagement: 'The ahistorical, apolitical aesthetic system championed by Santayana and [Van Wyck] Brooks was being put into practice by the new wave of modernist authors while the historical and political modes were not dying but being marginalized by critics as "lowbrow."'[33] Curiously, Willis's interpretation of Santayana's ahistorical influence and Cather's lack of 'radical' engagement with the environment comes from Cather's 'tendency toward abstraction, with its skyward environmental gazes'.[34] This is an interesting, quick interpretation of descriptions of extent as focusing on 'sky' rather than 'Earth', or the (however limited) view from above. From this perspective, her (and Santayana's) depiction may appear romantic, but as we will see in Cather's 'Earthward' descriptions, her engagement with environment is more subversive than Willis notices. Willis's emphasis on direct and overt political action is representative of the major error critics have made interpreting Santayana's strong critique of the genteel tradition and the colonial mansion as if he unequivocally endorses the 'American Will' embodied by industry and the skyscraper. On the other hand, Santayana is supporting the power of images to intervene in daily life, thus the need to turn attention toward literary forms of engagement rather than only overt political action. Consequently, in the essay, Santayana uses the environment as a path towards renewed appreciation of literary form.

The actual alternative conceptualisation of American culture that Santayana offers is a surprising turn away from culture, not as an evasion, as argued by Willis, but as a direct turn toward experience of the environment. The last section of Santayana's essay draws on his own imagination of the 'non-human beauty' of the material environment, specifically the Californian environment of the audience of this address delivered to the Philosophical Union of the University of California. This is a turn away from trust in any established viewpoint – either of the past embodied by the colonial mansion or the future in the skyscraper – and toward his own imagination and ability to transcend human institution to engage with the environment through the cultivation of his own 'inward landscape'.[35] This marks Santayana's main reason for critiquing the genteel tradition, and is his implicit critique of the 'American Will'.

What is most striking about separating out the genteel tradition from the 'American Will' through an architectural image is the potential for synthesis across categories real and imaginary. The everyday experience of two actual structures (mansion and skyscraper) what they symbolise (intellect and will) and their use (by women and men) is afforded at once in the juxtaposed structures. Because Santayana's essay focuses its criticism on the genteel tradition's dominance 'in religion, in literature, in the moral emotions'[36] the weighted attention seems to imply the inherent value of its opposite: the 'manly', the American Will, enterprise, and its embodiment in the skyscraper. But Santayana spends little time theorising the value of this second side of his binary.

Rather, his attention turns to the environment as a third term to break the opposition of the genteel tradition's hold on culture and the American Will as its accelerating engine:

> When you escape, as you love to do, to your forests and your sierras, I am sure again that you do not feel you made them, or that they were made for you. They have grown, as you have grown, only more massively and more slowly. In their non-human beauty and peace they stir the sub-human depths and the superhuman possibilities of your own spirit. It is no transcendental logic that they teach; and they give no sign of any deliberate morality seated in the world.[37]

Rhetorically, Santayana here appeals to his Californian audience. Inserting the natural environment at the end of his concise attack on the superficiality of American culture complicates his earlier, much more accessible and quotable architectural binary. His strong materialism comes out as he uses the environment and the wonder of the Californian frontier to further extend his criticism to attack not just American culture and philosophy but all its historical and ancient forebears:

> A Californian whom I had recently the pleasure of meeting observed that, if the philosophers had lived among your mountains their systems would have been different from what they are. Certainly, I should say, very different from what those systems are which the European genteel tradition has handed down since Socrates; for these systems are egotistical; directly or indirectly they are anthropocentric, and

inspired by the conceited notion that man, or human reason, or the human distinction between good and evil, is the center and pivot of the universe. That is what the mountains and the woods should make you at last ashamed to assert.[38]

Condemning anthropocentrism in 1911 is a fascinating, original point of view. At this point, the aesthetic function of his skyscraper/mansion image is overwhelmed by the thick description of environment. This a good example of how poetic images disrupt and unbalance reductive conceptualisations. In the context of literary narrative, descriptive passages function similarly.

It is not hard to understand, formally, how these three terms function: the 'big house' encloses and protects a careful definition of human space by limiting and controlling everything 'unnatural'; the skyscraper simultaneously denies and mocks natural forms by rising above; and 'your forests and your sierras' are constructed as a frontier from which humans explore with the intent to better both culture and nature. But, concretely, these images have further possibilities. Each affords a particular point of view: a regressive, hidden and grounded vantage to survey a controlled surround; a similar retreat above to survey a wide space; and the wandering viewpoint. Santayana, in part, is disdainful of the inability to rise 'high' enough in America to influence society through his unique perceptions. He wishes for the possibility to be detached from society not down in a colonial retreat or high up in a skyscraper, or even in the wilderness, but through the freedom to communicate what one imagines no matter one's position: a version of the original democratic vision of America.

Santayana's synthesis in *The Genteel Tradition* is an opening into the vast forests and mountains of the American West, where the duality of American philosophy embedded in the cultural forms of the mansion and skyscraper can be contemplated or, better, forgotten. In the end of the essay, Santayana is imagining this third option as freedom from the genteel tradition, where 'it is the yoke of this genteel tradition itself that these primeval solitudes lift from your shoulders. They suspend your forced sense of your own importance not merely as individuals, but even as men.'[39] This struggle to envision a non-anthropocentric worldview, particularly as a way of critiquing both the weight of tradition and the accelerating technologies of seeing, is also where Cather picks up her method of displacing human narrative plots with aerial description.

Environment in Cather Criticism

I will show a brief example of extent in aerial description from *O Pioneers!* and turn to how critics read environment in Cather before developing a final theoretical tool, the concept of architectural 'built form', for analysis of this early work compared to her later work, *Death Comes for the Archbishop*.

Aerial description and architectural images are a productive place to study environmental imagination. Cather's experiments with the novel use aerial description as the contrasting space of the form of environment and the development of human means of controlling the environment. This is evident in both global extradiegetic narration and local instances of zero focalisation. We can, for example, see how the latter plays out in a brief passage from the beginning of *O Pioneers!*:

> From the Norwegian graveyard one looks out over a vast checkerboard, marked off in squares of wheat and corn; light and dark, dark and light. Telephone wires hum along the white roads, which always run at right angles. From the graveyard gate one can count a dozen gayly painted farmhouses; the gilded weather-vanes on the big red barns wink at each other across the green and brown and yellow fields. The light steel windmills tremble throughout their frames and tug at their moorings, as they vibrate in the wind that often blows from one week's end to another across that high, active, resolute stretch of country.[40]

Here there is a mix of descriptive language: 'Vast' is key here, as it suggests the kind of continuity associated with extended aerial views. There are several abstract metaphors, though the land as 'checkerboard' is immediately given concrete referents (squares of wheat and corn) and a repetition of hues that pattern the landscape ('light and dark, dark and light'). This leads to further concrete description: geometrical lines of wires and roads. The spatial anchor is repeated as the graveyard is mentioned once again in a kind of rhythmic patterning; this time it is indeterminately placed in the vastness of many farmhouses spread out in the landscape. The anthropomorphisation of the 'winking' barns is immediately undercut by more concrete description, a surprising reversal of the assumption that 'checkerboard' and 'light and dark' signalled monotone: as the image unfolds, the fields are given colour. Finally, the image becomes dynamic and extends in a further dimension as spatialised time. 'One week's end to another across that high, active, resolute stretch of country' contradicts the sense of finite time and replaces it with a kind of non-quantitative establishment of time stretching, physically, across the extent of the Great Plains that extend without apparent end.

The description from the slight elevation of the graveyard is afforded by the extent of the aerial view. The normal qualities of agency and representation in realism are reversed: the environment is not mutated and reduced by description and representation but it is positively and uniquely manifest in literary form. This relationship between environment and text has been noticed by other Cather critics, but I would like to push their claims further to apply to aerial description in literary narrative, generally. For example, Guy Reynolds notes that Cather's work explores the connection between shaping and being shaped by the environment, which goes beyond the thematic level: 'Cather's reasoning might be termed "organic modernism." The environment of Nebraska is used as an analogue for novelistic form; landscape might even *create* form.'[41]

Taylor Eggan presents an interesting middle ground between the ideological interpretations of landscape description from Williams or Moretti and this material interpretation in Reynolds. He moves to distinguish between what is normally considered as the formal definition of 'focalisation' – the perspective or point of view of figures in a narrative – as actually only discrete 'microfocalisations' always working within a 'macrofocalisation', or the general ideology constructed through the work. His analysis of the former is original: 'In the context of fictional narrative, landscape does more than simply "set the scene" or conjure the "spirit of place" within which a story plays out. Rather, landscape is a descriptive practice that actively gathers unfamiliar space into a viewing subject's beloved place.'[42] But when he turns to a theorisation of 'macrofocalisation' the benefits of this approach to landscape in literary narrative falters. For Eggan, once the ideological frame for literary description of landscape is considered, it no longer stands on its own as an expression of landscape, work that 'actively gathers unfamiliar space', but instead is subordinated to narrative:

> Far from being purely mimetic, landscape description actively manifests the storyworld; it frames the natural setting and shapes it into an ideological space for its characters. For this reason, landscape is never merely a setting or a backdrop. [. . .] Landscape is an object that is produced and framed – that is, focalized – and hence intrinsic to the narrative structure.[43]

He still strongly denies the conventional interpretation of subordinating descriptions of environment in the reading experience – it is not just 'backdrop' that the reader can skip to get to the 'actual' story more quickly – but in doing so he subordinates landscape description to ideology.

Inattention to the form of environment has consequences for analysis, and shows why foregrounding narrative or ideology is useful, but should not be the primary mode of interpretation. Not coincidently, this plays out when Eggan interprets a description in Cather that foregrounds extent. Turning away from signals of 'microfocalisation' leads Eggan to misrepresent the material details of the landscape descriptions he analyses. In Cather's novel *The Professor's House* Eggan imagines the scene in which Tom Outland is having his final moments in the Blue Mesa, ecstatically seeing what he has lost, for the final time, 'whole', as if Outland 'stands atop the Mesa overlooking Cliff City'.[44] But in the scene, Outland is actually laying at 'the wide bottom of Cow Canyon', where he experiences a subdued religious epiphany of the Cliff City as it would have been seen from below:

> I lay down on a solitary rock that was like an island in the bottom of the valley, and looked up. The grey sagebrush and the blue-grey rock around me were already in shadow, but high above me the canyon walls were dyed flame-color from the sunset, and the Cliff City lay in a gold haze against its dark cavern. In a few minutes it, too, was grey, and only the rim rock at the top help the red light. When it was gone, I could still see the copper glow in the pinions along the edge of the top ledges. The arc of the sky over the canyon was silvery blue, with its pale yellow moon, and presently stars shivered into it, like crystals dripped into perfectly clear water.[45]

Though a very subtle and normally inconsequential misreading, it is significant that Eggan imagines this scene as if it is an aerial description. It shows the way that extent works as a basic aesthetic form. Because we associate the perception of extent with looking *up* at a starry sky (Santayana's example) or *down* and *across* in the view from above (my examples), when we are dealing with the imagination of extent, the critical construction of an ideological 'macrofocalisation' can impede close attention to perspectival detail on the level of the images of the environment. Here we can see Eggan's assumptions that the view from above is equivalent to dominant perception, and so when the latter is present in his interpretation of the novel, he assumes the former. If the experience of extent is an immediate experience of material and form, then a third term, such as Eggan's ideological 'macrofocalisation', focuses one at the expense of the other; in this case Eggan misreads the form of the focalisation itself because he foregrounds ideology.

In addition, Eggan's push away from any apparent essentialism undermines clear definition of what he means by landscape or environment. He claims: 'Instead of innocently depicting the natural world, landscape description "worlds" nature. Hence, critics should pay closer attention to how landscape metaphysics transforms natural spaces into aesthetically and ideologically charged places.'[46] Two fallacies stand out. First, there are very few critics, even in the first-wave ecocriticism he targets, who would argue that literature is 'innocent' in its depiction of the environment.[47] Second, Eggan shifts from the positive, constructivist metaphor of 'narrative architecture' toward 'transformation' of reality into representation, the very mimetic position he disavows throughout the essay.

I am sympathetic to the slippage in the latter problem with Eggan's argument, and I will follow Eggan's architectural metaphors by developing Christian Norberg-Schulz's theories of the relationship between architectural built forms and their environments. Rather than 'transformation' we can think about how actual environments extend into fictional storyworlds as literary descriptions and function as an articulation of the latent affordances of environment. In this sense, literary description is a 'built form' in its relationship to the environment in the same way that architecture is a more immediately concrete 'built form'.

Built Form

Reynolds links Cather with Frank Lloyd Wright, another Midwesterner. Cather is a similar 'architect', in that her constructions articulate the environment in poetic images: 'For Cather and Wright both believed that in the Midwest the "hard molds" of received form (architectural and narrative) would be broken up and remade. And so, using environmental logic, a new language of flow, organicism, and flexibility entered their aesthetic lexicon.'[48] He argues that her use of 'strangely abstract, painterly shapes within the land' given in her descriptions of the environment from above mark her as similarly radical as modernist painters experimenting with shape, colour and landscape.[49] One can take this a step further, though, and argue that Cather was not just playing with 'received form' in the sense of high modernist experimentation, but she was using these modernist techniques to examine the other, non-aesthetic ways in which the environment was being shaped, in this case, by technology. She opposes technological progress and specifically the 'official' perception offered by aerial photography by offering up poetic images as 'built forms'.

There are two ways description presents built forms. The first is the establishment of built forms as we would normally consider them, as architecture. But the second is the specific construction of aerial description: a built form in the chiasmic sense that the description is afforded by the environment it is imagining.

The modernist architect and theorist Christian Norberg-Schulz developed a framework for thinking about architecture as continuous with environment. Norberg-Schulz begins with the level of experience: 'Architecture is not a result of the actions of man, but rather it renders concrete the world that makes those actions possible.'[50] In this case, architectural built forms are autonomous and directly related to the environment in which they are embedded. Norberg-Schulz contrasts this with the way that culture (not art or architecture) uses the environment:

> Culture means to transform the given 'forces' into meanings which may be moved to another place. [. . .] We understand that the given economic, social, political, and cultural conditions do not *produce* the meanings concretized by a man-made place. The meanings are inherent in the world, and are in each case to a high extent derived from the locality as a particular manifestation of 'world.' The meanings may however be *used* by the economic, social, political, and cultural forces. This use consists in *a selection among possible meanings*.[51]

Norberg-Schulz appears to privilege some kind of buried meaning, but it is clear this is not an idealised 'truth'. The 'deeper roots' are simply the concrete arrangement of a local place or 'world' that is necessarily reduced or 'selected' in social and political expression. The interpretations of these cultural institutions are often mistaken for meaning itself, Norberg-Schulz notes, which is functional as an efficient way of building society. But these selections of meaning from the environment must be stabilised by concrete reminders of the 'actual conditions', before interpretation. This is the role of architecture:

> Countries, regions, landscapes, settlements, buildings (and their sub-places) form a series with a gradually diminishing scale. [. . .] At the 'top' of the series we find the more comprehensive natural places which 'contain' man-made places on the 'lower' levels. [. . .] In other words, man 'receives' the environment and makes it focus in buildings and things. The things thereby 'explain' the environment and make its character manifest. Thereby the things themselves become meaningful. That is the basic function of detail in our surroundings.[52]

Most importantly for the present analysis of literary description, the 'things' that Norberg-Schulz values for their articulation of detail are not just 'buildings' located on this architectural hierarchy, but are available in aesthetic objects in all media:

> all of the things that configure the environment, are found both on the earth and under the sky. These two relationships entail horizontal extension and a vertical elevation or, as I have previously said, 'rhythm' and 'tension.' These are expressed in space and form, and despite the flow of changes, they are manifested in the figure as something durable, that is to say, as a *Gestalt*. The significance of the figure lies in this manifestation, and this is applicable for every sort of 'figure,' ranging from music figures to poetic figures.[53]

This is an effective way to measure how 'figures' as descriptions afford certain modes of access to the environment. The architectural built form that 'receives' its surroundings is a meaningful articulation of environment, focusing its nonhuman form into a human form. Similarly, literary description functions as a built form to articulate some quality of the environment, in this chapter 'extent' – which Norberg-Schulz calls 'rhythm' – in the American Mid- and Southwest, notably also identified by Norberg-Schulz, a century after Santayana, as basic to all organisations of space and form.

There is a transgression, though, when this series of diminishing scale is disrupted by technology. This is what Cather articulates when highlighting 'the relentless mechanical gear which directs every moment of modern life toward accuracy' as opposed to her values of 'dreamy indefiniteness' in literary form and historical fictions. It is also what motivates Santayana's turn away from the architectural built forms of modernity to foreground encounter with nature. The aesthetic relationship between environment and architectural figures is broken by a functional relationship: the aerial view presents all nonhuman and human built forms at once from one point of view on the same scale.

The flattening of the perceived aerial image is something that literary description cannot replicate and so subverts, as language cannot present a flat, totalising image. Description is most often interpreted as discrete representation embedded in narrative, part of a figure–ground relationship, and so is a 'pause' in narrative discourse. But thinking of description as a built form that 'receives' the environment and so is a presentation of possibility rather than action, literary description of landscape articulates the environment, disrupting narrative form rather than simply pausing it. Regardless of whether a reader backgrounds description in their experience and subordinates it to narrative discourse or foregrounds it as an articulation of environment, its qualities oppose the simultaneity of technologies of aerial vision, such as photography. This is clearly played out in Cather's fiction and the aerial images that define this break between literature and photography.

Farmland Extent in *O Pioneers!*

Often in Cather's work, aerial description is not given with any reference to verticality but is apparent because of patterned description of the vast surround that I have been calling extent. Two examples from early in *O Pioneers!* make this clear. First is the opening, an example of Santayana's 'multiplicity in uniformity', where the same image is repeated in each of the first four sentences:

> One January day, thirty years ago, the little town of Hanover, anchored on a windy Nebraska tableland, was trying not to be blown away. A mist of fine snowflakes was curling and eddying about the cluster of low drab buildings huddled on the gray prairie, under a gray sky. The dwelling-houses were set about haphazard on the tough prairie sod; some of them looked as if they had been moved in overnight, and others as if they were straying off by themselves, headed straight for the open plain. None of them had any appearance of permanence, and the howling wind blew under them as well as over them. The main street was a deeply rutted road, now frozen hard, which ran from the squat red railway station and the grain 'elevator' at the north end of the town to the lumber yard and the horse pond at the south end. On either side of this road straggled two uneven rows of wooden buildings; the general merchandise stores, the two banks, the drug store, the feed store, the saloon, the post-office.[54]

The prairie houses as well as the surrounding environment are unified in this description, but this uniformity does not hold a stable image of either element. Rather, the image multiplies itself, reinforcing their interrelation through rhythmic repetition that makes this description a built form that implies this pattern extends throughout the other settlements in the Nebraska tableland. Two elements are repeated: dwellings that are minute and indeterminately placed, and the land that extends around the town. The 'little town of Hanover' is 'anchored', it is a 'cluster of low drab buildings huddled', and the houses are 'set about haphazard'. These sentences seem to conventionally introduce the pioneer town setting of the novel, but this description and re-description suspends the town strangely in space rather than providing depth or detail for the reader to recognise a referential environment. This is emphasised in the second part of each of these sentences where the wide environmental surround, like the cluster of houses, is described three times: The Nebraska tableland threatens to blow the town 'away;' the town is set 'under a gray sky', though the slow flakes 'curling and eddying' suspend this over the land/under the sky division; and again the houses seem to be sucked out into the 'open plain', though not just by the wind but 'as if they were straying off by themselves'. The next sentence underlines the image: 'None of them had any appearance of permanence, and the howling wind blew under them as well as over them.' Though this is a reference to the fragility of the pioneer dwelling-house, as the culmination of this poetic image of the vast land with scattered, indeterminately placed human structures, the verisimilar reference to the cold house with an above-ground foundation is subordinate to the strange agency of the environment repeatedly reaching in and out of the human structures.

The description in this opening is a patterned repetition that functions to block familiar identification with the human organisation on the land and instead foregrounds the environment that refuses to be organised. Emphasis on how the indeterminate clusters of dwellings are 'anchored', 'huddled', and 'set' is contradicted by the environment's ability to blow them away, wrap them in snow and wind, and draw them out into the open plain. There is no perceptual reality to this image, both in the sense that the perspective is heterodiegetic and so constructed of an 'impossible' position from without, and in its suspension of realism through repetition. This image implies extension not in mimetic description but through a strange, rhythmic style that implies the extent of the environment repeats this pattern if one continued to 'zoom out'.

The next sequence moves with the extent of this first image of the centre of town toward the periphery, a more specific locale, the Bergson farm. This description also functions as the transition of power from John Bergson to his daughter, Alexandra. Here the description is more recognisably an aerial view, which functions to further emphasise how the extended form of environment is revealed in its confrontation with the edges of the human:

> On one of the ridges of that wintry waste stood the low log house in which John Bergson was dying. The Bergson homestead was easier to find than many another, because it overlooked Norway Creek, a shallow, muddy stream that sometimes flowed, and sometimes stood still, at the bottom of a winding ravine with steep, shelving sides overgrown with brush and cottonwoods and dwarf ash. This creek gave a sort of identity to the farms that bordered upon it. Of all the bewildering things about a new country, the absence of human landmarks is one of the most depressing and disheartening. The houses on the Divide were small and were usually tucked away in low places; you did not see them until you came directly upon them. Most of them were built of the sod itself and were only the unescapable ground in another form. The roads were but faint tracks in the grass, and the fields were scarcely noticeable. The record of the plow was insignificant, like the feeble scratches on stone left by prehistoric races, so indeterminate that they may, after all, be only the markings of glaciers, and not a record of human strivings.
>
> In eleven long years John Bergson had made but little impression upon the wild land he had come to tame. It was still a wild thing that had its ugly moods; and no one knew when they were likely to come, or why. Mischance hung over it. Its Genius was unfriendly to man. The sick man was feeling this as he lay looking out of the window, after the doctor had left him, on the day following Alexandra's trip to town. There it lay outside his door, the same land, the same lead-colored miles. He knew every ridge and draw and gully between him and the horizon. To the south, his plowed fields; to the east, the sod stables, the cattle corral, the pond, – and then the grass.[55]

Unlike the opening passage, here there are explicit signals that this image is from a lifted vantage anchored by the focal point of the Bergson farm. As this image unfolds in the second paragraph, it is ostensibly given a seat in Bergson's consciousness, as his thoughts are framed more clearly when he is introduced lying in bed, presumably looking out the window, defying the non-anthropocentric description in the previous paragraph before this break 'into' his mind. A conventional interpretation is to background the initial description in the first paragraph as 'setting' or to treat it retroactively as a bleak projection from Bergson's dying consciousness onto an unfriendly landscape, as internally focalised. Or, this can be read through Reynolds's emphasis noted above that, in Cather's fiction, landscape creates form.

The description before the break 'into' the Bergson house is assertively negative. It presents an oscillation of what is possibly seen, what is unlikely to be seen, and what is impossible to determine as 'seen'. While the first part of the description establishes 'seeing' this view from above, visual primacy is dropped after the organising feature – the creek – is introduced. This manifests in an identifiable shift in tone that starts with 'Of all the bewildering things'. The creek destabilises all the other 'human' lines on the land. The rest of the description escapes a binary between a/perspectival focalisation as it emphasises that, from the focal point of the land, all lines on the surface are indeterminate marks, whether it be creek, road, ploughed fields or the glacial record. In the next paragraph focalisation is reflexively staged, in the sense that its normal ability to organise the material environment into realistic description fails because it accounts only for human perception and not the indeterminacy of the environment surrounding the farm. At this point in the novel, human perspective-taking fails, alongside human attempts at organising the form of environment into agricultural forms.

The most significant instance of aerial description in *O Pioneers!* comes when Crazy Ivar, a kind of amicable, though feared, outcast in the community (and later taken in by Alexandra as part of the Bergson family), imagines a bird's perspective of the divide as he answers a question about how the ducks know that Ivar is not a typical human who would see their interest in his pond as an opportunity to hunt them:

> Ivar sat down on the floor and tucked his feet under him. 'See, little brother, they have come from a long way, and they are very tired. From up there where they are flying, our country looks dark and flat. They must have water to drink and to bathe in before they can go on with their journey. They look this way and that, and far below them they see something shining, like a piece of glass set in the dark earth. That is my pond. They come to it and are not disturbed. Maybe I sprinkle a little corn. They tell the other birds, and next year more come this way. They have their roads up there, as we have down here.'[56]

Unlike what we will see later in the novel, there is no reference to the gridded tracts normally associated with cultivation in the Midwest. Instead, linear organisation is projected into the sky, and Ivar invites

Emil, Alexandra's brother, to imagine himself as a part of the flat, dark earth. If the previous description of the Bergson farm implicitly marks the extent of the environment as unframeable and indeterminate, here an explicitly nonhuman perspective is foregrounded, which affords a different mode of access to the form of environment. The two previous aerial descriptions quoted above offer a nonhuman perspective that is conventionally naturalised and so perhaps ignored by the reader because they are from the familiar perspective of an extradiegetic narrator. But here, embedded in dialogue, a similar aerial description is more accessibly presented from a nonhuman perspective. The similarities between these aerial descriptions become a pivot from which the reader can begin to read how the form of environment pushes through description into the discourse.

Though Ivar does conventionally anthropomorphise the birds as in the midst of a journey, telling other birds about good waypoints, this is a rhetorical tool to communicate to his child interlocutor that the environment is organised in ways beyond human perception. Like the previous passage, where space is seemingly well-organised into navigable lines by roads and farms, from another point of view – specifically, an aerial view – these lines are 'faint tracks', 'scarcely noticeable', 'insignificant', 'indeterminate' 'feeble scratches'. The aerial view – here an imaginary bird's-eye view – foregrounds the extent of the environment, how Ivar's pond is just one waypoint among many repeated stops along the birds' journey; the same effect implaces the Bergson farm, from an elevated perspective, as a mere instance of 'feeble scratches' on the land that extends in time to prehistory and in space across the uncultivated expanse of the American West.

Of course, it did not take long for this environment to be cultivated and finally, at least temporarily, successfully organised by agricultural form. But rather than represent this as a triumph, in Cather's fiction the human imposition of agricultural form onto the land becomes another element that compounds complexity in her fiction, an enaction of Caroline Levine's principle that 'what narrative form affords is a careful attention to the ways in which forms come together, and what happens when and after they meet',[57] in this case the forms being description and environment. Whereas I have argued that it is basic in all fictional narrative for this collision to be primarily the play between descriptive forms and environment form, in *O Pioneers!* this play becomes thematised as well. The collision multiplies to include the conflict between figures who try to describe the environment in a way that maintains indeterminacy (Alexandra, Ivar), or describe the environment in the modern, determinate, gridded way (particularly,

Alexandra's defiant brothers), and most importantly the prevailing resistance of the form of environment to ideology. As has been argued throughout this chapter and the rest of the book, aerial description offers a prime place to study this collision as it foregrounds a moment of suspended narrative, and, as Philippe Hamon puts it, 'description is the point where the narrative comes to a temporary halt, while continuing to organize itself'.[58] In the case of O *Pioneers!*, description shows how the environment continues to organise itself outside human perception, just as the characters feel like they have gained some control over it.

Between the polar perspectives of Alexandra and her brothers stands her childhood best friend Carl, less sure of his perspective and without as much direct experience with their changing environment, as he left Nebraska for school. When he returns to visit Alexandra and witnesses how she has transformed the land after her father's death, he is less ambivalent than his childhood friend about the meaning of the results because he simply cannot comprehend what he is seeing. Curiously, the reflection on the environment and description from his perspective comes as a *non sequitur* in response to a question about his own attempt at representation, through watercolour paintings:

> She put her hand affectionately on his shoulder. 'You owe me a visit for the sake of old times. Why must you go to the coast at all?'
> 'Oh, I must! I am a fortune hunter. From Seattle I go on to Alaska.'
> 'Alaska?' She looked at him in astonishment. 'Are you going to paint the Indians?'
> 'Paint?' the young man frowned. 'Oh! I'm not a painter, Alexandra. I'm an engraver. I have nothing to do with painting.'
> 'But on my parlor wall I have the paintings—'
> He interrupted nervously. 'Oh, water-color sketches – done for amusement. I sent them to remind you of me, not because they were good. What a wonderful place you have made of this, Alexandra.' He turned and looked back at the wide, map-like prospect of field and hedge and pasture. 'I would never have believed it could be done. I'm disappointed in my own eye, in my imagination.'[59]

Here the 'dark earth' from the bird's-eye view that Ivar presented is juxtaposed with the 'wonderful' transformation actualised by Alexandra. A brief description of the landscape disrupts Carl's response to her question and splits his attribution of agency to Alexandra with an expression of his confusion to its veracity. The 'wide, map-like prospect of field and hedge and pasture' is much different from the indeterminate scratches before Alexandra took over the farm, but the description retains an extended form. Rather than through a textured description of the environment, extent is shown indirectly through Carl's response. His glance over the extended environment causes a shift from complementing Alexandra to sudden doubt. Belief, perception and imagination are all challenged when he looks out at the fields; it seems to appear to him as even more indeterminate as it escapes clear identification of the domesticating forces of agricultural form.

This exchange is interrupted by Alexandra's brothers, but it continues the next day:

> That evening after supper, Carl and Alexandra were sitting by the clump of castor beans in the middle of the flower garden. The gravel paths glittered in the moonlight, and below them the fields lay white and still.
>
> 'Do you know, Alexandra, [. . .] I've been thinking how strangely things work out. I've been away engraving other men's pictures, and you've stayed at home and made your own.' He pointed with his cigar toward the sleeping landscape. 'How in the world have you done it? How have your neighbors done it?'
>
> 'We hadn't any of us much to do with it, Carl. The land did it. It had its little joke. It pretended to be poor because nobody knew how to work it right; and then, all at once, it worked itself. It woke up out of its sleep and stretched itself, and it was so big, so rich, that we suddenly found we were rich, just from sitting still.'[60]

Since the previous discussion, Carl has reconceptualised his reaction to the map-like environment into the same kind of representational engraving process of his own work. But once again, his attempt at rationalising what he sees is defied by an image. Strangely, the 'sleeping landscape' that originates in extradiegetic description finds its way into Alexandra's explanation that it 'woke up out of its sleep'. In addition, Carl's exaggerated, typical, almost managerial gesture with his cigar toward the 'white and still' fields that lay below them becomes an ironic framing of the landscape and shows the inability of the environment to be contained. Alexandra's response concurs, and though it may be a romanticisation that erases the agricultural form she worked to impose on the land, her explanation is similarly ironic, juxtaposing her comparative stillness to its sweeping expanse.

Foregrounding the short, intrusive descriptions of the environment is a counterpoint to arguments such as Melissa Ryan's, which emphasise how *O Pioneers!* and the other early novels present a process of taming the land: 'Alexandra's conquest of the wilderness is represented as a process of domestication. She makes a home on and of the plains by bringing order to the landscape.'[61] Undoubtedly, Alexandra's response above is an attempt to background this process of domestication. But it is significant that the descriptions of the environment remain consistent in defying anthropocentrism. Despite being partially re-formed by agriculture, the extent of the environment only re-appears in different ways, here through irony and negation. Alexandra's ironic description of the dormant landscape is a curious echo of a descriptive, extradiegetic voice that continues to emphasise the consistent built form of the extended environment.

The final chapter of *O Pioneers!* is a vortex of previous images from the novel, a different one being recalled in each paragraph, either by references in dialogue or through description. The most significant is the famous apostrophe that ends the novel: 'They [Alexandra and Carl] went into the house together, leaving the Divide behind them, under the evening star. Fortunate country, that is one day to receive hearts like Alexandra's into its bosom, to give them out again in the yellow wheat, in the rustling corn, in the shining eyes of youth!'[62] This is a de-anthroporphisation of an earlier kind of apostrophe, which uses second-person address to invoke the absent reader:

> When you go out of the house into the flower garden, there you feel again the order and fine arrangement manifest all over the great farm; in the fencing and hedging, in the windbreaks and sheds, in the symmetrical pasture ponds, planted with scrub willows to give shade to the cattle in fly-time. There is even a white row of beehives in the orchard, under the walnut trees. You feel that, properly, Alexandra's house is the big out-of-doors, and that it is in the soil that she expresses herself best.[63]

Other instances of the second-person in the novel follow Brian Richardson's identification of 'you' as a replacement for the third-person 'one' (what he calls 'the hypothetical form'[64]), but here it is used to make immediate the perspective of what Monika Fludernik calls the 'survey perspective'.[65] It differs, though, because it offers not a panoramic sweep, but rather an image of extent. It is not about perception, as in other passages, but a feeling of 'order and fine arrangement' that recurs throughout *O Pioneers!*[66] It puts on display how it is not Alexandra's physical house that works to 'focus' the environment, but this description itself, directed toward the reader, that functions as a built form to organise the imagination of environment. In doing so, it becomes a unique version of what Richardson calls the 'autotelic form' of second-person address 'that is at times the actual reader of the text and whose story is juxtaposed to and can merge with the characters of the fiction'.[67] The reader is interpolated through the reminder that their feeling is directly related to how the environment is described. In this way, it functions like Santayana's turn to nature from the skyscraper and colonial mansion images to defy conventional modes of perception through a turn toward a kind of 'new animism'.[68] The aerial descriptions in O Pioneers! defy the ability of Alexandra's story or the reader's conception of narrative enclosure to constrain the form of environment. Instead, it converts the human form of 'hearts like Alexandra's' into the nonhuman elements of 'yellow wheat' and 'rustling corn'.

Descriptive Re-implacements in *Death Comes for the Archbishop*

The ending of O Pioneers! embodies the 'dreamy indefiniteness' Cather values by synthesising narrative form with the form of environment in its final apostrophe. After 'the world broke in two', though, the challenge to directly present imaginary built forms became more pronounced. Aerial photography moved toward the primacy of perception over imagination and became a more accessible mode of depicting the environment in popular culture. Earlier practices of depicting landscape through 'fictional' means such as mapping and landscape painting were subordinated to official means of reimagining the ideal Jeffersonian grid into an official way of breaking up property. This is Cather's primary starting point for *Death Comes for the Archbishop*. She looks back even further than the turn of the century, to the early and mid-nineteenth century, and an environment, New Mexico, that never had an idyllic grid projected from an aerial view. As such, Cather is utilising an open narrative of the first Western missionaries after the occupation of New Mexico to challenge the stable, official perception of the environment. She foregrounds how it is the form of environment and its objective built forms of literary description that destabilise the official mode of managing the environment.

Like *O Pioneers!*, *Death Comes for the Archbishop* is about the effects of attempting to control the land, but it more closely focuses on the inability of humans to adapt to an uncontrollable environment. *Death Comes for the Archbishop* is another instance where landscape creates form, in this case as the extent of the environment overwhelms the characters and so leads to narrative fragmentation. Reynolds calls these forms 'folds' and, increasingly in Cather's late fiction, 'fissures' that disrupt conventional narrative. In the case of *Death Comes for the Archbishop*, these gaps are 'radical structural disjunctions' in the terrain of the novel 'in which Cather showed scant regard for preserving unities of place or time or point of view'; both forms interrupt with 'a sundering of the realist text by other voices'.[69] While Reynolds focuses on literal voices and what he calls the 'parables' that interrupt the narrative, we can say the same thing about nonhuman 'voices' and the form of environment that is afforded by description.

The landscape that creates fissures in the novel is 'the intrusive omnipresence of the triangle',[70] as the form of the American Southwest is described in the novel. The main focaliser, Bishop Latour, is 'sensitive to the shape of things',[71] and so descriptions of this extensive, repeating environment begins to influence the shape of the narrative. The novel is an episodic, nine-part account of mid-nineteenth-century French missionaries Bishop Latour and his vicar Joseph Vaillant travelling across their new diocese in recently annexed New Mexico. The novel is a reversal of *O Pioneers!* and Cather's other early novels, which show how the environment changes first, and then the people adapt; here, the environment is supposed to change once the spirits of the natives and pioneers are converted. It also differs because the environment remains resistant to the end: 'The old countries were worn to the shape of human life, made into an investiture, a sort of second body, for man. [. . .] But in the alkali deserts, the water holes were poisonous, and the vegetation offered nothing to a starving man.'[72]

European Built Forms

The prologue to the novel presents not only a narrative frame for Bishop Latour's travels, but it offers a contrast to the shifting tone of description from *O Pioneers!* through the only similarly romanticised aerial description in the novel. In the prologue, a young Spanish bishop hosts a luncheon to discuss whom the cardinals have chosen to send to New Mexico. He holds some strong national stereotypes as well as romanticised ideas of the environment, quickly confronted as the novel progresses: 'Oh, the Germans classify, but the French arrange! The French missionaries have a sense of proportion and rational adjustment. They are always trying to discover the logical relation of things. It is a passion with them.'[73] Latour, the French missionary chosen to take over the new diocese, is later confronted by the impossibility of arranging the environment. In addition, the Spanish bishop builds his image of the American Indians from romantic novels. After telling a story in which he transposes New England and Plains tribes onto the Pueblos whom the new diocese will serve, he is gently corrected, "'Down there the Indians do not dwell in wigwams, your Eminence;'" but he responds, "'No matter, Father. I see your redskins through Fenimore Cooper, and I like them so.'"[74] This is a notable instance of architectural built forms and the relevance of their arrangement in the environment. In addition, it becomes a kind of metafictional commentary on the reductive effects of romance's overt subordination of description to narrative; the Spanish bishop likes thinking about wild yet resourceful and helpful natives in the context of pioneering and colonisation. That the other bishop feels compelled to correct not the Spanish Bishop's overt stereotype of the 'redskins' themselves, but of their method of dwelling in the environment, becomes a signal of overt connection between images of the environment, dwelling and people that *Death Comes for the Archbishop* will foreground.

His interlocutors' gentle correction and quiet acceptance suggests an irony in the Spanish bishop's wilful ignorance, which is also apparent in the framing of aerial description.[75] In this opening, the reader is confronted with a typical pastoral European countryside, with its views that extend straight towards centres of power:

> The villa was famous for the fine view from its terrace. The hidden garden in which the four men sat at table lay some twenty feet below the south end of this terrace, and was a mere shelf of rock, overhanging a steep declivity planted with vineyards. [. . .] Beyond the balustrade was the drop into the air, and far below the landscape stretched soft and undulating; there was nothing to arrest the eye until it reached Rome itself.
>
> It was early when the Spanish Cardinal and his guests sat down to dinner. The sun was still good for an hour of supreme splendor, and across the shining folds of country the low profile of the city barely fretted the skyline – indistinct except for the dome of St. Peter's, bluish grey like the flattened top of a great balloon, just a flash of copper light on its soft metallic surface. The Cardinal had an eccentric preference for beginning his dinner at this time in the late afternoon, when the vehemence of the sun suggested motion. The light was full of action and had a peculiar quality of climax – of splendid finish. It was both intense and soft, with a ruddiness as of much-multiplied candlelight, an aura of red in its flames. It bored into the ilex trees, illuminating their mahogany trunks and blurring their dark foliage;

it warmed the bright green of the orange trees and the rose of the oleander blooms to gold; sent congested spiral patterns quivering over the damask and plate and crystal.[76]

Here, as in *O Pioneers!*, the description of dynamic light and colour affords the experience of extent. This aerial view presents the 'folds of country' not just as the perception of a vast spatial distance, but the uniformity of the 'soft and undulating' land foregrounds the temporality given by the progressing sunset. This transforms the environment into an intense but indistinct ground of 'ruddiness' and 'blurring' that creates a direct connection between the villa, the land below and the final reflection of light off of St Peter's, as the built form that focuses both the spatial and temporal 'climax' or 'splendid finish'.

Though these are the first paragraphs of the novel, the description is not a mere establishing shot. The aerial description emphasises the antiquity of the bishop's attempt to ignore the form of environment through dining in his hidden garden only during the hour in which it appears most brilliant, terminating in a view of the Vatican. The extensiveness of the view is afforded by the waves of redness across the hills. This image is given as a foreshadowing of later descriptions of the environment, as one of the cardinals describes the new diocese to the Spanish bishop: '"[In Santa Fe] the very floor of the world is cracked open into countless canyons and arroyos, fissures in the earth which are sometimes ten feet deep, sometimes a thousand. Up and down these stony chasms the traveller and his mules clamber as best they can. It is impossible to go far in any direction without crossing them."'[77] In the desert, the extent of the environment cannot be so easily collapsed into a beautiful aerial view, as its chasms are not seas of reddened ilex but are seemingly bottomless canyons.

Southwestern Environmental Forms

The cultural built forms that help the perceiver organise the landscape – such as St Peter's in the prologue – are not present in the recently occupied American Southwest. Instead, ancient mesa villages and low, adobe 'New' Mexican towns are set amidst the 'countless' canyons and mountains in the Rio Grande Rift. The descriptions of the deserts and mesas defy the idyllic European landscape in the opening by presenting imaginative built forms that do not unify the perception of the landscape, but instead fragment the normal integration of what is seen into what one knows; or, on the level of narrative discourse, the description of the landscape into the progression of the plot. For example, amidst his year-long journey from Ohio to New Mexico, Latour's first impressions of the environment present complete indeterminacy:

> He had lost his way, and was trying to get back to the trail, with only his compass and his sense of direction for guides. The difficulty was that the country in which he found himself was so featureless – or rather, that it was crowded with features, all exactly alike. [. . .] They were so exactly like one another that he seemed to be wandering in some geometrical nightmare [. . .].[78]

This is a direct contrast to the pastoral Roman countryside in the dreamy prologue; the extent of the environment is multiplying 'featureless features' into a nightmare. Unlike in *O Pioneers!*, where imagining the environment from above became a productive, authentic mode of encounter with the environment, written over a decade of technological acceleration later, *Death Comes for the Archbishop* presents the inadequacy of supplanting this imagination with increasingly precise perception of the environment. Architectural built forms may effectively organise the environment of European and American cities, but once 'official' perception in the form of aerial photography began to present images of the rural Midwest in the same 'skyscraper' form that defined industrial urban centres, the extent of the environment became collapsed into top-down perception rather than the local imagination.

In her late novels, Cather turns to the more distant past of American history and a more isolated environment to show how it is the indeterminacy of imaginative built forms – in her case descriptions of the environment embedded in fiction – that should influence interaction with the land, rather than this top-down command. Bishop Latour realises this explicitly:

> just as it was the white man's way to assert himself in any landscape to change it, make it over a little (at least to leave some mark of memorial of his sojourn), it was the Indian's way to pass through a country without disturbing anything; to pass and leave no trace, like fish through the water, or birds through the air. It was the Indian manner to vanish into the landscape, not to stand out against it.[79]

From the beginning, the narrative discourse is fragmented by descriptions of the environment that Bishop Latour at first tries to control, but immediately realises he must step back to let the environment control him. Thus the rest of the novel breaks the framing of the prologue, which introduces the ambitious goals of the European bishops, to 'cleanse' the 'Augean stable' of the Mexican diocese,[80] and instead becomes a detailed description of 'the topography of the diocese'[81] rather than a conventional narrativisation of its transformation, symbolised by the reference to Cooper. The essential feature of Latour's diocese is its ever-expanding extent: 'Bishop Latour leaned back in his chair and locked his hands together beneath his chin, "I wish I knew how far this is! Does anyone know the extent of this diocese, or of this territory? The Commandant at the Fort seems as much in the dark as I."'[82] His partner, Vaillant, is less concerned with confronting the mystery, and Latour's repeated question is answered by the narrator through a proleptic description:

> The Bishop again shook his head and murmured, 'Who knows how far?'
> The wiry little priest whose life was to be a succession of mountain ranges, pathless deserts, yawning canyons and swollen rivers, who was to carry the Cross into territories yet unknown and unnamed, who would wear down mules and horses and scouts and stage-drivers, tonight looked apprehensively at his superior and repeated, 'No more, Jean. This is far enough.'[83]

Vaillant will later be sent to the edge of the ever-extending diocese, in Denver, after he and Latour have attempted to reach each church in New Mexico. As such, the narrative voice embeds a description of the future environment into the narrative present, again juxtaposing the limited frame of the human figure – 'far enough' – with the yet unknown environment that will not be contained by a conventional narrativisation of the missionary journey.

Once Latour has established himself after a long confrontation with the previous leader of the region, a Mexican bishop, he begins the tour of his new diocese. Here he joins his guide, a Pecos Indian, Jacinto, who becomes the principal 'fold' in the narrative – informing Latour about the history of the land and the indigenous people living and ancient – which balances the 'fissures' presented by descriptions of the environment. These wrinkles quickly become primary, as both embedded stories and descriptions of the environment become the methods to simulate realism in the transversal of what appears to be a historically realistic span of time and space.

Cather's descriptive form from her early novels is retained and amplified in this later novel, and it is worth comparing how the descriptions foreground what is imagined much more than what is seen. Rather than abstract reflections on environment, the descriptions become imaginary structures – or built forms – that focus the form of environment. Here is a description as Latour passes between Laguna and Acoma:

> This mesa plain had an appearance of great antiquity, and of incompleteness; as if, with all the materials for world-making assembled, the Creator had desisted, gone away and left everything on the point of being brought together, on the eve of being arranged into mountain, plain, plateau. The country was still waiting to be made into a landscape.[84]

Compare with this much commented-upon passage from *My Ántonia*:

> There seemed to be nothing to see; no fences, no creeks or trees, no hills or fields. If there was a road, I could not make it out in the faint starlight. There was nothing but land: not a country at all, but the material out of which countries are made. No, there was nothing but land – slightly undulating, I knew, because often our wheels ground against the brake as we went down into a hollow and lurched up again on the other side. I had the feeling that the world was left behind, that we had got over the edge of it, and were outside man's jurisdiction.[85]

Whereas in *My Ántonia* this reflection on environment is framed by Jim's romantic look back on his childhood, the description from *Death Comes for the Archbishop* is embedded in Latour's spiritual framework, placing the environment not in the progressive history of American development but in the eternal formation of Earth. Jim only has access to the country from his own perspective, which attempts to embed what he has seen within the narrative he is telling. The reflection and the description of the environment from *Death Comes from the Archbishop*, though, attempts to present the environment concretely. The subtle conceptual differences in these passages enforce this. The same three elements of environment are recognised in both the early and late novels – land, country and world – but their relationship to one another, and the focaliser, is much different. Latour does not include human-made things in the 'material' of environment. From his perspective, the world exists in the desert in its basic form, even if it is not a whole 'landscape'. One can still perceive the mesas – 'piles of architecture' – as 'assembled', though not unified. The environment, then, affords a description beyond what is perceived and extends into poetic image: 'The desert, the mountains and mesas, were continually reformed and re-colored by the cloud shadows. The whole country seemed fluid to the eye under this constant change of accent, this ever-varying distribution of light.'[86] 'To the eye' signals perception, but rather than perceiving a unified landscape, this description enacts the formation and reformation of one's image of the landscape.

Interestingly, the above reflection is interrupted by an aerial description from Latour's present perspective:

> Jacinto interrupted these reflections by an exclamation.
> 'Acoma!' He stopped his mule.
> The Bishop, following with his eye the straight, pointing Indian hand, saw, far away, two great mesas. They were almost square in shape, and at this distance seemed close together, though they were really some miles apart.
> 'The far one' – his guide still pointed.
> The Bishop's eyes were not so sharp as Jacinto's, but now, looking down upon the top of the farther mesa from the high land on which they halted, he saw a flat white outline on the grey surface – a white square made up of squares. That, his guide said, was the pueblo of Acoma.[87]

The experience of extent is illustrated in full as the description unfolds:

> It was very different from a mountain fastness; more lonely, more stark and grim, more appealing to the imagination. The rock, when one came to think of it, was the utmost expression of human need; even mere feeling yearned for it; it was the highest comparison of loyalty in love and friendship. [. . .] Already the Bishop had observed in Indian life a strange literalness, often shocking and disconcerting. The Acomas, who must share the universal human yearning for something permanent, enduring, without shadow of change – they had their idea in substance. They actually lived upon their Rock; were born upon it and died upon it. There was an element of exaggeration in anything so simple![88]

Latour is greatly impressed with how the Acomas have made concrete what he and the church have always considered an abstraction – Christ as Rock. He is disconcerted by the limitations of his own imagination (like Carl in O *Pioneers!*); he had to encounter the form of environment – the built form of this pueblo atop the mesa – before an apparent spiritual truth appeared real. This is elaborated as Latour then climbs up into the mesa, and finds lodging in the cloisters, up above the pueblo:

> Built upon the north-east corner of the cloister the Bishop found a loggia – roofed, but with open sides, looking down on the white pueblo and the tawny rock, and over the wide plain below. There he decided he would spend the night. From this loggia he watched the sun go down; watched the desert become dark, the shadows creep upward. Abroad in the plain the scattered mesa tops, red with the afterglow, one by one lost their light, like candles going out. He was on a naked rock in the desert, in the stone age, a prey to homesickness for his own kind, his own epoch, for European man and his glorious history of desire and dreams. Through all the centuries that his own part of the world had been changing like the sky at daybreak, this people had been fixed, increasing neither in numbers nor desires, rock-turtles on their rock. Something reptilian he felt here, something that had endured by immobility, a kind of life out of reach, like the crustaceans in their armor.[89]

This description uses the same material as the description of the sunset across Italy in the opening. But here the bishop is in a 'stone-age' cloister instead of a luxurious hidden garden villa, so his experience of extent is much different. Rather than the play of red colouring 'much multiplied candlelight' across rolling hills and focused by the copper dome of St Paul's Basilica, here, strangely, 'shadows creep upward' as the mesa-top candles go out. The same form of environment – Santayana's 'unity in multiplicity' – present in either undulating hills or scattered mesa tops immediately evokes a comparison to Latour. The equivocal form is what catalyses the contrast between the present and what Latour remembers of similar aerial views in 'his own part of the world'.

Latour's nostalgia even evokes a similar, though toned down, racialist flattening that the Spanish bishop in the prologue adopts more brazenly. The origin of the contrast Latour detects between the Acoma and 'European man' is the conflation that occurs when he experiences apparently 'infinite' space given by the extended aerial view, being erased by time. In this way, Latour's erasure of present indigenous life by equating it with the stone age turns into a critique of 'his own epoch', already parodied by the repetition of Cooper's native stereotypes in the prologue. The image of 'the wide plain below' and the changing light foregrounds the prior description of the land in the Southwest as continually reforming, strangely contradicting Latour's present feeling of immobility and timelessness and his nostalgia for the dynamic world of European culture. In this way, by focusing on the form of environment, the reader is given access to these juxtaposed attitudes; once Latour is lifted above the plain, atop the mesa that appeared from the ground as 'materials for world-making', he feels as if he is in the concrete position to do the world-making himself. But the view from above, as a space of indeterminacy, is too unstable for Latour to return to the dynamic experience of landscape he had on the ground. Vitally, for the reader, the extent of the mesa plain is a space of indeterminacy that affords the juxtaposition with the prologue as well as both Latour's responses: the numberless mesas that form and reform continually, and the vast plains as infinitely and terrifyingly repetitive and regressive.

Notably, this kind of colonial terror is not where Latour's experience with his diocese – both the people and the environment – ends. Directly following this aerial description, the next chapter opens an embedded narrative about a previous missionary in a time when 'all the missions now in ruins were active'.[90] This Spanish bishop was an indulgent despot, who used a painting of St Joseph to manipulate the Lagunas to tolerate his tyranny because he had magical control over the rain and their prosperity. The story offers another juxtaposition to Latour's brief feelings of homesickness and attendant dehumanisation of the Acoma. In the story, the bishop hosts an extravagant dinner for the bishops from the neighbouring mesas, who are jealous of his high 'air-bound seat'[91] atop the same Acoma mesa in which Latour reflects in the narrative present. After the bishop accidentally kills one of his servants for spilling sauce on him, his guests flee and the Acoma begin planning a revolt. The aerial description takes on a much different tone:

> The airy loggia, where he customarily took his afternoon repose, was like a birdcage hung in the breeze. Through its open archways he looked down on the huddled pueblo, and out over the great mesa-strewn plain far below. He was unable to fix his mind upon his office. The pueblo down there was much too quiet.[92]

Now, rather than the extended environment fixing the world in changeless time, the bishop begins to fear the changes below that the night conceals and that he can only imagine. He continues to watch the sun set and the moon rise: 'But tonight he wished he could keep the moon from coming up through the floor of the desert – the moon was the clock which began things in the pueblo. He watched with horror for that golden rim against the deep blue velvet of the night.'⁹³ The environment now is a signal of coming change rather than Latour's later feeling of immobility. The height that the bishop enjoys in this embedded story and of which the other padres are jealous becomes his demise; he is thrown off the mesa by the villagers, who then welcome a native, Mexican bishop as their next padre. Typical of the structure of the 'fold' and 'fissure' in *Death Comes for the Archbishop*, this story is embedded without contextualisation or commentary. The embedded story ends here and 'Book Four' begins. Most notably, from the perspective of the form of environment, the reader is afforded a juxtaposition of Latour's temporary, racialist nostalgia prompted by aerial description with a brief narrative recounting the kind of potential change that Latour, at this point, cannot perceive in his diocese.

When Latour is constructing a cathedral after he has retired from his travels, he encounters the same issues with his imagination of the environment as he considers his own imposition of architectural order onto the landscape. Latour realises the absurdity of his typically Western desire to impose a cultural form he is used to – the Romanesque cathedral – onto the land:

> In the working of silver or drilling of turquoise the Indians had exhaustless patience; upon their blankets and belts and ceremonial robes they lavished their skill and pains. But their conception of decoration did not extend to the landscape. They seemed to have none of the European's desire to 'master' nature, to arrange and re-create. They spent their ingenuity in the other direction; in accommodating themselves to the scene in which they found themselves. This was not so much from indolence, the Bishop thought, as from an inherited caution and respect.⁹⁴

He is aware that his attempt to focus the landscape may not be a careful articulation of the 'deep roots' of meaning embedded in the environment in which the Acoma 'accommodate' rather than conceptualise. He resists the idea that his structure will break the continuity of extent in the environment, and instead decides upon a way for the material of the cathedral to articulate its environment. If the experience of extent is a basic aesthetic sense, 'allied to the material' as Santayana puts it, the description in which Latour encounters the material for his cathedral illustrates how aerial description can directly relay the form of environment to the reader:

> At about four o'clock they came out upon a ridge high over the Rio Grande valley. The trail dropped down a long decline at this point

and wound about the foot of the Sandias into Albuquerque, some sixty miles away. This ridge was covered with cone-shaped, rocky hills, thinly clad with piñons, and the rock was a curious shade of green, something between sea-green and olive. The thin, pebbly earth, which was merely the rock pulverized by weather, had the same green tint. Father Latour rode to an isolated hill that beetled over the western edge of the ridge, just where the trail descended. This hill stood up high and quite alone, boldly facing the declining sun and the blue Sandias. As they drew close to it, Father Vaillant noticed that on the western face the earth had been scooped away, exposing a rugged wall of rock – not green like the surrounding hills, but yellow, a strong golden ochre, very much like the gold of the sunlight that was now beating upon it. Picks and crowbars lay about, and fragments of stone, freshly broken off.[95]

This is a return to the foregrounding of built form from the prologue that parallels the opening description of the relationship between St Peter's Basilica, the environment and its description. His absurd project of building the Romanesque cathedral in the desert becomes an instance of Norberg-Schulz's articulation of the land. With this nonanthropocentric frame in mind, the reader can reflect on how the cathedral in the desert is simultaneously a colonisation and an act of re-formation; it is an equivalent built form to the description of landscape in a novel such as *Death Comes for the Archbishop*. Rather than acting as a symbol that is the terminus of a certain way of perceiving the environment – as the cathedral in the prologue – Latour's cathedral acts to *extend* the environment by integrating itself into its form using physical materials locally available. It both disrupts the environment and emphasises its particular form.

The construction of these two structures – the extended landscape and the story that culminates in the building of the cathedral – are Cather's protest against modernisation. The pioneer's mode of transforming the environment is the limit, for her, and once industry took over through urbanisation, indeterminacy, folds and fissures and 'dreamy indefiniteness' lost their influence. The immediacy of aerial photography and the attendant technologies of flight decayed the development of the imaginative resources that mediate humans and environment. Cather takes Santayana's implicit critique of the 'American Will' concretised in the skyscraper and embeds it in her descriptions of the environment, consistently rejecting the determination of the perceptions offered by the aerial view. Instead, she follows Santayana's approach toward a third term, nature, as a way of recovering the view from above for the imagination, in literary images and aerial description. The experience of extent becomes the primary mode for the presentation of the form of environment as it is most 'allied to the material'. This is where the world broke in two for Cather: when official perception of the environment replaced the imagination of the environment afforded by literary description. In her novels, she experiments with literary technique, foregrounding description as a built form to oppose the organising force of narratives of modernisation.

Notes

1. Merrill Skaggs, *After the World Broke in Two*, ix; Bill Goldstein, *The World Broke in Two*, 1; Eric Haralson, 'Modernism', 216–17; Guy Reynolds, *Willa Cather in Context*, 125.
2. From a letter dated 23 November 1927. See Willa Cather, *Willa Cather on Writing*, 12.
3. See John J. Murphy, 'Compromising Realism to Idealize a War'; Skaggs, *After the World Broke in Two*, 35.
4. Lawrence Buell, *The Future of Environmental Criticism*, 39.
5. Caroline Levine, *Forms*, 19.
6. George Santayana, *The Genteel Tradition*, 39.
7. Cather, *Not Under Forty*, 99.
8. Ibid., 99; 96.
9. Ibid., 99; 100.
10. Lacey Fosburgh, 'Why More Top Novelists Don't Go Hollywood', n.p.
11. Jason Weems, *Barnstorming the Prairies*, ix.
12. Ibid., xii.
13. Ibid., x.
14. Ibid., 107–08.
15. Ibid., 137.
16. Ibid., 256–57.
17. Weems does include images from this *National Geographic* issue but does not pursue detailed analysis.
18. John A. Macready, 'The Non-stop Flight Across America', 70.
19. Ibid., 86.
20. This also reflects Roland Barthes's use of the view from the Eiffel Tower, described in my introduction: 'the bird's-eye view, on the contrary, represented by our Romantic writers as if they had anticipated both the construction of the Tower and the birth of aviation, permits us to transcend sensation and to see things *in their structure*'. See Barthes, *A Barthes Reader*, 242.
21. Macready, 'The Non-stop Flight Across America', 34.
22. Weems, *Barnstorming the Prairies*, 116.
23. Ibid., 116.

24. Ibid., 130.
25. Santayana, *The Sense of Beauty*, 103.
26. Ibid., 98.
27. Ibid., 100.
28. Ibid., 98.
29. Raymond Williams, *The Country and the City*, 281.
30. Franco Moretti, *Atlas of the European Novel*, 113.
31. Lloyd Willis, *Environmental Evasion*, 76.
32. Ibid., 75.
33. Ibid., 76.
34. Ibid.
35. Santayana, *The Genteel Tradition*, 64.
36. Ibid., 39.
37. Ibid., 62.
38. Ibid., 63.
39. Ibid.
40. Cather, *O Pioneers!*, 29.
41. Reynolds, 'Modernist Space', 180; emphasis in original.
42. Taylor Eggan, 'Landscape Metaphysics', 398.
43. Ibid., 401.
44. Ibid., 406.
45. Cather, *The Professor's House*, 226–27.
46. Eggan, 'Landscape Metaphysics', 410.
47. See Greg Garrard, *Ecocriticism*, 3–5.
48. Reynolds, 'Modernist Space', 180.
49. Ibid., 181.
50. Christian Norberg-Schulz, *Architecture*, 45.
51. Norberg-Schulz, *Genius Loci*, 170; emphasis in original.
52. Ibid., 16.
53. Norberg-Schulz, *Architecture*, 133.
54. Cather, *O Pioneers!*, 1.
55. Ibid., 7–8.
56. Ibid., 16–17.
57. Levine, *Forms*, 19.
58. Philippe Hamon, 'What is a description?', 332.
59. Cather, *O Pioneers!*, 41.
60. Ibid., 45.
61. Melissa Ryan, 'The Enclosure of America', 277.
62. Cather, *O Pioneers!*, 122.
63. Ibid., 30.
64. Brian Richardson, *Unnatural Voices*, 29.
65. Monika Fludernik, 'Description and Perspective', 466.
66. Cather, *O Pioneers!*, 14.
67. Richardson, *Unnatural Voices*, 30.
68. Santayana, *The Genteel Tradition*, 57.

69. Reynolds, *Willa Cather in Context*, 21; 20.
70. Cather, *Death Comes for the Archbishop*, 17.
71. Ibid., 18.
72. Ibid., 275.
73. Ibid., 5.
74. Ibid., 6.
75. This irony recurs in Cather's treatment of the environment; see Robert Azzarello, *Queer Environmentality*, 87–88.
76. Cather, *Death Comes for the Archbishop*, 3–4.
77. Ibid., 7.
78. Ibid., 17.
79. Ibid., 232–33.
80. Ibid., 5.
81. Ibid., 265.
82. Ibid., 40.
83. Ibid., 41.
84. Ibid., 94.
85. Cather, *My Ántonia*, 11–12.
86. Cather, *Death Comes for the Archbishop*, 94.
87. Ibid., 94.
88. Ibid., 95.
89. Ibid., 102–03.
90. Ibid., 103.
91. Ibid., 108.
92. Ibid., 111.
93. Ibid., 112.
94. Ibid., 223.
95. Ibid., 238–39.

Chapter 3

Verticality and Empty Thematics in Paul Bowles's Novels

Alongside the frontier landscapes of the Great Plains and the Southwest in Willa Cather's novels, one expects that the descriptions of desert environments in Paul Bowles's work from another colonial frontier, North Africa, will similarly emphasise extent. In this chapter, I will highlight a more prevalent element in his fiction that is the most basic and recognisable aspect of the view from above: verticality. That a figure must obtain a focal point higher than what is described is a definitional feature of aerial description – perhaps its only essential component. The process of getting to a lifted vantage point and the phenomenology of being up high is usually effaced by the immediacy of the view that is afforded by the climb. Conventionally, the transition from low to high takes the form of representations of transportation that open up a new setting for the plot to advance, prolonging time for extended representations of interiority. Often, the representation of travel will be skipped altogether. Here I will highlight the function of transition from down below to up above, while maintaining a focus on the form of environment that structures the climb and the eventual view.

Postclassical narratology (particularly approaches that utilise cognitive science) conceptualises space by drawing equivalencies between psychological processes of perceiving space and the linguistic construction of space in narrative discourse. Similarly, Bowles criticism has developed a psychologised spatial dynamic through its repeated emphasis on interiors and exteriors in both Bowles's fiction and his symbolic proximity to the American literary canon. These systems lack meaningful theories of verticality, or what makes the view from above different from 'grounded' perception and its representation. In this way, conventional analyses of description emphasise the ways that description helps construct or form the narrative story logic. But by turning attention to images of the environment, it becomes clear that descriptions have an opposing effect.

If narrative theory does focus on the vertical relationship between seer and seen, it often takes for granted the significance of transportation and the trip upwards in its construction of types of narration and description. In this sense, aerial description is reduced to the ways they function to exemplify some property of the narrator, not the ways the environment interacts with the human subject. By flattening the vertical imaginary into what is constructed as what I will call the 'horizontal' form of story logic, narrative theory is able to justify separating description as bumps along this path rather than essential to the experience of narrative. I discussed this in Chapter 1 in regards to Gérard Genette and classical narratology, and in this chapter I will discuss Monika Fludernik's postclassical formulation of spatiality. José Manuel Lopes calls spatial descriptions 'masters of disguise' that 'reveal a "narrativized" form of internal arrangement, when not building actual narrative bridges across discrete segments', and that description is 'far more pliable and versatile than narrations, since, unlike the latter, they are free from the constraints of logic and narrative grammar'.[1] I take this somewhat forgotten contribution to description in narratology as my starting point.

Similarly, Philippe Hamon shows how description and its attendant 'empty thematics', or content that does not directly relate to the thematic dynamics of plot – such as open windows, clear air, idling, etc. – reveal the unmanageability of narrative discourse. Descriptive excess is managed and its role in narrative discourse has historically been minimised by critical concepts.[2] I alluded to this theoretical argument about 'unmanageability' in Chapter 1, and here I will further develop how it functions in analysis. Aerial description is an excellent example of unmanageable language, as it reveals character-environment as a second dyad – alongside narrative-description – that marks another accidental casualty of narrative theory. First, I will introduce an example of ascent and empty thematics from Bowles, and then I turn my attention to Bowles criticism – an oddly biographical specialty – to highlight the impact of verticality in spatial analysis of fiction. I will develop this concept through focus on the imagination in Gaston Bachelard and description in Hamon, before showing how this analysis applies to Bowles's novels.

Literary images have an essentially negative function: they short-circuit not just the familiar content of perception but also what is considered possibly perceivable. Bachelard opens *Air and Dreams* by claiming this deforming power for the imagination:

> We always think of the imagination as the faculty that *forms* images. On the contrary, it *deforms* what we perceive; it is, above all, the faculty that frees us from the immediate images and *changes* them. If there is no change, or unexpected fusion of images, there is no imagination; there is no *imaginative act*. If the image that is *present* does not make us think of one that is *absent*, if an image does not determine an abundance – an explosion – of unusual images, then there is no imagination. There is only perception, the memory of a perception, a familiar memory, a habitual way of viewing form and color.[3]

We can make a similar claim about the prosaic form of the literary image: description deforms narration. The conditions of description extend beyond the description itself; the form of description includes the blurry or 'empty' boundary between text-types that is the narrative armature that makes a particular description possible. Foregrounding the form of environment as afforded by description reverses conventional, rational constructions of story logic, which state that it is the progression of plot that determines what kinds of descriptions are included in the discourse. Instead, this can be reoriented to foreground the material conditions for description, how the necessity of descriptive images in realism demands a multiplication of empty thematics, to the extent that description has the potential to overwhelm narrative.

'Deforming' is a useful negative construction that accounts for how descriptive images function for the reader without assuming that its experience during reading implies a subordinate position. This is different from other theories of space and description. In David Herman's landmark *Story Logic: The Problems and Possibilities of Narrative*, description's function is wholly positive and constructive. Spatial descriptions 'create mental representations of space'; 'help readers map'; 'enable readers to identify an action structure'; and 'configure [. . .] the storyworld'.[4] For Herman, the structural necessity of spatial description in narrative story logic thus becomes the key to making actions and events perceivable in an abstract space reliant on the reader's already-present cognitive schemas of visual space. This allows him to make a claim for the renewed focus on description in narrative discourse: 'far from merely providing descriptive background or ornamentation for the primary action in a story, spatial reference helps constitute narrative domains'.[5] Despite a focus on description, this is a positive conceptualisation for description that is not tenable in the realm of the literary image. 'Constitute' implies the formation of the narrative storyworld, while my adaptation of Bachelard's main claim is that description deforms narrative and the reader's experience therein. Hamon shares a similar idiosyncratic focus on images, but rather than a poetics, as in Bachelard, he instead develops a highly organised schema for the form of description in literature. The main overlap between the two is an emphasis on non-geometrical space and the 'empty' or 'airy' space introduced into the text by descriptive images.

If the effort to ascend is included in literary narrative, it takes the form of Hamon's 'empty thematics'. This is his term for transitions in realist literature when a description becomes necessary but the narrative demands of realism cannot abide a discrete interruption. It can take four forms: the introduction of 'transparent media' (such as clear air or the view from above), specialist characters (artists who see impressionistically, engineers who can describe technical detail), idle scenes (being early to a meeting, looking down from above) or 'psychological motivations' (traits that include intense looking).[6] These structures are ironically 'empty' for Hamon, as they reveal the primacy of description as a text-type in literary fiction. It is not just experimental or anti-realist literature that can play with these ideas. As I have been arguing, a readerly focus on the ways that environment clashes with human narrative forms also reveals the subversive force of description in literature. This multiplies indeterminacy because of the inevitable interruptions when narrative form and the form of environment collide.

These two opposing theories of description coexist because of different assumptions about referentiality in literature. In the present case where I am foregrounding the form of environment, the notion of positively forming a narrative domain is less salient than the idea of deforming our perceptual norms of encountering the environment, which allows a focus instead on how the environment reveals itself in its imaginary valence through descriptive images. Thus the critical foregrounding of description can happen in a much different way from Herman's story logic, not as a structure or construction (a logic) but as another form clashing with narrative within the novel (a poetics).

Negations of Colonial Narratives

As with the form of an extended landscape described from above, discussed in Chapter 2, the verticality assumed by height is essentially indeterminate. Key to this is the difference between perceiving and imagining being above the environment. In Bowles's fiction (and aerial description in general) the imagination is presented as primary, and, in his novels, characters are very often ascending. Descriptions of human figures climbing and looking down from varying heights deform the plots as the environment moves to the foreground. Consider how this plays into a description from Bowles's novel *Let It Come Down*. The protagonist, Dyar, here at the end of the novel, believes he has escaped what he calls 'the cage of cause and effect' that controlled his life from his previous job as a bank teller in New York until the point when he moves to Morocco and decides to steal and exchange a large sum of illegal British pounds. He has recruited a Moroccan, Thami – with whom he has developed a trying companionship – to guide him out of the International Zone to a hut above a mountain village in the Spanish Zone where he can rest and decide how to proceed. The intrigue of Dyar's developing angst and execution of the theft forms the novel into an ironic heist plot that never actually develops into something generically recognisable, as it subverts any kind of stability of character or motivation and instead is organised around a few central aerial images.

For example, the descriptions during his hike blend imagination and perception:

> Once before, two days ago, he had become intoxicated upon emerging into a world of sun and air. This morning the air was even stranger. When he felt it in his lungs he had the impression that flying would be easy, merely a matter of technique. [. . .] It was a question of starting to walk and continuing to walk. Slowly the contours of the valleys beneath shifted as he went along. He paid no attention to the path, save to note that it was no longer the one by which he had come yesterday. He met no one, nothing. After an hour or so he sat down and had two pipes of kif. The sun still had not climbed high enough to strike this side of the mountain, but there were eminences not far below which already caught its rays. The bottoms of the valleys down there were green snakes of vegetation; they lay warming themselves in the bright morning sun, their heads pointing downward toward the outer country, their tails curling back into the deep-cut recesses of rock. He continued with less energy, because the smoke had cut his wind somewhat, and his heartbeat had accelerated a little. In compensation, however, he felt a steadily increasing sense of well-being. Soon he no longer noticed his shortness of breath. Walking became a marvelously contrived series of harmonious movements, the execution of whose every detail was in perfect concordance with the vast, beautiful machine of which the air and the mountainside were parts. By the time the sun had reached a point in the sky where he could see

it, he was not conscious of taking steps at all; the landscape merely unrolled silently before his eyes. The triumphant thought kept occurring to him that once again he had escaped becoming a victim. And presently, without his knowing how he had got there, he found himself in a new kind of countryside. At some point he had wandered over a small crest and begun going imperceptibly downward, to be now on this upland, sloping plain, so different from the region he had left. Long ago he had ceased paying attention to where he was going.[7]

The vertical system constructed in this passage is a blend of imaginary and perceptual signs, introduced by Dyar's strange feeling that 'flying would be easy, merely a matter of technique'. This is basically a metafictional moment, as the passage shifts from a familiar description of walking to a defamiliarised walking-as-flight. It is also a reminder of the axiom from Bachelard quoted in this book's introduction; imaginary flight negates the need to rationalise the possibility of flight, as the imagination's essential dynamic is felt-lightness. The description is positive when describing what is possibly seen far below – the contours and the bottom of the valley and the landscape, generally. The lowness of the environment below proliferates through the image of a snake: 'eminences not far below', at 'the bottoms of the valleys' with 'their heads pointing downward' and 'their tails curling back into the deep-cut recesses of rock'. But the description negates what is expected of the narrative – he pays no attention to the path, it is not the path from the previous chapter, he meets 'nothing' along the way, he is not conscious of taking steps. The inclusion of these negated elements makes the environment dynamic in an unconventional way: the concrete descriptions of what is seen from above take precedence over any interior reflection they may prompt.

The description of the hike goes on for four more pages, but when Dyar's interiority starts to overwhelm the discourse, like many characters in Bowles, its ability to influence the form of the character's story (his own view of himself as man-on-the-run, or his generic typification as a fugitive in a heist plot) is totally dismissed, his thought 'evaporates' into an image of the environment:

The years he had spent in the bank, standing in the teller's cage, had been real, after all; he could not call them an accident or a stop-gap. They had gone by and they were finished, and now he saw them as an unalterable part of the pattern. [. . .] And so everything turned out to have been already complete, its form decided and irrevocable. A feeling of profound contentment spread through him. The succession of ideas evaporated, leaving him with only the glow of well-being attendant upon their passage. He looked among the pebbles for the beetle; it had disappeared along the path.[8]

Dyar is suspended in this vertical world, and his progress towards an unknown goal is not linear. The experience of looking downward and encountering the image of valley-as-snake is miniaturised in a view of looking down at an actual beetle. Again, his realisations are reflexive; just as Dyar realises he can easily (though tragically) dismiss the relation of his past self as a working man in New York to his current self trying to escape with stolen money through North Africa, so the identifiable form of the plot as a generic heist embedded within the imperialist romance mode is overtly signalled, recognised and subverted. Against any generic expectations, Dyar would much rather sit still and look down than run away. Here, the form of environment clashes with narrative form to displace the human character from the reader's generic expectations.

Critics note that this negation is how Bowles deconstructs the romantic colonial novel, much like Joseph Conrad. Nearly all of Bowles's characters, like Dyar, never make it back home to establish a clear perspective on the differences between home and abroad. In *The Sheltering Sky*, Kit exemplifies the terror of the dead-end structure in Bowles's fiction as she attempts to send a telegram back home after she has been abducted and becomes the concubine of a desert trader: 'CANNOT GET BACK'.[9]

Richard Patteson uses the spatial metaphor of the domestic interior and the wild, native exterior to argue that Bowles's novels represent 'the antithesis of the end-centered imperialist romance'.[10] Patteson focuses on this failed return home rather than the significance of navigating through the environment for the concepts associated with cultural homelands and journeys out and back. In *A World Outside*, he argues that Bowles subverts the colonial perspective of the imperialist romance by making the return home impossible and the domestication of foreign space unthinkable. These are two 'horizontal' trajectories that Patteson tracks to develop his theorisation of spatiality in Bowles's fiction.

Contra Patteson, in Bowles's fiction the journeys are not just *out* but *up*. Foregrounding description and environment invites a flip of the axis of imaginary movement to focus on aspects of vertical perspective in Bowles's images. To argue that Bowles is subverting the imperialist romance by simply cutting its form in half (disallowing its conventional ending) necessitates a limited theorisation of the 'horizontal' relationship between subject and environment, journeying toward or away from home with the landscape – and consequently description – as the backdrop. But there is a strong vertical imagination that affords descriptions of the environment from above that becomes an even more radical subversion of the imperialist romance form, by way of foregrounding the material environment and description rather than just tracking the interior and exterior journey of the focalising Western subject. Description, in this way, deforms narrative.

Outside/Inside Space in Bowles Criticism

Perhaps excepting Ernest Hemingway, there is no modern American writer with a higher proportion of criticism centred on biography. Bowles's work remains even more buried, though, because other than *The Sheltering Sky*, he never became as widely popular as someone like Hemingway, which adds to the 'outsider' mystique that seems to easily transfer from his biography to his fiction and vice versa. In the second *Review of Contemporary Fiction* special issue to focus on Bowles (the first of which was mostly dedicated to biography), Ann Foltz puts it succinctly: 'The mere fact of being Paul Bowles has greatly overshadowed his artistic achievements.'[11] The constant impulse to refer back to Bowles's life creates a vicious tautological loop that compromises formal criticism from the start. [12] The existing criticism focuses on Bowles, Bowles's Tangier, Bowles in Bowles's Tangier, Bowles writing about Bowles in Bowles's Tangier, fictional Bowleses that represent Bowles writing about Bowles in Bowles's Tangier, and so on. Not only is Paul Bowles constructed and reconstructed in these analyses, but this egocentric approach to his own view of North Africa only causes room for factual disagreement rather than critical insight.[13] It is worth spending time on the movements of Bowles critics in this study, as the constant tendency to either write generic critical biography or develop biographical analysis of his stories buries the aesthetic and philosophical value of his work.

Patteson's aforementioned *A World Outside* is the strongest critical treatment of Bowles's fiction. Consequently, he also uses Bachelard as a touchstone in his analysis, but his interest lies in Bachelard's work on intimate spaces and the home in *The Poetics of Space*. Patteson's primary work is to explicate an 'architectural form' in Bowles's fiction that seems to repeatedly and violently reject any attempt by an outsider to construct a comfortable space within a foreign place. Even though Patteson uses this potentially strong spatial dynamic as its organising principle, the metaphorical 'outside' he is studying can only be a symbol – most of the time a symbol for chaos.

Patteson commits a conceptualisation error as he uncritically inherits previous spatial frameworks. His architectural model is a direct response to Wayne Pounds's earlier study, *Paul Bowles: The Inner Geography*, which is a psychoanalytic interpretation of the exteriorisation of fictional characters' psyche into an alien landscape. Pounds reads Bowles as 'part of the larger development through which American literature has sought to assimilate the experience of the frontier',[14] and then supplies Jungian and Freudian overlays to explain the historical inevitability of an expatriate like Bowles writing stories about such intense alienation and terror.[15] Though Patteson wishes to flip Pounds's terms to foreground the places described in Bowles through an explicit focus on the 'exterior architecture' (and not the 'inner geography'), his model stretches beyond its reasonable applications for concrete description. He identifies Bowles's 'implicit model of human experience: an interior presumed to be secure, and an exterior known to be hostile' and pulls his central interior/exterior dynamic from an anecdote in Bowles's autobiography *Without Stopping*, in which his father attempts to kill him as a baby by placing him in a basket on an open windowsill during a snowstorm.[16] Though the subtleties of Patteson's argument are important and are discussed below, this initial thrust into Bowles's fictional imagination is troubling: his claimed material, spatial reading of fictional environments originates from psychoanalytic processes and repressed structures, a decidedly egocentered approach to space.

Patteson's 'architectural form' has the potential to prioritise vertical space (a structure built *up* in imaginary space instead of *across* narrative time), but his conceptualisation runs into another dyad – exterior/interior, instead of vertical/horizontal. In Bowles's fiction,

> the effort to enclose is even more important than the effort to exclude, for the space that is inside was once out; it is exterior space domesticated, brought into the house. This profounder function of architectural form (profounder because it implies transformation, not just exclusion) can be readily seen in the typical Arabic enclosed courtyard, with its greenery (cultivated, not wild) and its carefully contained running water or fountain: the outdoors brought in, the wild made tame.[17]

Here Patteson attempts to recruit the Arabic 'enclosed courtyard' as both a recurrent image in Bowles and an actual architectural form. There are many descriptions throughout Bowles that describe this courtyard – which is best conceptualised from above – but Patteson ignores these examples and the imaginary structure Bowles uses and instead relies on his own abstract architectural structure.

As I highlighted in my first example from *Let It Come Down*, Bowles's vertical imagination is pronounced because of his extended descriptions while characters are in the midst of transportation, a proliferation of non-narrative discourse that does not become recognisable as a prototypical, linear journey because of its emphasis on the form of environment. Where other critics interpret this as a simple subversion of the generic spatial structure of the journey by removing a clear goal or attempt to return home, Bouchra Benlemlih sees it as more ambiguous: 'How Bowles transforms the real substance of Morocco into an interior journey is better explored in the ambivalent and richly suggestive space between interior and exterior, between imagination and reality.'[18] Rather than the novels devolving through the inevitable failure of maintaining interior, 'safe' space within exterior, 'hostile' space, Benlemlih focuses on the description of liminal space and the process of mediation in-between these two categories in the experience of the traveller, who is always Bowles's protagonist.

Most importantly, she emphasises that his is a wholly imaginary spatial structure, one that does not recruit conventional story logic for its progression but instead constantly destabilises perspective. This takes place on the level of description, replacing the schema of visual perception standard in realist prose through techniques she describes as typically baroque:

> The very incoherence and fluidity of the baroque worldview prompts geographical displacement and the morphing of form(s). [...] It opens our eyes to many scopic/observational devices, such as mirroring, the labyrinth, distortion, instability, and fragmentation, a surplus of images which seems to opt for movement and to advocate the irrational at the expense of the rational.[19]

In Bowles, the imaginary is primary, and this involves recruiting descriptive technique that is not recognised by previous critics who are more focused on the anthropocentric relationship between inside and outside. Benlemlih sums up her general theory of Bowles's fictional system as a constantly shifting imaginary geography – both through defamiliarised images of movement and through unstable focalisation. For her, 'Bowles's imaginative strategy is to set up the characters' journeys as self-discovery, but to integrate into the narrative alternating perspective upon those journeys'; 'All these journeys can be read as journeys of Western angst, yielding to reverie.'[20] She points out that Bowles constructs these journeys in order to negate them; they do not lead to discovery or understanding, nor violence and destruction, but they more strangely foreground indeterminate relationships between both the displaced Western characters and diverse North African peoples. This is not only a unique critical move in Bowles criticism, but is reminiscent of Bachelard's theorisation of the fluidity of everyday experiences like 'Western angst', afforded by the oneiric quality of poetic images.

Vertical Imagination

Bachelard's most popular work is *The Poetics of Space*, and it has been vastly influential across disciplines. Here, I draw mostly on *Air and Dreams: An Essay on the Imagination of Movement*. I am interested in Bachelard's phenomenology of imagination rather than his poetics of space. Though space and images are closely bound throughout his work, emphasis – especially for narratologists – has focused on his study of intimate spatiality associated with the home in *The Poetics of Space*.[21] While this is valuable research on the poetics of interior spatiality, Bachelard is only heuristically isolating intimate, interior spaces in *The Poetics of Space*. In a refreshing though incidental use of nomenclature now popular in contemporary criticism, Bachelard states that his overall interest is a 'slower ontology': one that does not read categories of being so immediately and superficially into spatial language, 'one that is more certain than the ontology that reposes upon geometrical images'.[22] Any complete study of spatial experience in literature must integrate both the structure of interior and exterior space, and, more importantly, the types of movements that connect them and the points of view they afford. This new focus collapses the assumption that the laws of rational geometric categories translate into the form of poetic images. Not only does my addition of verticality allow us to think more precisely about the variety of experiences of space in literature, but it opens up literary theorisations of space to study of the form of environment.

Air and Dreams focuses on the conjunction of spatial imagination and movement, specifically imagined movement and what Bachelard calls the *upward élan*. This is his argument that all imaginative activity is essentially tied to physical momentum and felt lightness: 'Dynamic imagination really only creates images of impulse, *élan*, and soaring; in short, images in which *the motion produced takes its direction from the force* that is imagined actively.'[23] The most productive place to study imagination is in poetic images and literary objects, the main concretisations of this upward tendency. Bachelard is careful to assert the autonomy of the image; its existence is not secondary to this impulse and it does not function only to express ideas, illustrate abstractions, or expedite metaphorical or analogical connections. The imaginary exists 'before' its expression in literary production: 'Literature is not merely a substitute for some other activity. It brings a human desire to fruition. It represents an *emergence* of the imagination.'[24] He even argues that the imaginary has primacy before human cognition and affect and asserts that we can 'put the image not only before the thought, before the account of it, but even before all *emotion*'.[25] Thus, for Bachelard, the image is the primary mode of access to the world: 'Imagination, which is both material and dynamic, is in no way *selective*. It does not *designate*; it *lives* abstract values.'[26] It is notable that Bachelard locates the power of this imaginative autonomy above the Earth and in the air.

Bachelard's theory of imagination maintains an anthropocentrism and idealism that seems to slip under his prevalent materialism.[27] But a similar account of the autonomy of images can be developed without a reliance on 'human spirit'. Instead of analysing the images themselves – just as it is necessary to integrate study of the poetics of interior spaces with exterior spaces – the focus must also turn to the situations in which they are embedded. In the case of the novel, aerial images are embedded in narrative storyworlds, and this aerial imagination is always an interaction between a focaliser and its environment, articulated by description and encountered by the reader.

Bachelard argues that the objects of his analysis are 'the product of an inner impression of *growing lighter*. The exterior world cannot give it to us.'[28] In his own subject-centred analysis, this is an inevitable point, but the *upward élan* is not necessarily something that is disconnected from the material environment. In some sense Bachelard is right: images rely on the subjective phenomena of felt-meaning.[29] But paradoxically, he has cut off the body from the environment, the source of the experience of air and heights. Following his abstraction, the environment is most often flattened and schematised into 'setting', limiting its meaning to a traditional idea of 'surround' rather than a structure that affords action and motion. In fictional narrative, description holds these affordances in readiness. The aspects of described objects in literary texts, for

Roman Ingarden, are part of the 'pulsating mode of experiencing' typified by encounter with indeterminacy in fictional texts.[30] If we use James J. Gibson's or Caroline Levine's language of 'affordances' in place of 'aspects held in readiness', we can begin to think about these aspects as a part of the spatial form of environment, and not gaps or places which must necessarily be 'filled in' by the reader.

Because of Bachelard's anthropocentrism, much of his analysis skirts a study of the environment. As such, his definition of the spatiality of environment differs from the definition in this book. For Bachelard, if the material environment is not the archetypal source of symbols and creates the bounds by which the space of the subject and imagination are defined, then it remains a stage for human ideals. The pattern of his analysis of aerial imagination consistently moves away from the specific position from which aerial imagination is available – or the environment in which it is embedded – and towards its integration into the structure of human spirit. For example, explicating some brief lines from surrealist poet Paul Éluard:

> Before a sky from which objects have been banished, there will be born an imaginary subject whose memories have been banished. The distant and the immediate form a bond. What is distant from the object is immediate to the subject. This is another proof that the common bond between spirit and matter [. . .] is even more perceptible if one is willing to take his stand in the realm of imagination rather than in that of representation, and if he is willing to study – together – imaginary matter and the imagining mind.[31]

Bachelard's imagining subject is 'before a sky', in the unique space of reverie where subject and object can meet directly. There are no representations here because the connection between the two is immediate and material. Though it may seem that this is due specifically to the imaginer's position, Bachelard reduces this space even more, to a single dimension, 'only a depth dimension [. . .] one without a within'.[32] The dreamer hanging before a sky is only spirit – its stand-in is an 'imagining *mind*' – unembedded, disembodied and ultimately positionless. In addition to the body, the potential embedded in the sky itself is a casualty of this attempted recuperation of a 'view-from-nowhere' phenomenology of imagination. All the images of the environment Bachelard studies are disqualified from a similar positive interpretation of a dimension 'without a within' as benefits the subject: the human spirit and not the material environment is described and foregrounded from Bachelard's perspective.

Bachelard notably deviates from this ego-centric perspective when looking closely at narrative, not poetry. Poetic images integrated into a different structure – both the logic and the environment of a story-world – demand a less symbolic, more concrete analysis. On describing figures above a deep abyss in Honoré de Balzac's *Séraphîta*:

> we notice that the abyss loses its distinctive features because we move away from it. One who ascends sees the obliteration of the abyss' characteristics. For him, the abyss dissolves, becomes hazy, and grows more obscure. [. . .] Anyone who rises sees the heights become more clearly delineated and differentiated. The dynamic imagination is subject to an extremely powerful finalism. The human arrow lives not only its *élan*, but also its goal. It lives its sky.[33]

To be sure, like his associative interpretation of Éluard's poetry, this is not exactly a close reading of Balzac's novel. Here we have an original seed for a further and more generally applicable theorisation of aerial description. Bachelard lays out a basic perceptual reality: what is below becomes less physically visible for a figure positioned above. Naturally, then, the immediate surround ('the heights' and 'the dynamic imagination') becomes 'delineated and differentiated'. There thus seems to be a vertical scale for experiencing the shift from perception to imagination: the environment affords both, and the focaliser's position in regards to it largely determines which aspects of its form are foregrounded by description. That is, the environment (earth) moves from perception into imagination as the narrative agent tries to retreat from it (into air).

Vertical images have an autonomy separate from 'horizontal' narrative story logic, always enveloping the subject, either carefully characterised and typified or as transparent as the empty centre of zero-degree focalisation: the blending of the environment in which the characters are embedded and the environment that is the intentional object for the reader. Both the *élan* and the 'finalism' are determined by the way a subject is embedded in the environment. Rather than aiming analysis toward what this can tell us about the imagining subject, a phenomenology of imagination – specifically, of the reading experience – must also include the form of environment. This perspective is accessible through engagement with the description of the environment in narrative fiction.

Where Bowles critics utilise Bachelard to construct a dichotomy between home and abroad, inside and outside, intimacy and alienation, my approach moves away from these psychologised and anthropocentric interpretations of description and points to the forms of vertical organisation of the environment. Bachelard's poetics of space should not be considered the field onto which the various representations of textual space are mapped, such as the privacy and inaccessibility of the character's mind linked to the intimacy of containers like drawers, rooms and the home. Rather, what spatial description affords is a comparison of the form of environment being described and the form of description itself.

Empty Thematics and Aerial Description

Recent trends in place- or environment-centred geocriticism and ecocriticism have begun to develop similar theories of literary form as it relates to descriptions of space. Wai Che Dimock notes that a consequence of backgrounding concrete places has ignored one 'important part of modernist aesthetics', what she calls the 'Calypso effect'.[34] In a study of James Joyce's inclusion of images of Gibraltar in *Ulysses*, she notes that Joyce creates 'a veil, replacing flood-lit information with a barely illuminated fuzzy sketch [. . .] one that sacrifices sharpness of resolution in order to preserve the uncrystallized condition of possibility just prior to it'.[35] Though Joyce thoroughly researched Gibraltar, including what could possibly be seen of the Strait and Morocco from the Sierra Nevada, he restricts and distorts what he knows in the description focalised by Molly Bloom in order to present 'a deliberately wide-open, off-focus image of a world that would otherwise have been sharply and starkly marred by conflict'.[36] Dimock emphasises openness and possibility throughout her analysis and points to the oddity that the novel that is perhaps more closely associated with a single place than any other novel includes 'this conspicuous foray [. . .] to a place so obviously outside that orbit'.[37] The description of Gibraltar (and, interestingly for the subject of this chapter, Morocco) deforms the narrative story logic that organises *Ulysses* about, around and in Dublin.

It is not a coincidence that Dimock has chosen a distanced, aerial view for her example of this modernist form of spatial representation that is recognisable in its 'all-encompassing scalar indeterminacy'.[38] The current chapter paints with much narrower strokes than Dimock, focusing on the construction of verticality in descriptive images, as these images too are marked by indeterminacy. Bowles also contributes to this characteristically modernist form, though not in the ways

Dimock briefly alludes to in her conclusion; she wonders: 'Could there be a Morocco present on its own terms, not refracted to stand for something else or to stand against something else?'[39] She argues that Bowles's work in particular shows how narrative as a medium distorts the possibility for the place to be presented as it is.

To contrast, I am considering the ways description – not narrative – does indeed articulate a relatively 'unrefracted' environment. Consider the description as it continues from the previously quoted passage from *Let It Come Down*:

> Little by little the uncertain trail led downward across regions of rough pastureland and stony heaths. It was with astonishment that he saw on a hillside a group of cows grazing. During the morning he had grown used to thinking of himself as the only living creature under this particular sky. If he were coming to a village, so much the worse; he would continue anyway. [. . .] If the cows had surprised him, the sight now of a dozen or more natives working in a remote field did not. Only their minuteness amazed him; the landscape was so much larger than it looked. He sat on a rock and stared upward. The sky seemed to have reached a paroxysm of brilliancy. He had never known it was possible to take such profound delight in sheer brightness. The pleasure consisted simply in letting his gaze wander over the pure depths of the heavens, which he did until the extreme light forced him to look away. Here the terrain was a chorus of naked red-gray valleys descending gently from the high horizon. The clumps of spiny palmetto, green nearby, became black in the distance. But it was hard to tell how far away anything was in this deceptive landscape. What looked nearby was far off; the tiny dots which were the cattle in the foreground proved that – and if his eye followed the earth's contours to the farthest point, the formation of the land there was so crude and on such a grand scale that it seemed only a stone's throw away.[40]

The description is a clear example of empty thematics; Dyar is driven by hunger to wander from an empty cabin on top of a mountain to find any nearby town. Whereas a conventional realist narrative may use this empty thematic of hunger to be logically satisfied by food, and so ending the scene after the description, Bowles's work dwells in the emptiness by prolonging description.

This is a clear and identifiable spatial trajectory that links Dyar's movement with the plot in the novel. Thami, the Moroccan native Dyar has travelled with to the Spanish Zone, has left earlier in the morning to placate his wife's family, who own the cabin and are not happy a white man is being housed as he illegally travels out of the International Zone. Dyar hates being dependent on Thami, so he decides to go off on his own to find food in a town whose location is unknown to him. Though this is a logical link that should reunite the lost protagonist and his native companion, his journey plays out much differently. Dyar decides to smoke kif as he walks, erasing his hunger and so any conventional motivation to wander away from home: '"With this you don't need food," he said. Soon enough he had forgotten his hunger; there were only the multiple details of the bright landscape around him.'[41] The transition to an engaging, 'full thematic' (a journey alone into the unknown) that should follow the logically realistic satisfaction of hunger is displaced by an empty thematic (frequent stops to look around at the environment). The description thus deforms the narration. The use of kif in place of food again emphasises the primacy of imagination. The vertical dynamics in this passage rapidly shift away from any geometrical sense of distance, size and scale, as the view from above affords the reversal of the typical habit of perception that 'grand scale' objects, such as rolling mountain ranges, are unreachably far away. Instead, the description affords the paradoxical image of the grand, seemingly at-hand. This follows the strange flip from looking 'upward' at the brilliant sky by gazing 'over' the heavens. The vertical imaginary developing in this description is detached from 'up' and 'down' and follows what Bachelard calls the 'soft plasticity' of reverie and images rather than the 'hard geometry' of rational discourse.[42] The valleys are described as 'descending gently from the high horizon' and the colours of the palmetto from near and far are juxtaposed as if they stand on the same plane.

Vertical Images in *The Sheltering Sky*

In Bowles's fiction there are many other examples of characters orienting their worlds via images of the environment from above.[43] In addition to these examples from *Let It Come Down*, I will show a few descriptions of aerial images in *The Sheltering Sky*, before moving to how Bachelard's theory of imagination and Hamon's theory of description – thoroughly vertical ideas – contradicts the 'horizontality' of narratology.

In *The Sheltering Sky*, Port and Kit Moresby are in the midst of their travels around the world, now in North Africa, where their strained marriage that has relied upon proximity is tested by a growing spatial distance. Early in the novel, Port chooses to go on a walk without his wife:

> Slowly the street began to descend; this surprised him because he imagined that the entire town was built on the slope facing the harbor, and he had consciously chosen to walk inland rather than toward the waterfront. The odors in the air grew even stronger. They were varied, but they all represented filth of one sort or another. This proximity with, as it were, a forbidden element, served to elate him. He abandoned himself to the perverse pleasure he found in continuing mechanically to put one foot in front of the other, even though he was quite clearly aware of his fatigue. 'Suddenly I'll find myself turning around and going back,' he thought. But not until then, because he would not make the decision to do it. The impulse to retrace his steps delayed itself from moment to moment. Finally he ceased being surprised: a faint vision began to haunt his mind. It was Kit, seated by the open window, filing her nails and looking out over the town. And as he found his fancy returning more often, as the minutes went by, to that scene, unconsciously he felt himself the protagonist, Kit the spectator. The validity of his existence at that moment was predicated on the assumption that she had not moved, but was still sitting there. It was as if she could still see him from the window, tiny and far away as he was, walking rhythmically uphill and down, through light and shadow; it was as if only she knew when he would turn around and walk the other way.[44]

First, Port is moving downward. But this is a surprise to him, as his image of the city is always oriented downward toward the ocean: now that he is walking away from the ocean, he feels he should be walking uphill. This is a difficult spatial arrangement to hold in our minds as readers. The salience of what Port imagines (the city as slope downward toward the water) is difficult to reverse as he confronts the opposite of this trajectory in his actual movement (the city sloping down away from the water). This contradiction is reconciled through spontaneous reverie, the strange autonomy of an image Port conjures of another's downward gaze so that he can feel like he really exists in the world and not in the negated environment of his imaginary trajectory upward. For the reader, this is now an embedded image (being Port's), but it is easier to access than the initial description of the environment, as the focalisation is strangely handed over midsentence through the 'as if' locutions to Kit, who is high up and immediately exposes his wandering, tiny figure in the midst of the city. Port's contradictory image of upward momentum on a path that is actually headed downward shifts to the description from Kit's perspective that is a view from above and blends the empty thematic into the narrative story logic: the walk (and this walking scene) will end when Kit (the new 'narrator' of Port's actions) decides it will.

Kit gazing out of the window at Port and the dynamic perspective shift into a reverie that gives way to aerial description is a curious twist on Hamon's empty thematics. Port's relationship to the city is not valid unless he can imagine himself embedded within it; this is the persistent, anxious goal of the traveller in a foreign land. But his embeddedness within the environment is not accomplished through what could be called a 'full' thematic (that is, events that develop as themes that stretch across time through narrative form) but rather through a characteristically 'empty' thematic (an idle woman looking out a window down at the town through the clear air). In this early scene, description and its forms of existence take precedence over narrative story logic.

Indeed, it is the prevalence of images of the environment from above that begin to dominate the novel. The vertical dynamics of this scene – the *élan*, the imaginary momentum – is continually upward. Even as the focaliser actually and apparently consciously moves downward, following the path down into the medina, his sense of agency is passed to someone spectating above him. The perspectival shift from Port to Kit, as the passage shifts from description of the city to Port's tiny figure embedded in the city, represents an imaginary shift in focalisation 'into the air'. Here we have the first description of the topography of North Africa in the novel – unpredictably hilly terrain with tiny figures moving up and down – which establishes a vertical rather than a horizontal form of environment.

Though this vertical form is apparently evident in the central image in the novel, 'the sheltering sky', the sky as a conceptual anchor is not as simple as it seems. In criticism of the novel, the sky is often treated as a symbol of opacity that forces Port and Kit to adopt a habit of superficial interpretation. As Brian Edwards summarises, 'with a solid sky as the focal point, the Saharan landscape takes on an exaggerated two-dimensionality; sky reflects earth, where both are solid screens'.[45] While it may seem like a screen/projection metaphor is how the characters in *The Sheltering Sky* encounter the landscape, an analysis, such as Edwards's, which reduces Port's cognition (characterised by treating all surfaces – landscape, faces, language – as screens and masks) into discrete images of the landscape fails to account for the way the form of environment affords movement in three dimensions. In this example, Port is only able to imagine himself as a real part of the environment by wandering up, down and through its topography, even going so far as recruiting Kit's wandering, lifted perspective to further emphasise the depth of encounter that he is feeling as he walks. Though this is an urban environment rather than the Saharan sky that Edwards is defining, here there is a dynamic focalisation switch that is predicated on movement and exploration of an environment rather than detached observation and interpretation. Just as walking (and, later, riding in a car) provides opportunity for these dynamic, aerial images to develop for Port, so for the reader this movement of focalisers develops a depth to the presentation of the environment. Alexa Weik von Mossner argues along similar lines to the present chapter that 'the ecological shape of the Sahara and Bowles's emotional relationship to it did not only shape but partially generated *The Sheltering Sky*'.[46]

Movement emphasises the verticality of images in *The Sheltering Sky* and provides a way of thinking about the function of other aerial images in the novel. Soon after this walk, Port continues to explore without Kit and eventually ends up far outside the city, with a local as his guide, who has led him into an intimate scene in a tent to have tea with a woman, Marhnia. The guide, Smaïl, tells what is to Port an inscrutable story about three poor women whose greatest desire is to have tea in the Sahara. The women eventually receive enough money for a tea set and journey into the desert to find 'the highest dune so they can see all the Sahara'.[47] The three spend two days climbing from one dune to another, always spotting an even higher dune in the distance. They finally die in their sleep on top of the highest dune, where they decided to rest before they had tea with a view of all the Sahara below them. Port is unable to understand the significance of the story and replies, 'It's very sad', in an attempt to please Marhnia, who requested the story.

The juxtaposition of the former image of Kit looking down on Port, guiding his actions, and the latter image of the women on top of the highest dune looking down on the desert, to fulfil their dreams, begins to develop the pattern of multifocalisation that makes *The Sheltering Sky* a productive case for studying descriptions of the environment. Though these apparently represent what Bertrand Westphal categorises as 'exogenous' and 'endogenous' points of view – the 'vision of the traveler' and 'an autochthonic vision of space', respectively – Bowles's technique is to synthesise these two perspectives into an 'allogenous' perspective, 'characteristic of those who have settled into a place, becoming familiar with it, but still remaining foreigners in the eyes of the indigenous population'.[48] Critical to understanding the form of environment is attunement to multifocal presentation of place. These two views from above afford two distinct ways of encountering the environment: projected *into* imagination in the case of Port passing off his agency to an imaginary force, and fatally projected *from* dreams into the real world in the case of the embedded story of tea in the Sahara. Crucially, both images are framed within embedded stories. Port constructs a narrator of his actions, able to control his tiny figure from above, and Smaïl tells the story to Port at the request of Marhnia, presenting to Port a virtual scenario of his earlier imaginary one that propelled him to reach Smaïl and Marhnia in the first place.

The Sheltering Sky is notable for the death of Port in the middle of the novel. As is apparent from his inability to integrate these two perspectives into one that is multiform and allogenous rather than discrete and categorical, the vertical imaginary of the novel makes this death, and thus a shift to a more adaptive focaliser, Kit, inevitable. Port's limitation is described directly in an extended and vivid description as he is leaving Tangier by car and looking down at the tents in which he was listening to the story in the earlier scene with Smaïl and Marhnia:

> He ceased listening. They had left the town, traversed the valley, and were climbing a large, bare hill on the other side. As they swung around one of the many S-curves, he realized with a start that he was looking straight at the Turkish fortress, small and perfect as a toy at this distance, on the opposite side of the valley. Under the wall, scattered about on the yellow earth, were several tiny black tents; which one he had been in, which one was Marhnia's, he could not say, for the staircase was not visible from here. And there she was, doubtless, somewhere below in the valley, having her noonday sleep in the airless heat of a tent, alone or with a lucky Arab friend – not Smaïl, he thought. They turned again, mounting ever higher; there were cliffs above them. [. . .] Again and again the valley came into view, always a little smaller, a little farther away, a little less real. The Mercedes roared like a plane; there was no muffler on the exhaust pipe. The mountains were there ahead, the sabkha was spread out below. He turned to get a last look at the valley; the shape of each tent was still discernible, and he realized that the tents looked like the mountain peaks behind them on the horizon.
>
> As he watched the heat-covered landscape unfold, his thoughts took an inward turn, dwelt briefly on the dream that still preoccupied him. At the end of a moment, he smiled; now he had it. [. . .] The particular meaning with regard to his own life scarcely mattered. For in order to avoid having to deal with relative values, he had long since come to deny all purpose to the phenomenon of existence – it was more expedient and comforting.[49]

Port is unable to think with the irony of this aerial description. He instead, once again, constructs a viewpoint (this time, an 'inward turn' into a dream he had been trying to recall) in an attempt to efface any intentional relationship between himself and 'the phenomenon of existence'. Unlike the women in the story, Port has his tea at the *bottom* of the valley, and so it is ironic that he is now climbing up to a point that affords him the view that is fatal in the story from the previous night, on the threshold of the Sahara. But, already, this image is more than he can understand, and it becomes the first moment in the novel where aerial description foregrounds the form of environment at the expense of character – who will, in Part Two, die high up in a French military fort that 'dominates the town' of Sbâ, and feels like 'a separate town, alien to the surrounding landscape'.[50] His death is not just the result of his inability to adapt to the environment as he becomes physically sick, but it is his rejection and this inability to adapt to the imaginary form of the Saharan environment that leads to his even more significant existential death.

In this passage, the mobile, dynamic perspective of objects down below blends with the surround as the image unfolds, before it is finally folded back inward into Port's reverie. This is different from the dynamic perspective-switch of the previous passage because rather than an imaginary upward movement there is an actual Mercedes climbing upward. For the reader, like for Port, this is a moment for a conventional 'objective' view from above to be subverted by precisely the law Bachelard sets out: 'we have great difficulty imagining what we know'.[51] Alone (without his companion), Port has the opportunity to organise what has happened the day before – both the night out, a dream and presumably the 'Tea in the Sahara' story. This opportunity for retrospection is given via a material connection to his environment, the upward 'S-curve'. We have the distinct transition from the previous night, which was a plunge further and further down into an unfamiliar city under the walls in the valley, to the *upward élan*: the valley appearing 'a little less real' with each new, higher perspective up the S-curve along the hill. The description of the landscape similarly becomes less and less diegetically precise: from the perspectival focusing of Port's sudden 'start', the valley as 'straight across', the fortress placed 'perfectly' and an accessible image of the toy castle, the tents scattered like dots. But as Port climbs and tries to locate the previous night's events in this vivid landscape, the images are not integrated in this perceptual, downward 'knowledge', but start to climb into imagination. The description culminates in the rich poetic image of the mountains and the tents at their feet appearing equivalently formed. This is enough to set Port directly into the other 'events' – though unreal – of a previous night, the strange dream of 'a train that went always faster' that he only wishes to encounter as a puzzle, with no desire to integrate it into his actual world, keeping neatly separate what he knows and what he imagines.

A conventional interpretation of this passage focuses on the insight in his psyche (or the crisis that is set off) as Port dismisses a mysterious dream. This follows an interpretation of the novel that views the environment as a 'screen' on which the characters project their own psychological problems and existential dilemmas. But as analysed above, the continuity of these three images of the environment presents a progression of how its form becomes the direct cause of Port's eventual fate, not the blank slate onto which he projects terror and that reveals to him his sickness unto death. Nor is this an example of the 'openness' that Patteson implies (really meaning 'blankness', not potentiality) when he argues that Bowles's main problem is 'how to represent metaphysical vacancy in fictional form'.[52]

This can be rephrased more basically: the proliferating description of the environment in Bowles's novels is already an example of 'emptiness' overwhelming 'fullness' with respect to the function of description to deform narrative discourse. Foregrounding descriptions of the environment also shows how the environment structures movement – literally, in these examples as Port wanders up and down as he tries to escape the city, but also in the movement of the plot, as focalisation shifts to foreground verticality.

'Horizontality' in Narratology

This analysis of *The Sheltering Sky* is distant from most theorisations of the relationship between spatial description and narrative storyworlds. Aerial description and the images given in the midst and at the terminus of ascent foreground both the materiality of the reader's relation to narrative (through the experience of images of the environment) and the imaginary structure of the storyworld (through metaphors of experience as landscape). The imaginary structure – meaning the affordances of description of the environment – has been disregarded in most models of storyworlds developed by narratologists. Instead of following the distinct spatial phenomenology of the reader navigating through imaginary environments in fictional narrative, narratologists are typically more interested in a universal or abstract logic (or geometry) that seems to integrate the total function of description into the process of constructing representations of perception.

Narratologists often focus on the story logic that Hamon critiques for disregarding empty thematics. Monika Fludernik, for example, has developed a psycholinguistic model of spatial description ported from Holly A. Taylor and Barbara Tversky. Fludernik argues that it is important to consider that 'focalization and (a)perspectivism need not coincide'; or, 'focalization [. . .] need not correlate with spatial parameters'.[53] Meaning, a description can be given from the point of view of a character within a story without any graspable spatial arrangement of the objects or scene. By making focalisation an even more precise term, Fludernik opens up description to both ideological and cultural content communicated rhetorically and without a concrete form. Thus the existence of descriptions that are impossible to draw or map but simultaneously seem to communicate a precise perspective 'inside' the storyworld and not from an outside authorial narrator. Rather than turn to a phenomenology of this paradox of unmappably precise space, Fludernik reconceptualises focalisation through psycholinguistic categorisation in order to explain the experience of these at once indeterminate and yet rooted spaces. From Taylor and Tversky she pulls three types of perspectivism in natural language processing: survey, gaze and route.[54] The *survey* seems to be a direct parallel to aerial description as defined here – a 'bird's-eye view' describing something below and at a distance. A *gaze* is a fixed and specific perspective of a surround from the point of view of a character, and a *route* is a dynamic, mobile description, also from a precise perspective. Fludernik wants to further differentiate focalisation and perspective to show that something can be aperspectival in terms of deictic reference in conventional focalisation, but is still experienced as perspectival because of a more basic, human psychological spatial element that she locates in the three kinds of psycholinguistic spatiality.

In contrast, another critic who is interested in distinguishing perspective from focalisation is Westphal. For him, the more generative conceptual move is to consider multifocalisation rather than further differentiate subspecies of one, unitary category. This shifts emphasis from the quality of the subject's point of view to the form of multiple descriptions of a place collected from a wide variety of descriptions and narratives over time. An example of this would be the disparate accounts of Port's view from above the valley and Smaïl's story of the Moroccan women's view from the dunes.

Two key points – in the form of two reversals – should be emphasised here. First, space for Fludernik still has something like a geometry: there are vectors that either point or they do not, in some direction or another, from some determinate origin or not. These vectors, though characters, narrator-figures or authors, remain abstract. Westphal's multifocalisation makes the origin of this analysis material space itself, a geography. Meaning, multifocalisation is a given from the perspective of a specific space (or type of space, such as the summit, high point or lifted vantage being studied here) because of the variable ways of representing its form. Second, narratologists make distinctions about one single '*uni*focalisation' at a time, and these theorisations of focalisation are necessarily ego- or anthropocentric. In this case, ego is generalised in the narrator as the representation of a human figure with perceptual capabilities at least analogous to our own.[55] Thus, narration is primary, as it develops a superficially 'grounded' relationship between subject and the environment. Description gets short shrift because it often does not necessarily adhere to anthropocentric perspective.

As an example, we can make a parallel from the habitual theorisation of the function of description as representation (such as Herman develops in *Story Logic*) to the different modes of descriptive language in travel narrative. Westphal argues that the emphasis on representation has led to a proliferation of criticism on exogenous point of view, where description 'exudes exoticism' and subsequent criticism responds to the formal elements of the representation of the Other.[56] Not only does this subordinate other modes of travel writing – 'endogenous' and 'allogenous' – but it prioritises spatial metaphor over material spatial relationships available when an egocentric point of view is abandoned for a nonanthropocentric perspective. The ego-centric bias multiplies rhetoric associated with the 'outsider' looking 'in'. This is an abstractly constructed perspectivism that subsequently requires nuanced study of subjective focalisation (such as in Fludernik) rather than the form of environment given in multifocalised description. The most important point here is that narrative theorists have extended these spatial abstractions and have lost the environment in which the studied texts are embedded. This removes the most original feature of individual narratives: the way that description functions to open up a particular environment. Aerial description in *The Sheltering Sky*, for example, is notable not because of its innovative use of point of view, but because it subverts human points of view by allowing the form of environment to structure the narrative.

Axes of the Environment in *The Spider's House*

As in *Let It Come Down* and *The Sheltering Sky*, spatiality in *The Spider's House* is not definable through empirical psycholinguistic categories because the work is not organised by a narrator who represents perceptual experience in realistic deictic perspective but rather is organised by its vertical images from a variety of focalisers. Nor is it possible to centre meaning in the novel around superficially spatial categories such as inside and outside, other than abstractly and through a default subject-centred mode of literary analysis.

A comparison of two aerial descriptions of the city of Fez will tease out this point that description of the environment is not limited to anthropocentric positioning. *The Spider's House* alternates focalisations from a Moroccan boy, Amar, and an American writer, Stenham. Once they meet in Book Three, the focalisation is more variable, either free of any character or of their third companion, Lee, who has escaped her husband and has been travelling around the world alone, meeting Stenham in Fez. This first description is Amar's:

> The next morning he felt perfectly well. He got up very early and went out onto the roof to look over the wall at the city spread out around him. Fog lay in the valley. A few of the higher minarets pushed up from the sea of grayness below like green fingers pointing skyward, and the hills on both sides were visible, with their raw earth and their rows of tiny olive trees. But the bowl where the center of the city lay was still brimming with the nocturnal, unmoving fog. He stood awhile looking, letting the fresh early air bathe his face and chest, and he said a few holy words as he turned his head in the direction of Bab Fteuh. Beyond the gate was the waste land by the cemetery where he played soccer, and then the village of reed huts where there were many goats, and then the wheatfields leading gently toward the river, and then the mud villages under the high clay cliffs. And if you went farther there was a sort of canyon-land all made of clay, where in the spring after the rains the water rushed through, often carrying with it drowned sheep and even cows.[57]

This description would ostensibly fall under the category of Fludernik's 'gaze' perspective, as it includes the distinct – and oddly precise – motion of Amar turning his head (suggesting a hyper-precise deictic centre), amongst other subjective cues. But after this shift, the description becomes a 'route' perspective, which then makes it unclear if what is being described is actually available perceptually to Amar on his rooftop. 'And then . . .' 'and then . . .' 'and then . . .', along with the second-person address, opens up the extent of this aerial description through a kind of unnatural, nonstop motion spun out from Amar's head-turn. With this isolated example, it seems possible to say that the description from the 'outer' world given by aerial description turns 'inward' once the focaliser begins to imagine instead of see.

But Amar (or any figure of internal focalisation) cannot be some kind of embodied barrier by which to mark the crossing of external and internal. Rather than trace how the images are possibly 'inside of' Amar or even 'interior to' his perspective, the continuity of perception and imagination here suggests that the image is wholly an affordance of the environment, before Amar's perception. Meaning, this image of the city as bowl brimming with fog – pushing out over the sides with a momentum that pushes Amar into the imaginary – is not an aspect of any single focalisation, but is part of the form of environment, available to the reader through a distinct multifocalisation; Stenham later is the focaliser of a similar description of the city.

As it is articulated by multiple narrators, the environment here is shown to be organised not by perception, but by its imaginary, vertical form. The bowl image is held in readiness for the reader to be opened up later, when Stenham and Moss – a shady British financier staying at the same hotel – are making their way out to another hotel to meet a friend of Moss:

> Eleven hundred years ago the city had been begun at the bottom of a concavity in the hills, a formation which had the contours of a slightly tilted bowl; through the centuries as it grew, a vast, eternally spreading construction of cedar wood, marble, earth and tiles, it had climbed up the sides and over the rim of the bowl. Since the center was also the lowest part, all the passageways led to it; one had to go down first, and then choose the direction in which one wanted to climb. Except the paths which followed the river's course out into the orchards, all ways led upward from the heart of the city. The long climb through the noonday heat was tiring. An hour after they had started out they were still struggling up the crowded lanes of the western hill. The mist had been totally dissipated, the sky had gone blue, hard and distant. [. . .] [Stenham] knew perfectly well where he was going, but the fun consisted in seeming to be wandering until the last minute, and then making a sudden virtuoso turn which would bring Moss out into a place that would be all the more startling for being completely familiar.[58]

The 'bowl' image immediately ties this description to Amar's view of Fez from above at the beginning of the novel, but now it is not fog that overflows the bowl, but the city itself. Again, if we applied the psycholinguistic terms Fludernik suggests, this is simply a 'survey' perspective, as the suggested 'wandering' route perspective at the end of the passage is adeictic and contains no concrete description.

So how does the image transform from fog-as-liquid to city-as-liquid? It would be wrong to attribute this to the loss of subjectivity in the description in the latter passage. Rather, we can think of it in terms of the objectivity of the environment being described. The alteration of the description of Fez from above in these two passages begins to suggest that certain dynamic elements of navigating Fez are only available in the view from above, and this view is only available because it is a part of the form of environment in Fez. The storyworld opens up two kinds of movement afforded by the environment, and the plot develops under these two types. First, a succession of discrete, familiar spaces are described from Amar's perspective. Then a series of web-like upward paths structure Stenham's image of Fez, which are not imminently narratable but appear in aerial description.

At one point, the reader is confronted with both ways of accessing the environment when Stenham is imagining his time above the networked paths wandering Amar's mud villages and canyon-lands:

> Stenham arranged his chair so that he could lie far back in it, staring into the blue afternoon sky. [. . .] He was not sleepy, but he felt an utter disinclination to move or think. In his mind's eye he began to see vignettes of distant parts of the town: arched stone bridges over the foaming river, herons wading in shallow places among the reeds and cane, the little villages that the very poor had recently built at the bottoms of the ancient quarries – you could stand at the top and look down vertically upon their houses made in building-block patterns; the people were not so impoverished that their terraces could not be spread with orange and magenta rugs being aired, and women sat in tiny courtyards that were pools of shade, out of the venomous sun, thumping on their drums of clay. [. . .] It was all these strange and lonely spots outside the walls, where the city-dwellers unanimously advised him not to walk, that he loved. Yet their beauty existed for him only to the degree that he was conscious of their outsideness, or that he could conjure up the sensation of compactness which the idea of the Medina gave him. It was the knowledge that the swarming city lay below, shut in by its high ramparts, which made wandering over the hills and along the edges of the cliffs so delectable. They are there, of it, he would think, and I am here, of nothing, free.[59]

Stenham's idea of the city may be romanticised, but the reader has access to much more than his perceptions and judgments, and can here read his dreams. Amar's dreams and perceptions are also available, and the dynamic between them is less the relationship of colonial outsider and colonised insider and more a play between different ways of encountering the environment. Amar feels similarly free from his country when viewing it from above as Stenham does, despite their different origins. A non-egocentered approach is able to balance out the mediation of the environment in this neo-colonial situation and foreground that it is not just linear narrative (historical) plots that work into the colonial structure, but description and a 'vertical axis' of spatial relationships.

Patteson misreads this scenario as falling within Stenham's 'real' activity of constructing for himself (by travelling to further and further exotic, 'outside' places) an increasingly safer shelter through detachment from his life and the lives of others. He calls this Stenham's primary 'self-deception'.[60] This judgment of Stenham is accurate in regards to his refusal to understand the seriousness of Moroccan independence bubbling and about to break at this point in the novel, but associated directly here with a distinct image of the city from above, this self-deception applies more to the critic than his subject. In isolating the image of the city focalised by Stenham as delineated to the 'outside', Patteson cuts off comparison with Amar's (and others') own alienated affect. That is, by locating existential alienation with the spatial concept of 'outside', Fez itself as an environment is collapsed into a dimensionless 'inside', reproducing the same ego-centric error as Bachelard, only in reverse: here we have a within 'without a without', abstractly constructing categorically discontinuous viewpoints from which any foreigner's experience or any native person's experience of foreignness is ignored. In fact, this is a main theme of *The Spider's House*: the ambivalent relationship of Amar to his country's revolution.

Bowles's textual environments push against the discrete categorisation of 'insiders' and 'outsiders' and presents – through descriptions of ascent – the integration of the view from above with the process of reaching this perspective. In this chapter, I have foregrounded these transitions in order to show the primary effects of deformation that empty thematics obtain. In regards to the form of environment, this accidental feature of realism becomes an organising feature rather than a mere piece of story logic to be explained through mimetic psycholinguistic categorisation. Instead, empty thematics present the vertical imaginary of the environment as a negation of perception in order to decentre human plots. It is notable that the flexible fog images in *The Spider's House* echo the newspaper-fog of the Harry

Mathews story explicated in my introduction: just as the expectations of climbing to a height to see a view can be frustrated by the environment, so can the form of environment frustrate the habits of narratology and literary criticism.

Notes

1. José Manuel Lopes, *Foregrounded Description in Prose Fiction*, 5.
2. Philippe Hamon, 'Rhetorical Status of the Descriptive', 25.
3. Gaston Bachelard, *Air and Dreams*, 1; emphasis in original.
4. David Herman, *Story Logic*, 263; 281; 283.
5. Herman, *Story Logic*, 285.
6. Hamon, 'What is a description?', 318.
7. Paul Bowles, *Let It Come Down*, 251–53.
8. Ibid., 256.
9. Bowles, *The Sheltering Sky*, 245.
10. Richard Patteson, *A World Outside*, 71.
11. Anne Foltz, 'Paul Bowles', 82.
12. Much critical work on Bowles acknowledges a pilgrimage to Morocco and thanks him for his insight and clarifications. There has been only one critical monograph in English on Bowles since his death in 1999.
13. See Brian T. Edwards, *Morocco Bound*, 86, for details about the debate over Bowles's in/appropriate representation of Moroccan politics and Bouchra Benlemlih *Paul Bowles's Literary Engagement with Morocco*, 40, 70, on his translations of illiterate Moroccan storytellers.
14. Wayne Pounds, *Paul Bowles: The Inner Geography*, 1.
15. A similarly flat interpretation of affect and response is available in Leslie Fiedler's famous quip that Bowles is 'a pornographer of terror, a secret lover of the horror he evokes' and his dismissive criticism: 'The whole impact of his work is the insistence on the horrible, and his stories seem only literary by accident, despite their having appeared in very little magazines, and despite the astonishing ease and rhythmical beauty of the style. Like the tales of the science-fictionist, his work denies the world of our everyday living for landscapes more easily allegorized for his purposes; his mythic North Africa and Latin America has its reality in the nightmare, like the trans-galactic worlds of space fiction.' See Fiedler, 'Style and Anti-Style in the Short Story', 170.
16. Patteson, *A World Outside*, 2–3. Patteson points out there is additional anecdotal evidence for this organising principle in *Without Stopping*, when, as a child, Bowles dreams a burglar entered their home through a window and wakes to find it has actually happened.
17. Ibid., 32.
18. Benlemlih, *Paul Bowles's Literary Engagement with Morocco*, 73.
19. Ibid., 81.

20. Ibid., 122; 124.
21. See Marco Caracciolo, 'Leaping into Space', 256; Katrin Dennerlein, *Narratologie des raumes*, 17; Marie-Laure Ryan et al., *Narrating Space / Spatializing Narrative*, 41.
22. Bachelard, *The Poetics of Space*, 215.
23. Bachelard, *Air and Dreams*, 94; emphasis in original.
24. Ibid., 249; emphasis in original.
25. Ibid., 101; emphasis in original.
26. Ibid., 69; emphasis in original.
27. Marlene Marcussen has similar reservations as she turns to Heidegger and Casey from Bachelard because of the 'hidden psychology' that always informs his study of material space, as he was primarily influenced by Carl Jung. See Marcussen, 'Reading for Space', 76. My reservations are less severe because this psychologism is mostly exclusive to his study of interior spaces.
28. Bachelard, *Air and Dreams*, 60.
29. For the use of 'felt-meaning' as a term, see Eugene Gendlin, *Experiencing and the Creation of Meaning*, 6.
30. Roman Ingarden, *Cognition of the Literary Work of Art*, 269.
31. Bachelard, *Air and Dreams*, 168.
32. Ibid.
33. Ibid., 60.
34. Wai Che Dimock, 'Gibraltar and Beyond: James Joyce, Ezra Pound, and Paul Bowles', 61.
35. Ibid., 63.
36. Ibid., 60–61.
37. Ibid., 60.
38. Ibid., 61.
39. Ibid., 66.
40. Bowles, *Let It Come Down*, 254.
41. Ibid., 253.
42. Bachelard, *The Poetics of Space*, 168.
43. Even in Bowles's nonfiction, in his autobiography *Without Stopping*, there is the presence of these images of the environment as organising forms: 'The house was high on the side of a mountain, with a vast view of Los Angeles, the Santa Monica Strait, and Catalina Island beyond. I had not realized that the United States could offer such impressive landscapes. The interest lay not in the detail, but in light effects seen at great distances. What created the beauty, in effect, was the extraordinary clarity of the air. It is strange to think that in the few intervening years the entire area should have been permanently ruined.' See Bowles, *Without Stopping*, 182–83.
44. Bowles, *The Sheltering Sky*, 18.
45. Edwards, *Morocco Bound*, 110.
46. Alexa Weik von Mossner, 'Encountering the Sahara', 224.
47. Bowles, *The Sheltering Sky*, 30.

48. Though Westphal points to Bowles and Tangier as an example of these perspectives, he does not elaborate on how this multifocalisation functions in his fiction. Westphal, in fact, uses Tangier as an example for equalising the study of the three different forms of multifocalisation he develops. The Moroccans whom Bowles translated present an endogenous view of Tangier; the exogenous view is present through the writings of the beat generation – including Allen Ginsberg – who made Bowles a travel destination. Bowles's writing is in the middle, *allogenous*, because he settled in Morocco for over fifty years, 'but still remaining [a foreigner] in the eyes of the indigenous population'. See Westphal, *Geocriticism*, 129.
49. Bowles, *The Sheltering Sky*, 57–58.
50. Ibid., 161.
51. Bachelard, *Air and Dreams*, 92.
52. Patteson, *A World Outside*, 84.
53. Monika Fludernik, 'Description and Perspective', 474; 471.
54. Ibid., 466.
55. Or, in the case of 'unnatural narratology', perceptual capabilities totally different from our own. (See Jan Alber, *Unnatural Narratology*.) But this remains within a human/inhuman binary that does not positively theorise the *non*human, for one (see Caracciolo, 'Beyond Other Minds'), and also results in an impoverished and secondary theorisation of material space (see Marcussen, 'Reading for Space').
56. Bertrand Westphal, *Geocriticism*, 128.
57. Bowles, *The Spider's House*, 32.
58. Ibid., 148–49.
59. Ibid., 165.
60. Patteson, *A World Outside*, 36.

Chapter 4

'Only Scenery': Scale, Whole-Earth Images and Don DeLillo's 'Human Moments in World War III'

There is a commonplace that people became bored of the moon after Apollo 11 landed on its surface.[1] Matthew Tribbe points to 'the fact that Americans were never as keen on the moon program as current public memory and myth suggest'[2] and an anecdote from a 1973 essay in the *New York Times Book Review* by Hugh Kenner, a conversation between himself and the owner of a science fiction bookstore:

> 'I wonder,' I asked, 'whether the classic stuff lost its bite when we got so used to the real thing. Men on the moon on everyone's home screen. Fiction couldn't keep up.'
> 'On the contrary,' Mr Jolly replied, 'reality couldn't keep up. When your image of interplanetary adventure becomes a man in a huge white diving suit stumbling over a boulder, when you've lived through the excruciating real time of those slow motion excursions, then crystalline cities on Venus lose their believability.'[3]

As it is posed here, the borders of reality began to shift for fiction writers in the late 1960s and 1970s. With expert and complex technology entering popular culture in the form of a media barrage promoting the moon shot, the basic function of representation went into question. This is one of the explanations for the drift in literary fiction from modernism to postmodernism, so posed by Brian McHale's argument that there was a shift from epistemological to ontological concerns in the mid-twentieth century, an 'ontological shock [. . .] of recognizing that there are other worlds besides this one'.[4] No longer was progress headed toward opening up new ways of thinking and conceptualising the expanding world (as its space had been exhausted) it was opening up actual new worlds – spaces such as the moon. Joseph Tabbi calls the literary techniques used to express this new form of the unfamiliar the 'postmodern sublime'.[5]

Two images that exemplify the tensions between reality and representation during this period are the *Earthrise* and *Blue Marble* photographs, two of the few unplanned artefacts of the tightly planned NASA engineering spectacle. As Richard Lewis points out in a 1974 book about the Apollo program: 'the story of each mission was known in advance. It is prewritten in the flight plan that tells precisely what each astronaut is expected to do at a particular moment. It would be hard to find any aspect of human experience that is more regimented than manned lunar exploration.'[6] Because the narrative is fixed, the aesthetic artefacts that disrupt the flight plan come from an emerging counternarrative. Stewart Brand – who started the *Whole Earth Catalog*, the cover of which was adorned by early images of the 'whole Earth' from space – is by some counts the impetus for NASA to turn their cameras around with his somewhat tongue-in-cheek, conspiracy-toned button campaign that asked, 'Why haven't we seen a photograph of the whole Earth yet?'[7] The existence of the *Earthrise* and *Blue Marble* images taken during Apollo 8 and Apollo 17, respectively, is an aesthetic supplement to the scientific plan executed by NASA in the 1960s and 1970s, and indeed it has been interpreted under every rubric of the sublime.

The images' existence presents one of the only indeterminate artefacts in a nearly fully closed, determinate system; unlike the moon rocks that are subject to geophysical science or even the humans and plants returning as biological specimens, there were no theories to prove in regards to photography from the moon. The precariousness of their appearance is often backgrounded by the apparent inevitability of their existence. Turning the cameras around to Earth was unnecessary in a series of missions that was burdened with justifying each step as necessarily scientific. Robert Poole points out, 'Like the crew of Apollo 8, NASA was so preoccupied with the Moon that it too forgot about the Earth. Photographs of Earth hardly featured at all on the official mission plans; they belonged in a miscellaneous category labelled "targets of opportunity."'[8] A variety of contingencies are structured into their existence; for example, James L. Kauffman points to a scientist's testimony at the 1962 Senate hearings arguing against even the necessity of humans, much less human photography, aboard the Apollo missions, because regardless of the astronauts' agency they are still reliant on tools, computers and systems for which 'it would be necessary ahead of time to decide what feature of the unexpected should be anticipated'.[9] This tight form of contingency planning points out precisely how closed and determinate the Apollo systems were.

The question of whether images of the Earth are more significant scientifically or philosophically was a recurring theme in print and TV journalism during the 1960s and 1970s. Their precariousness became one of the reasons why their reception was so varied, as the 'general lack of preparedness had one important effect on all concerned: the sight of Earth came with the force of a revelation, a sense which deepened as the excitement of Apollo faded'.[10] As a scientist trying to capture images of the universe asks in Don DeLillo's novel *Ratner's Star*, 'Are we dealing with physics or metaphysics?'[11] The problem was indeed posited through this binary, its simple form determining the apparent simplicity of the problem: do we learn anything about ourselves now that we have risen above and perceived what Apollo's eye sees? The astronauts universally opted for the metaphysical route to describe their experience of the 'whole Earth', as did many people who only saw the photographs in magazines and televised images.[12] The media and popular reaction to these images is well-documented, and will be alluded to here, but in this chapter I will focus on some of the anomalies related to how these images are re-implaced in literature and their unique, though rarely exercised, function of affording an aesthetic encounter with the form of environment at such an apparently unprecedented and vast scale.

I will look at one of the only pertinent examples of extended description of the 'whole Earth' in literary narrative, DeLillo's short story 'Human Moments in World War III', published in *Esquire* in 1983. 'Human Moments' takes place some sixty years after World War II, inferable because the two-man crew of the *Tomahawk II* begins intercepting World War II radio transmissions that have been bouncing around outer space. The unnamed first-person narrator is a three-mission veteran and his partner, Vollmer, is on his first mission at age twenty-three. The ship is in low-Earth orbit, at 150 miles above the surface.[13] Though claiming that the story is notable for being one of the few 'whole Earth' literary texts could be accused of unfairly exploiting and exaggerating the generic divide between literary and science fiction – as cosmic, 'whole-Earth' images are more common in the latter – this is a pragmatic decision motivated by the relative lack of study of astronautical subjects in literary fiction compared to generic science fiction.[14] Aerial description set in this 'final frontier' follows the line the previous chapters trace in literary fiction from the American West and North Africa as 'frontiers' in their respective parts of the twentieth century.

Scale is a vital critical term for studying images of the 'whole Earth'. My approach differs from previous studies of scale in that I do not foreground scale as a new method for literary and cultural criticism, but read it as part of the form of environment. In this chapter, I will engage with recent theories about scale in criticism and literature by Timothy Clark and will elaborate on the rhetorical context of the reception of the Apollo images. Then I will discuss the reasons why the images were prevalent in poetry but absent from literary fiction. I argue that the existence of the 'whole Earth' in poetic images marks the transition of this aerial view from 'unnarratable' to 'unnarrated'. I will then turn to the scale of the 'whole Earth' as an unnarrated space of indeterminacy in DeLillo's 'Human Moments in World War III'.

Literary Criticism Without Scale

Throughout this book, I have been pushing against the dominant strains of ideological interpretations of the view from above. Critiques of the view from above are often complicit in the objectivity they criticise through a critical narrative not unsimilar to God's-eye- or, in this chapter, 'whole Earth'-holism. My argument is literary, and so description as a unique form is what breaks this narrative both in the fictional texts I am studying as well as the theoretical and critical background that informs this book. This is not to deny the genuine theoretical import of postcolonial criticism of the view from above nor the reality of historical applications of the view from above for globalism and imperialism and, as was shown in the previous two chapters, modernism. But I am opening up the 'local' experience of reading literary fiction in opposition to the hegemony of the narrative of aerial vision as a way to supplement these interpretations with a focus on experience. We must be conscious that the discourse communities that critique the historical applications of aerial imagery are also historically situated. How do we explore, as Benjamin Lazier puts it, the 'structural tensions between organism and artifact'[15] anew when considering 'whole-Earth' images re-implaced in literary narrative? Does the case of the 'whole Earth' alter the previous understandings of aerial description on 'smaller' scales?

In a sense, the previous two chapters have defined two imaginary axes of spatiality in descriptions of the environment by exploring extent and verticality. Even though they are careful to avoid the geometrical associations of 'horizontal' and 'vertical', these two concepts are difficult to untangle from experiences of repetitive extent or imaginary vertical ascent. What follows logically in a discussion of spatial form is thus a rational 'expansion' of this grid in a zoom out or in, that is, the concept of scale. This reasoning largely defines both the daily and critical concepts of scale.

The 'whole-Earth' images discussed here are the first version of the 'smooth' scaling images of the Earth that have led to both civilian and military uses of Google Earth as a representation of the Earth.[16] (I discuss these images and the smooth zoom in my conclusion.) Reading this image otherwise, from the imaginary origin of the 'whole-Earth' photographs, offers a different perspective that does not inevitably lead to concepts of scale that concentrate on the human act of 'zooming' in and out, but rather foregrounds inter-objective aspects of scale that the reader can access in the literary work. Literature exists within this 'scale variance' of reality that Timothy Morton develops:[17] its particular value is that it offers an articulation of scale without reference to human perception, instead foregrounding the imaginary. These aspects are difficult to access in daily life because of the fixed scale of human perception, and perhaps impossible to access with scale tools like Google Maps and Google Earth, as they embed smoothness rather than difference and discontinuity.

My utilisation of scale varies from this conventional figuration, which has been critiqued across disciplines concerned with globalisation and, particularly, climate change. The main difference is that I start not with the concept of scale and use it as the lens from which to look into the text, but rather read how the text itself articulates scale as a form in its specific existence. This conceptualisation of scale is already present in contemporary geographical methodology. My approach in this chapter is a version of 'literary criticism without scale', following the critique of scale in an influential essay as it pertains to geography, 'Human Geography Without Scale:'

> Levels of scale suggest an epistemological hoist – a methodological leg-up. These aerobatics – implying a transcendent position for the researcher – cannot help but undermine attempts at self-reflexivity. How, we might ask, can a researcher write seriously about situated positionality after having just gone global?[18]

Marston et al. get to the heart of my critiques of ideological interpretations of the view from above. Like Caroline Levine in the context of literary theory, the authors are interested not in predetermined concepts for how structures are organised, but in a dynamic analysis of how forms change once they are recontextualised and put into juxtaposition with other forms. Even more radical than Levine, in this geographical context the affordances of form are not stable, as their articulation may also be indeterminate: 'Whereas we embrace potentialities for creative forms of change and fluidity, we note that these moments are always occurring with varying degrees of organization.'[19] From this perspective, it becomes apparent that Levine herself is making an assumption about the stable pre-existence of 'wholes', for example, that depend on an 'epistemological hoist' that ordains the critic with the appropriate scalar tools to evaluate the text as 'whole' with separate 'whole forms' that clash within it.[20] The kind of horizontal separation between inside and outside that Marston et al. critique is available only through a further vertical separation between critic and text; they even go as far as to say 'if the difference between the horizontal and vertical terms rests solely upon the "point of view" from which space is marked, then there is no added value in maintaining their separation'.[21]

What would literary criticism without scale look like? This question comes as scale is being reconsidered for world literature, inaugurated by Wai Chee Dimock in *Across Other Continents* and solidified by Ursula Heise in *Sense of Place and Sense of Planet* and Susan Stanford Friedman in *Planetary Modernisms*. At worst, these approaches advance a positivistic and ironically geometrical notion of scale: as if the 'big' problems of globalisation and climate change require a similarly 'big' approach such as this 'wider', ecological scale of analysis. As Martson et al. suggest for geography, and as Michael Tavel Clarke and David Wittenberg acknowledge may also be a problem for literary studies, 'If the privilege ascribed to the global over other scales is an effect of the dominance of neoliberal globalisation and discourses linking size and power, one might justifiably ask whether academic disciplines prioritizing the global scale are serving or resisting the forces of capitalism.'[22] While the use of scale does present complex ideological problems, I am arguing here that it additionally obscures basic experiential insights from the act of reading.

Theories of increasing the scale of analysis by taking account for 'deep' time or space (as in Dimock or Heise) risk burying the subversive power of representations of the 'human' scale or other possibilities for interpreting 'large-scale' phenomena. When applied specifically to the problem of scale in relation to the concept of the 'whole Earth', Kelsey similarly points out that representations at this scale are much more radical than they are given credit for:

> Perhaps the most questionable aspect of the critical literature on Earthrise and Blue Marble is a tendency to underplay the radical significance of their retrospection. The critics, in an effort to locate these images within a history of territorial expansion and geographical prospect, tend to finesse the problem that the imperial gaze, almost by definition, did not look back. [. . .] The eradication of signs of empire in images that ostensibly include its centers of power throws a wrench into any neat ideology critique along these lines. In these iconic NASA photographs, the centers of imperial power disappear into an equalizing representation of terrestrial colors and forms.[23]

Mary Louise Pratt's 'seeing-man' is implicated here, as this figure resolutely surveys looking forward and down at 'virgin' land; by contrast, aerial description as it pertains to the 'whole Earth' affords, phenomenologically, a new form with which to construct description. As we will see with 'Human Moments in World War III', the material details of the Earth from this vantage are not only related to ideologies of scale, but directly related to the form of its presentation.

The most sophisticated conceptualisation of scale in literary studies is Timothy Clark's *Ecocriticism on the Edge*, which includes both a discussion of scale in relation to ecocriticism and a discussion of scale and 'whole-Earth' images directly relevant to the present chapter. For Clark, the image is a way to contextualise the method of interpretation, bracketing the 'default', human scale in order to record its effects. He argues that the 'whole Earth' is often reduced to a ready-made text for interpretation rather than a catalyst for developing new processes for interpretation: 'Always mediated in image or discourse, [the whole Earth's] eventhood is always being neutralized [. . .]. A new reading must try to respond to, and keep open, that peculiar eventhood, its challenge to the seemingly absolute reality of the "normal" human scale.'[24] Once viewed as an object constantly unfolding to the imagination, it now functions as a tool for reflexive awareness where 'the terrestrial measure constitutive of my world becomes defamiliarized and even deranged when the Earth as a whole is viewed as an object in that world'.[25] Denying the 'epistemological hoist' of the view from above allows Clark to redefine scale as not just a tool or an objective reality, but an effect:

> To contemplate the sight of the whole Earth is to think the disjunction between individual perception and global reality, a disjunction that has now become so consequential in the Anthropocene. The scale at which one speaks of oneself as a person-with-a-world may be constitutively opaque to understanding beyond a now dangerously narrow spatial-temporal window. [. . .] The phenomenal self-evidence of my singular world is itself a scalar effect unable, so to speak, to see itself as such.[26]

Here, Clark deconstructs the terminology associated with scale as it is assumed in critiques of globalisation. He argues that in the context of climate change – which creates new categories of objects – it is more pertinent to discuss 'scale effects:' 'phenomena that are invisible at the normal levels of perception but only emerge as one changes the spatial or temporal scale at which the issues are framed'.[27] For example, overpopulation is only representable via models in statistics or even literary art, but the model then becomes an indeterminate object rather than a determinate representation of overpopulation as such.[28]

In the context of literary criticism, I understand scale effects to be the determinations that follow critique based on the scale one chooses for analysis. Like the present chapter, Clark performs a close reading of a single short story to exemplify three different scales at which one can read: 1) A personal scale, which can be typified by 'naïve' readings on the level of character and plot as an expression of local character or psychological types. 2) A contextual scale, the norm for literary criticism, that draws a small circle around the text to explain its existence and intent within historical and national contexts (now increasingly becoming transhistorical and 'global' contexts as the circle slightly expands). 3) A new scale that Clark proposes is the appropriate form of critique in the present, which converts characters into 'physical entities' equivalent with all other nonhuman agents in the text and interprets plots on the millennial trajectory of outsized human population growth, extraction and combustion of natural resources, and destruction of the planet.[29]

I would like to extend Clark's critique to suggest that scale – like extent and verticality – is part of the form of environment. Clark makes similar strong phenomenological claims for his concept of scale effects: 'A given scale is not part of a world in the sense of [. . .] some recognized nexus of significances or field of meaning; rather, it inheres in any world as a dimensionality that is all-structuring.'[30] The scale at which a physical entity lives determines their experience of the world. Thus it is also used as or is part of an interpretive system, including human storytelling and literary criticism. Clark critiques scale as the unrecognised assumption that always defines the other in relation to itself. He defines his concept of 'scale effects' as the consequence of this assumption, which provides an awareness of scale that opens up a new form of critique, that is, ecocriticism. Continuing this progression, I am proposing that scale effects and the awareness thereof is a signal that there is something beyond human perception that destabilises an anthropocentric conception of scale; this 'something' is accessible in literary images, the form of environment as afforded by literary description.

Defining 'literary criticism without scale' is a recognition that scale is not only a theoretical tool for phenomenological analysis, but something to be examined as part of literary form as an articulation of the environment. As Marston et al. put it: 'For one encounters these "structures" not at some level once removed, "up there" in a vertical imaginary, but on the ground, in practice, the result of marking territories horizontally through boundaries and enclosures, documents and rules, enforcing agents and their authoritative resources.'[31] This is also Bruno Latour's call for the return 'down to earth' where there is 'No away. No escape. [. . .] [We] can still feel the sublime, but only for what is left of nature *beyond* the Moon and only when we occupy the View from Nowhere. Down below, no longer any sublime.'[32] Even Clark's sophisticated theorisation of scale effects still depends on a critical 'outside' and a view from nowhere, the implicit construction of which determine the interpretations of scale much more than any of the theoretical problems he attempts to solve. But a critical perspective that is 'down to earth' recognises that it is not just our human conceptualisations of scale that have agency in this situation, but the scale of the Earth itself that is articulated in literary images. This has been my motivation to focus on description rather than narration and foreground the ways that the form of environment clashes with the form of the text through aerial description as a space of indeterminacy. In 'Human Moments in World War III', description again plays a key role in the way the story unfolds, even more evident in the condensed form of a short story than the novels previously analysed.

An issue with Clark's conceptualisation is its assumption that scale effects can only be visible via representations and so literature as a model renders scale effects as eminently narrated and so readable. Despite his interest in Derridean play, he presents very few gaps in the texts he studies, instead locating the gaps between the scales at which one can read: the gaps between individuals and culture, culture and world, world and Earth. In order to continue my study of these spaces of indeterminacy that I locate primarily in the form of the text and the form of environment, I will point out how the 'whole-Earth' image is *unnarrated* in 'Human Moments' through emphasis on description; because, as Mieke Bal puts it, 'description is a form of *un*-writing the reality-claim of fiction'.[33] In 'Human Moments of World War III', in which two characters float in a vessel above the Earth in low-Earth orbit, the narrator fixates on 'human moments' that recur in he and his partner's work. As the narrator plays the explicit role of interpreter in this story, like a critic, we can think about his point of view as restricted to Clark's first, personal scale of interpretation. This is significant, as it stages the possibility for the reader to read beyond this point of view through the recognition that the narrator is leaving much of the story unnarrated. Before turning to the short story, I will describe the context for the 'whole Earth' that the images in the story negate.

Constructing the 'Whole Earth'

There are a variety of interpretations for why the two 'whole-Earth' images developed such immediate popularity. But the indeterminacy of their existence as well as the rhetorical context in which they were interpreted is much more interesting than any single interpretation. NASA photo AS08-14-2383 (*Figure 4.1*) was taken on 24 December 1968 by Bill Anders aboard Apollo 8 with a handheld Hasselblad camera during the first manned orbit of the moon.[34] It was not the first image of an 'Earthrise', but it was the first to be widely reproduced as such (*Figure 4.2*). A prior black-and-white image was captured by the unmanned Lunar Orbiter 1 in 1966 and Apollo 8 also captured earlier, live televideo and a black-and-white photograph of what is now called *Earthrise*.[35] NASA photo AS17-148-22727 (*Figure 4.3*) was taken on 7 December 1972 by the crew of Apollo 17 as they travelled toward the moon. Like *Earthrise*, it was also not a new image, despite the presentation of novelty. Rather, its popularity was the result of careful editorial work, though NASA is not responsible for the 'Blue Marble' title (*Figure 4.4*). Several satellites had already captured full-colour 'Blue Marble'-like images, the first being DODGE, a US Air Force satellite, in 1967.[36] Kelsey argues that it was inevitable that these nearly identical earlier images did not gain popularity: 'Only photographs taken by humans could signify our bodily arrival, our actual presence, at the extraterrestrial vantage that had underwritten the scientific imagination.'[37]

The differences between the original images (*Figures 4.1 and 4.3*) and their reproduced versions (*Figures 4.2 and 4.4*) are somewhat mundane, readily explainable via aesthetic and anthropocentric constraints, such as the symmetrical frame, recognisable horizon and colour correction. Denis Cosgrove points out a significant aspect of these images, one, in fact, that has nothing to do with the above material history of the images nor their reception, but with how they

Scale, Whole-Earth Images and Don DeLillo's 'Human Moments' 133

Figure 4.1 Original NASA photo AS08-14-2383. Image courtesy of the Earth Science and Remote Sensing Unit, NASA Johnson Space Center. eol.jsc.nasa.gov.

Figure 4.2 NASA photo AS08-14-2383 reproduced as *Earthrise*. Image courtesy of the Earth Science and Remote Sensing Unit, NASA Johnson Space Center. eol.jsc.nasa.gov.

Figure 4.3 Original NASA photo AS17-148-22727. Image courtesy of the Earth Science and Remote Sensing Unit, NASA Johnson Space Center. eol.jsc.nasa.gov.

Figure 4.4 NASA photo AS17-148-22727 reproduced as *Blue Marble*. Image courtesy of the Earth Science and Remote Sensing Unit, NASA Johnson Space Center. eol.jsc.nasa.gov.

are represented: 'Writings about them have paid little attention to their pictorial form and content; they have assumed instead that the pictures are so familiar that they do not require reproduction.'[38] He provides precise and beautiful descriptions of the images, noting that *Earthrise* is split into grey moon, blank space and blue planet, which function as an 'inversion of an intensely familiar representational theme: a nocturnal landscape illuminated by a half-moon'.[39] But the theme is primarily available once the horizon has been flipped from the vertical original to the horizontal (the image Cosgrove analyses). Careful description of the image reveals that, in fact, one is always describing the representation, no matter how concrete the description. Here we see the recurrence of Edward S. Casey's idea that description of the environment is always 'representation of representation'.

From the superficial edits and the inattention to the images themselves follow other interesting aspects of these images. The first, in fact, is that Cosgrove himself is projecting his three-dimensional geographical models onto this distinctly unique 'flat' image of the planet. It is not a spherical, explorable globe like one would find in a school classroom or a computer model, but a fixed presentation of one 'side' – necessarily the 'light' side – of this space at a specific time. Another significant aspect of these images' material form is that they are not conceptually 'global', not only because they highlight non-Western centres of power but, materially, they are constructed of segmented pixels that constrain the precision of the 'global' image. While this is literally true of the new 2012 *Blue Marble* series (NASA had to use composite images for the higher-resolution, 'updated' representations), Latour points out that this is true in both an abstract and a concrete sense:

> Despite the unanimous enthusiasm that it has aroused, the highly celebrated 'blue planet' has poisoned thought in a lasting way. It is a composite image that blends the ancient cosmology of the Greek gods, the old medieval form given to the Christian God, and NASA's complex network for data acquisition, before being projected within the diffracted panorama of the media.[40]

Even careful attention to description often leaves out a glaring detail about the images: they are dominated by clouds. In this way, expectations about what should be represented at this scale often occlude what is actually present. Kelsey points out the uniqueness of this scenario specifically in regards to space photography and its interpretation:

> A key source of historical tension in these images is the clouds. Although critics of the photographs often treat them as though they

were aerial photographs taken to a higher degree, they are not. Most aerial photography is taken through cloudless air to depict terrain with uniform clarity. The practice suppresses the very existence of a turbulent, moisture-laden atmosphere and brings aerial photography into alignment with the cartographic imagination, which excludes clouds from maps and globes. The vantage from space thwarted this habit and thus yielded unfamiliar images.[41]

It is this unfamiliarity that led to the variety of interpretations of the 'whole-Earth' photographs, each with varying degrees of precision according to what the images actually represented.[42] Literary texts have the opportunity to bring this blurriness between the reality of the images and their representation into the realm of fictionality. In doing so, aerial description continues the deformation process that is more readily ignored in popular discourse about the 'whole-Earth' images.

Literature and NASA

Norman Mailer was commissioned by *Life* magazine to write a series of essays on the Apollo 11 launch. In *Of a Fire on the Moon*, Mailer called the Apollo project and the colossal, coordinated effort to reach the moon a 'philosophical apocalypse'. This rhetoric is also used by David Ketterer in his 1974 study of science fiction to show how the trajectory of American literature's 'mainline apocalyptics' – Melville, Poe – are continued in science fiction.[43] He establishes the role of generic science fiction as the primary literary response to the new technological culture spawned by NASA.

Though Ketterer brackets realist literary fiction to claim ground for the seriousness of previously dismissed popular science fiction, in actuality, he may not have been ignoring much work at all. Poole notes, 'In the aftermath of the Apollo program the Aerospace Industries Association sponsored a study of the cultural impact of space exploration, and was disappointed to find that it had had "minimal influence on literature, especially poetry;" the poets' response was simply "years of silence."'[44] Though this conclusion is not correct as it pertains to poetry (as I explain below, the study was not interested in countercultural art), it is certainly true about literary fiction. This is not to say that NASA did not see the potential aesthetic impact of the Apollo project; from 1963 to the end of the program, NASA in conjunction with the National Gallery of Art commissioned dozens of artists to visit the NASA facilities and witness launches. A 1965 exhibition and 1969 book, *Eyewitness to Space*, collected paintings by James Wythe, Norman Rockwell and others. Robert Rauschenberg's largest print, *Sky Garden*, resulted from witnessing the Apollo 11 launch.

Writers, though, had a more difficult time than painters producing and promoting work about this period. James McElroy points to a material basis for this problem:

> Whatever else my imagination gropes for, it is neither easily familiar with nor easily insulated from structural steel, violent combustions and printed-circuit electronics. But in fiction – and I don't mean science fiction – how does one write about technology and its relation to people? Perhaps not directly at all, but rather in accord with some virtue of vision to be found in technology.[45]

But it is not just the materiality of technology that challenged writers; the problems originate from the aforementioned inherited problems about concepts of scale. Realistic, geometrical reproduction is more recognisable and approachable by popular audiences in visual media than alternative conceptions of scale that are not represented in space, as such, but to the imagination, as in literary art. Indeed, *Stoned Moon Book*, the poetic and photographic collage that Rauschenberg began during this time, was never finished nor published. This hybrid work of cut-up news stories and photographs related to Apollo 11 alongside Rauschenberg's correspondence and journals during his time at the launch could find neither audience nor completed form. Regardless, it contains a profound literary response to the Apollo missions:

> FOR THAT WHILE EVERYTHING WAS THE SAME MATERIAL.
>   THERE WAS NO INSIDE, NO OUT.
>   POWER OVER POWER JOY PAIN ECSTASY THEN BODILY TRANSCENDING A STATE OF PURE ENERGY. APOLLO 11 WAS AIRBORNE, LIFTING PULLING EVERYONE'S SPIRITS WITH IT.
>   NOTHING WILL ALREADY BE THE SAME.

The final line is presented vertically, parallel to a newspaper photo of the Apollo 11 rocket lifting off (*Figure 4.5*).

The cut-up poem and especially the final line – 'nothing will already be the same' – construct the essential paradox of 1970s space exploration: 'outer space' is only superficially on the outside when

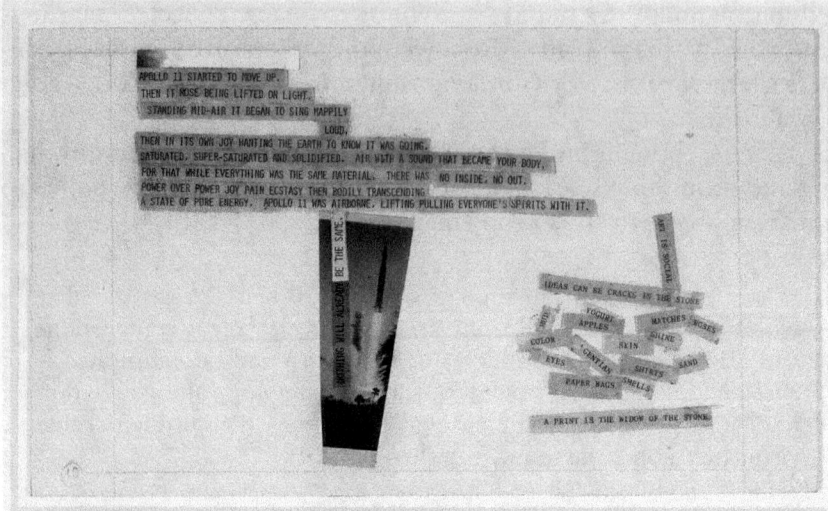

Figure 4.5 Robert Rauschenberg, *Stoned Moon Book*, Page 10, 1970. Image courtesy Robert Rauschenberg Foundation. Typewritten paper, Polaroid, acetate, coloured pencil, and graphite on illustration board. 9 ⅜ × 16 inches (23.8 × 40.6 cm). ©Robert Rauschenberg Foundation. RRF Registration# 70.D076.

one experiences the material effects of applied science and engineering at the very edges of progress. The sensation of the tangibility of 'outer space' is, by contrast, directly experienced in the bodily effects of rocket lift-off. Apollo 11, not just dependent on the successes of the previous Apollo missions but also all physical science before it, becomes a success even before touchdown on the moon, merely because it has come into being.[46] It is both already the same as these previous experiments because it is the conclusion of the theoretical proof, and it represents something different because it is not just a theoretical or imaginary object, but it obtains physical form. Curiously, Rauschenberg's line is presented in the future tense, which projects this impossibility furthermore into the future: what is to come will no longer be a surprise – because it will always be imaginatively predicated. It will be a *surprise at surprise* – because once it becomes a physical 'thing', the awe of its material form and its bodily effects leads one to forget that it already existed in another, imaginary form. This is the same experience that both predetermined and ignited the response to the 'whole-Earth' images.

The entirety of Rauschenberg's 'Stoned Moon' series (which also includes *Sky Garden* and other prints and collages that were finished and exhibited, unlike the book) presents a complex and changing relationship of American artists to the immediate wonder of the technological achievements of NASA. In his next project, Rauschenberg quickly turned on the official use of technology and the media's complicity in emphasising its destructive forms in the Vietnam War.

The technological complexities that Rauschenberg captured so efficiently in *Stoned Moon Book* were not as easily integrated into the structure of literary narrative. Tribbe notes:

> the hurdle for those writers trying to make sense of Apollo was larger than just an unfamiliar and puerile-sounding vocabulary more fit for vulgar science fiction than the serious literature that should be confronting the event. It went beyond the inevitable difficulties of working this new element of the human experience into the canon or injecting technology into the flesh- and spirit-oriented focus of contemporary literature.[47]

Mailer's *Of a Fire on the Moon*, for example, was not well-received: 'it often confused reviewers: space buffs found Mailer's philosophical ruminations insufferable, while readers expecting the Mailer of *The Armies of the Night* were baffled by the many pages he devoted to technical descriptions of the moon flight'.[48] This confusion was not just the result of readers' crossed expectations between a popular subject and a literary figure like Mailer, but the technological subject itself necessitated an overburdened literary style that had to both represent difficult material and interpret it simultaneously. William Atwill calls this the 'metadiscursive' response to space exploration in literature, which also includes Thomas Wolfe's *The Right Stuff*: 'Their texts are anxious about the limitations of language, claiming that technological subjects cannot be rendered comprehensible to those not part of the discipline, then contradicting that claim by creating a style, structure and syntax that do represent it.'[49]

This in part explains the empirical absence of literary fiction in response to the Apollo missions: writers found it difficult to render the contradictory nature of technological progress workable in a narrative structure, and readers more readily accepted narratives that mapped onto established tropes such as manifest destiny and the war hero. In these cases, as well as the international 'space race' narrative that the US government and NASA promoted, 'nothing will already be the same' becomes a repetition of these old tropes with new technology, rather than a prophesy about the material effects of technological and aesthetic artefacts.

NASA played a large role in shaping this discursive context in the 1960s and 1970s, which resulted in these unique 'metadiscursive' problems for literary authors. Kauffman argues that NASA used news media to simultaneously construct the narrative of the Apollo missions, convince the US government to fund the programs, and excite the public to understand and support the proposed goals. This was largely a result of replacing an old narrative with a more exciting one and moving the focus from scientific achievement to a necessary national act. A coordinated and consistent effort was required to code NASA not just as essential but as essentially American, even essentially 'human'. Most of this work was done rhetorically. From Mercury to Apollo, the language changed from experimental to explorational: astronauts were no longer called 'passengers', 'capsules' were now called 'spacecrafts', and they were no longer on 'rides' but were 'flying'.[50] This personalisation masked the shifting scientific and technological progress that may have benefited from the *absence* of manned flight, to the explicit agency of the human pilots who were carefully presented as the brain of the flight operation rather than the failsafe.

Kauffman argues this work was done largely by foregrounding the novelty of both the manned missions and their status as active exploration. This included an exclusive contract between NASA and Time Life for the astronauts' writings in order to promote the positive image of the prior Mercury missions.[51] The congressional hearings also relied on a frontier narrative that simultaneously downplayed and emphasised its scientific importance. Kauffman points out that two distinct rhetorical contexts allowed for the diverse narratives by which NASA convinced congress to provide unilateral support: the oral hearings included the Apollo missions as the continuation of the mythic American frontier to counter the recent USSR push into space, but the written committee reports did not allude to this narrativisation, exclusively including overwhelming technical and scientific arguments justifying the missions and their cost.[52] This means that the time for constructing a counternarrative passed after the committee hearings, and the written reports included a technological argument that could not be refuted by the non-expert congress members outside the committees.

This rhetorical context led to the existence and framing of the 'whole-Earth' images. But the attempt to map a clear and communicative narrative for the necessity of the Apollo missions also seemed to hinge on its internal contradictions, and this ambiguity was functionalised to easily shift across cultural contexts.⁵³ The conflicting mythic and aesthetic contexts enabled the control of the response through retrospective narrativisation: 'Both images owed much of their instant power to the way they tapped into a ready-made agenda: in the case of the "Blue marble" it was the eco-renaissance; in the case of Earthrise it was "Spaceship Earth."'⁵⁴ The force of these retrospective narratives downplayed any need to precisely describe the images, instead slotting them into pre-existing popular narratives.

Cosgrove differentiates two narratives that resulted from the *Earthrise* and *Blue Marble* images as 'one-world' and 'whole-Earth'. Cosgrove's commitment to the hegemonic, mythic narrative of the history of 'whole-Earth' images severely limits his interpretation of the historical events and is representative of most critical treatments of the images. Certainly, he is right to claim that 'the romantic association of (generally male) youth, power and will with the Apollonian perspective offered by air flight allowed for an heroic construction that attributed the airman with distinctively Modern qualities of scientific objectivity, technical mastery, global vision and, ultimately, mission'.⁵⁵ But this is the only perspective that Cosgrove considers, as if dissent did not occur. Though he notes the developing counterculture's response to the 'whole-Earth' image, most evident in Brand's *Whole Earth Catalog*, for Cosgrove this too seems to serve the direct relationship between technology and power, despite its insistence on 'appropriate technology' and the reduction of technology to the 'human scale'.

Negations of the Earth – Poetics of the Wrong World

For many artists, the image of the 'whole Earth' from moon orbit was a depiction of 'an entirely wrong world'. This is poet and critic Joe Luna's definition of what he calls the 'negative prosodic cosmography' that typifies responses by poets to the popularity of the *Earthrise* and especially the *Blue Marble* images.⁵⁶ Though the responses to these 'whole-Earth' images were varied, it is the immediate association of holism that unites political, ecological and aesthetic interpretations. Luna describes in great detail the response of the culture and counterculture to the Apollo images and develops a theory of the poetic response to the 'whole Earth'.

But why did the 'whole Earth' not appear in literary fiction? There are only a few works of literary narrative that have been consistently analysed as a response to the space race: Saul Bellow's *Mr Sammler's Planet*, John Updike's *Rabbit Redux* and the aforementioned *The Right Stuff* by Wolfe and *Of a Fire on the Moon* by Mailer. In the book about his experience on Apollo 11, astronaut Michael Collins wonders at the same problem: 'The pity of it is that so far the view from 100,000 miles has been the exclusive property of a handful of test pilots, rather than the world leaders who need this new perspective, or the poets who might communicate it to them.'[57] Collins foregrounds direct experience of the 'whole Earth', and not coincidentally singles out poets for their interpretation of this aerial view.

The 'whole Earth' became narratable, but only within the popular frameworks of mythic national narrative or romantic global holism. Poetry's main reaction was to recontextualise this image and show how, without the mythic narrative frame, it presented the wrong world. Once the 'whole Earth' had been perceived from space, these images offered affordances for further images of its negation. Luna argues that 'poetry was bound up in these events [. . .] through the way in which contemporary media made the adventures discoverable and desirable in language'.[58] The engagement with the 'whole-Earth' images and the reaction by poets was decisive and, as Luna argues, a continuation of Dante's apocalyptic images of the whole Earth from Satan's perspective in *The Inferno*, not the 'Apollo's Eye' image that Cosgrove promotes and was largely adopted by popular culture.

For example, Lawrence Ferlinghetti uses this image of a 'wrong world' in his 1973 poem 'Olbers' Paradox'.[59] He opens the poem with Walt Whitman's famous line 'And I heard the learned astronomer' but gives him a name: Heinrich Olbers. The poem constructs an image of a paradox hypothesised by Olbers that argues that the night sky should be light, not dark, if, as was argued during Olbers's life, the universe was infinite, static and so anywhere that one looks should be met by light from infinite stars. Ferlinghetti uses this cosmic perspective to imagine that, one day, this speculative space of infinite light will reach the Earth and reverse our experience of the night sky, where 'the part of day we call night / will have a white sky / with little black dots in it / little black holes / where once were stars'. Rather than the light reflected off the Earth and captured by the lens of a Hasselblad in *Earthrise* and *Blue Marble*, Ferlinghetti grounds the perspective to render not the 'whole Earth' but the 'whole universe' collapsed into and viewable as the lit night sky. Just like the typical usage of the 'whole-Earth' images, he renders his own reversed image as iconic in the last lines: 'And then in that symbolic / so poetic place / which will be ours / we'll be our own true shadows / and our own illumination / on a sunset earth.' While Luna focuses on Amiri Baraka and J.H. Prynne, Ferlinghetti's poem also resists the dominant claim that the 'whole-Earth' images are narratable, by showing how *everything* is outside the Earth and its collapse into our perception turns us into shadows, not new Apollos.

There are a host of studies in philosophy, intellectual history and the history of science that use *Earthrise* and *Blue Marble* to discuss changing ideas of the global in the twentieth century. By contrast, other than Luna's study, in literary criticism – especially focused on narrative – there have been relatively few comments. Even the most sustained literary critical approaches to the 'whole-Earth' images in Clark or Heise, for example, use them to frame larger cultural critiques and do not consider their existence or nonexistence in literary texts. This choice to frame the 'whole-Earth' images in a critique of climate change or globalisation discourse is indicative of the assumption that indeed the 'whole-Earth' scale is physically too 'large' for the literary text.[60]

Despite Clark's sophisticated and original interpretation of scale, the geometrical assumptions relating relative 'size' directly with scale remains. Unlike the present chapter, he does not start with the image and then discuss scale; the 'whole Earth' is considered a stable object (or artefact) to be interpreted and 'scale' seems to be the proper methodological tool to use. But the Apollo images of the Earth are by no means stable texts, as noted above. This is even more apparent in integrations of the 'whole Earth' into narrative, which do not obtain the reflexive commentary on the linguistic function of the 'whole-Earth' image as in poetry, but rather function to destabilise the image by re-implacing it in a fictional context.

The 'Whole Earth' from Unnarratable to Unnarrated

In 1970, Doubleday published an anthology of poems by US writers about the national drive into space, *Inside Outer Space*.[61] It is difficult to imagine a similar thematic collection of literary fiction. If the primary aesthetic reaction to the 'whole-Earth' images in the 1960s and 1970s was to deconstruct claims that the new perspective was unnarratable in any context other than a 'one-world' message, we should expect to find that literary narrative also interfaced with an apparently new and functional narrative form. This is not the case. Literary fiction does not integrate these images in any sustained way. Science fiction, of course, readily integrates these images into narrative, using them as a resource and appeal to the imagination of the reader. Space was a topic in popular literature in novels such as *Space* (1982) by James Michener and *Mysteries of Motion* (1983) by Hortense Calisher. Literary realism, though, did not develop a sophisticated response; based on Luna's interpretation of these images in poetry, this is ostensibly a missed opportunity: 'To describe the wrong world is already to appeal to something so far beyond our capacity to construe in practically responsible terms that it remains, in description, the closest thing to realism it is responsible to practice.'[62] If science fiction and other utopian fiction proposes a series of 'right worlds' – integrating the 'whole-Earth' images as recognisable references – description in realist fiction has the critical opportunity to respond by describing this 'wrong world'.

While these images in poetry make up the explicitly negative reaction to the 'whole-Earth' images, their empirical absence in literary narrative points to my arguments from the previous chapters: the primary feature of aerial description – of which the 'whole-Earth' image is the ultimate example – is to negate the perception of the environment. As this new point of view entered the realm of perception rather than its former existence in imagination, the simple recognition that it presents the 'wrong world' was not enough to make it narratable and integratable into narrative structures.

Rather, the 'whole Earth' has emerged from being previously unnarratable to presently unnarrated. Like all aerial description, it functions as an indeterminate gap that opens the reader up to the form of environment. The difference between what is *unnarratable* (impossible to represent in narrative) and *unnarrated* (a local instance in which something is outside the explicit content of a story) is a pertinent case as regards not just the concept of 'scale', but also aerial description, as we reach the limits of its definition once we consider this final aerial perspective. 'Unnarratable' scales could be considered those that are not amenable to human perception, which must be rendered using human tools to make them narratable and so affected by the human scale. By contrast, if we consider instances when scale is 'unnarrated', these gaps open up scale to be represented through their negation.

Gerald Prince considers the unnarrated to be primarily a temporal figure, but my conception brings it into the realm of spatial form.[63] While the unnarrated is a useful theoretical term, Prince also coins the term 'disnarrated' for the specific narrative technique that explicitly denotes negative space in a storyworld:

> terms, phrases, and passages that consider what did not or does not take place [. . .], alethic expressions of impossible or unrealized possibility, deontic expressions of observed prohibition, epistemic expressions

of ignorance, ontologic expressions of nonexistence, purely imagined worlds, desired worlds or intended worlds, unfulfilled expectations, unwarranted beliefs, failed attempts, crushed hopes, suppositions and false accusations, errors and lies, and so forth.[64]

The disnarrated is different from the unnarrated in that it is explicitly stated as *not* the case, rather than the unstated gaps between what *is* the case. With regards to scale, though, they function similarly, which also marks a limitation in Prince's theorisation: there will always be unnarrated gaps in which nonhuman scales (and forms) clash with human forms; disnarrating scalar relationships makes the limitations of human scale even more precise. For example, conceptualising the *Blue Marble* image as either 'one-world' or 'whole-earth' in Cosgrove's terms involves disnarrations that separate the world of the image from the world of phenomenological reality. Michael Collins eloquently captures this problem based on his experience as an astronaut on Apollo 11:

> Of course, we could always pass out whole-earth photographs and have everyone study them [. . .]. Unfortunately, it doesn't work that way. Seeing the earth on an 8-by-10-inch piece of paper, or ringed by the plastic border of a television screen, is not only not the same as the real view but even worse – it is a pseudo-sight that denies the reality of the matter. ('Oh, I've seen everything those astronauts have seen.') To actually be 100,000 miles out, to look out four windows and find nothing but black infinity, to finally locate the blue-and-white golf ball in the fifth window, to know how fortunate we are to be able to return to it – all these things are required, in addition to merely gauging its size and color. While the proliferation of photos constantly reminds us of the earth's dimensions, the photos deceive us as well, for they transfer the emphasis from the one earth to the multiplicity of reproduced images.[65]

Collins points out not only what is unnarrated in the typical narrative of one-world wholeness and fragility but, even more importantly, the way it denies reality, disnarrating the agency the 'whole Earth' asserts from this vantage. Collins specifically emphasises photographic reproductions as a problematic medium that simulates perception and thus makes the viewer feel like they can understand its meaning. Ironically, Collins then asserts a micro-narrative about what the experience was really like to contrast with the reductions of the photographs. Even though Collins explicitly asserts that he and his actual experience of the Earth from space are primary, he does so using the techniques of the imaginary, juxtaposing these two images in order to reimplace the 'whole Earth' for the reader of his memoir. Narratological tools help us see how these problems made narrativisation of the 'whole Earth' difficult to render coherently in official and media narrative.

'Human Moments in World War III' is, as far as I can tell, the only sustained aestheticisation of the 'whole Earth' in literary narrative after the Apollo images. Critique following Clark would show the different layers of scale effects available to an interpreter when teasing out the effects of different agents in the short story. This is functional, but the story is more radical: it stages the process of interpretation and renders it contingent upon the ideal of the simulated 'view from above' of the critic. The story takes place in low-Earth orbit, a prime space to experiment with descriptions of the 'whole Earth' as well as the local environment, and their synthesis affords experience of the form of environment, in this case, its scale.

Luna's 'negative prosodic cosmography' takes the form of the unnarrated and disnarrated in literary fiction. Most of the time – as is empirically evident from the lack of 'whole-Earth' images in literary narrative – this is figured as unnarratable. As DeLillo is writing in 1983, arguably after the peak of 'paranoid' fiction as it has been typified in his earlier works as well as in the novels of Thomas Pynchon, he has access to literary forms that now convert this unnarratable to the unnarrated. Previously, including in his 1976 novel *Ratner's Star*, the foregrounding of the unnarrated and the mystical intuitions of the paranoid figure in postmodern fiction was directed at governments, corporations and the scientific establishment. Transferring these forms to a presumably 'natural' figure such as the given environment is a new focus that DeLillo began in 'Human Moments' and continued in *White Noise*.

This conversion of encounter with the 'whole Earth' as unnarrated rather than unnarratable marks a decisive shift in the use of scale in fiction that is largely unprecedented, if only because of its use of a novel image. Just as Willa Cather and Paul Bowles were shown in the previous chapters to be at the frontiers of the unnarratable with respect to technologies and ideologies such as aerial photography and postcolonial geography, DeLillo foregrounds this indeterminacy by interacting with the technology of manned space flight and the point of view therein.

There are two stories in 'Human Moments', the second of which takes the form of what Porter Abbott calls a shadow story, or 'sensed possibilities of what might be the case, what might link the dots, however likely or unlikely'.[66] The narrator, though, readily provides an interpretation of this shadow story and, because he does so through the rhetorical context of the typical response to the image of the 'whole Earth' detailed above, he participates in the metadiscursive response to space exploration, and it becomes challenging to see just how unreliable he becomes through his apparent skills at reading 'scale effects'.

The narrator is not just unreliable; the story is an enactment of his encounter with the unnarratable. He puts on display the difficulties presented by scale effects, and this reflexivity is an opportunity for the critic to reflect on their own situation of being caught in the conundrum of having to choose the scale by which to analyse a text. The narrator picks a scale (human moments) and does not deviate; encounter with the environment (a 'nonhuman moment') becomes unnarratable except through Vollmer as a tool of vicarious perception. The reader, of course, is in an even more complex situation when confronted with this reflexivity, as the narrator becomes another vicarious tool for accessing the 'whole Earth' in the story. As Abbott puts it, 'How do we read what isn't there to be read?' – in this case, Vollmer's layered encounter with the 'whole Earth'.

My approach to the form of environment helps make what is absent in the story readable. It puts on display the inscrutability of the 'whole Earth' at this extremity of aerial description. By foregrounding scale as a distinct aspect of the form of environment, the critic has the opportunity to abandon scalar readings altogether, recognising that it is not the method of critique, but the subject. This solves a frustration in Clark's prescient theory of scale. That is, even as he deftly and originally identifies how prior literary method is inadequate for reading in the context of the Anthropocene, if one is to proceed, one still must choose a scale. Even with Clark's three carefully defined types of scales in literature, in the end – as he has more recently argued – perhaps scale is just a tool of deconstruction, a throwback to the continual indeterminacies of Derridean methods. Clark expands Derrida:

> Scale effects manifest materially the priority of alterity within iteration. They would thus add themselves to the series of related but not identical terms in Derrida's work, 'différance,' 'the trace,' the pharmakon, etc., each operating in a slightly different context. A scale effect is a thing, or force, or more precisely a difference of things and forces, with decisive effects while remaining 'that which in the presence of the present does not present itself.'[67]

Clark's return to Derridean play is perhaps not welcome in contemporary ecocriticism with its need for decisive responses and definite outcomes, but this type of critique becomes a window for more innovative formalisms to develop the tools – rather than definitive critique – for use.

Forms of Warfare

'Human Moments in World War III' has been interpreted as a story primarily about warfare, even didactically as 'a bleak warning of what happens when people become dissociated from war'.[68] This apparent dissociation shows how old and new styles of warfare are represented in literature, primarily because 'Vollmer still clings on to some aspects of the existential code'.[69] Elise Martucci argues that this dissociation is not just because of the new technologies of remote warfare, but also because of changing attitudes toward place: 'the characters view place as an abstraction or an idea rather than a concrete, physical location in which people are grounded. When they dissociate this way, they ignore the expressive energies of a place and, consequently, remain detached from the people who live there.'[70] These are, in fact, all scalar arguments, dependent on the apparent changes between the subject as a military subject no longer embedded within the battleground but rather physically above it or viewing a representation as if from above. 'Detachment' in this scalar reading is the interpretation of miniaturising the environment onto a screen or a window that implies a lack of physical proximity. This is put most directly by Michael J. Shapiro, who sees the 'target-viewing digitalization' of unmanned aerial vehicles or remote missile targeting predicted in 'Human Moments in World War III' because it functions to 'narrow' perception to an aerial view.[71] Importantly, the two characters in 'Human Moments' are citizen scientists under command of Houston; at some indeterminate point before the beginning of the story World War III is declared, 'Colorado Command' takes over, and their mission changes to inspecting suspicious satellites and tracking troops. In what has been written about the story, these concrete details are ignored, and the two civilian scientists are primarily considered to be military personnel. Equally important, in the story, all they ever perform are tests and training for the on-board weapons system, and there are no descriptions of warfare visible on the Earth's surface. Ironically, in this context, 'the banning of nuclear weapons has made the world safe for war'.[72]

Previous analyses of the story are nostalgic interpretations that graft the realities of perception onto the literary image in order to use the story as an artefact of the simulation-filled apparatus of modern warfare. This issue is approached more carefully by Fredric Jameson, who does not directly critique modern warfare because of this supposed change of scale but is interested in how this changes the situation of its representation. For him, the trope of the alienated soldier, despite being a recognisable narrative, cannot be the primary node of critique because it only maps one element of war's representation. Jameson offers a warning to diagnostic interpretations of representations of war, because the ability to present such a complicated network of narratives is less stable than any master critical-narrative can account for:

> The language of the existential individual already possesses an elaborate history with all kinds of stereotypes that it can be the task of representation to correct, disrupt, undermine, or metaphysically challenge. That of the collective does not yet exist. Group, nation, clan, class, general will, multitude – all these remain so many linguistic experiments for designating an unimaginable collective totality, a manifold of consciousness as unimaginable as it is real. War is one among such collective realities, which exceed representation fully as much as they do conceptualization and yet which ceaselessly tempt and exasperate narrative ambitions, conventional and experimental alike [. . .].[73]

This is the same reasoning behind my interest in 'affordances' and 're-implacements' of the environment rather than 'representations'. Just as war narratives are themselves a part of the existence of war, so are descriptions of the environment a part of the environment.

'Human Moments in World War III' is unique because it exploits the existential mode of war narrative at the direct expense of its reader's comprehension, by foregrounding unreliability and its proliferating unnarrated gaps. The former critiques of the story that readily pick up on this existential narrative miss the ways that foregrounding the 'human moments' is directly challenged by the scale produced by the story itself. Brad Congdon most precisely describes the story as a concentration of one of DeLillo's most recognised recurrent and original forms: the trope of 'men in small rooms'.[74] The 'small room' form – a kind of 'whole' to use Levine's term – structures DeLillo's novel *Libra* and has been read across DeLillo's work. But as it is re-implaced above the Earth in 'Human Moments in World War III', it offers a new way of understanding the representation of the environment. In the short story, the characters realise that, from above, there is no inside or outside. As such, the story is not an artefact of war but is part of the artefactual history of 'whole-Earth' images.

Human Moments and Human Scale

The narrator is fixated on the scale of 'human moments', and he narrates three stages that exemplify changes in imagining the 'whole Earth': first as a tool for imagination, then as a perceived object, and finally as the object of contemplation. In the end, he interprets Vollmer's apparent obsession with looking out of the window at the Earth as total satisfaction of his desires. Vollmer no longer has to speak about anything – neither his childhood nor the war – because he is busy contemplating the 'whole Earth'. But the 'whole Earth' is what the narrator sees, not Vollmer. The story is broken up by multiple aerial descriptions that are sometimes integrated into the narrator's discourse but, as the conclusion of the story shows, more often than not they disrupt the story entirely.

From the beginning, the narrator is fixated on Vollmer, who is the genius scientist to the narrator's professional role as the commander of the ship. The narrator focuses on what he calls 'human moments' in an explicit attempt to not 'think big thoughts or submit to rambling abstractions'.[75] As such, the primary details he notes are the orderly routines associated with their daily tasks as well as the mementos and memories they have brought from Earth, and he reduces the relationship between the two men to 'a housekeeping arrangement'. The narrator's explicit scalar dependency on 'human' details and the concrete acts of housekeeping are attempts at reassuring the reader that he is providing all the appropriate mimetic details required of an objective narrator. But by revealing both what is seen and the scale at which he sees it, he shows, from the start, that the narrative relies on this static interpretation of scale that does not allow the indeterminacy of scale effects and the ways that objects appear at different scales to affect reception.

His containment of their activity is an amusing if disturbing description, as the narrator is from the very start carefully delineating the scale at which the story will be told: he fantasises that it is not their job as scientists that brought them into close quarters, nor the war that keeps them there, but that it is 'an unlikely but workable setup caused by a housing shortage or spring floods in the valley'.[76] The narrator is aware of the absurdity of his relatively light-hearted conceptualisation:

> Earth orbit puts men into philosophical temper. How can we help it? We see the planet complete, we have a privileged vista. In our attempts to be equal to the experience, we tend to meditate importantly on subjects like the human condition. It makes a man feel universal, floating

over the continents, seeing the rim of the world, a line as clear as a compass arc, knowing it is just a turning of the bend to Atlantic twilight, to sediment plumes and kelp beds, an island chain glowing in the dusky sea.

I tell myself it is only scenery.[77]

Not only does the narrator reveal his consciousness of the relative, 'human' scale at which he is telling the story, but here he contextualises it as a reaction to the stereotypical cultural interpretation of 'whole-Earth' images. In the face of a 'universal' view, the narrator makes clear that this is not a perspective he wishes to adopt. Thus, his almost obsessive descriptions of Vollmer are coded in this reflexive awareness. From the scale of human moments, the narrator is focused on the ways that Vollmer's thinking and behaviour is changing. Vollmer does not attempt to deny the 'philosophical temper' afforded by his view of the Earth, but he also – at least in his few speeches and the indirect dialog – does not evade it through metaphysics. The narrator sees the 'housekeeping' scale within the *Tomahawk II* as separate from the scale of the Earth – and it seems like Vollmer does initially as well – but once the image begins to pervade the story, this apparent stability begins to break down.

Vollmer also sees the Earth as 'only scenery', but this materiality is precisely what makes it significant for him:

A note about Vollmer. He no longer describes the earth as a library globe or a map that has come alive, as a cosmic eye staring into deep space. This last was his most ambitious fling at imagery. The war has changed the way he sees the earth. The earth is land and water, the dwelling place of mortal men, in elevated dictionary terms. He doesn't see it anymore (storm-spiraled, sea-bright, breathing heat and haze and color) as an occasion for picturesque language, for easeful play or speculation.

At two hundred and twenty kilometers we see ship wakes and the larger airports. Icebergs, lightning bolts, sand dunes. I point out lava flows and cold-core eddies. That silver ribbon off the Irish coast, I tell him, is an oil slick.[78]

Importantly, though the narrator authoritatively states that 'The war has changed the way he sees the earth', this is unsubstantiated, a tinge of the unnarrated breaking through. Later, the narrator expands:

I try to keep our conversations on an everyday plane. I make it a point to talk about small things, routine things. This makes sense to me. It seems a sound tactic, under the circumstances, to restrict our talk to familiar topics, minor matters. I want to build a structure of the commonplace. But Vollmer has a tendency to bring up enormous subjects. He wants to talk about war and the weapons of war. He wants to discuss global strategies, global aggressions. I tell him now that he has stopped describing the Earth as a cosmic eye he wants to see it as a game board or computer model. He looks at me plain-faced and tries to get me into a theoretical argument: selective space-based attacks versus long, drawn-out, well-modulated land-sea-air engagements. He quotes experts, mentions sources. What am I supposed to say?[79]

The narrator's question here is an example of the disnarrated, where he poses his response to Vollmer's behaviour as an impossible and unrealised reaction. From this, we can determine the first two movements in Vollmer's point of view, as the narrator interprets it: 1) he appears to be overwhelmed and excited by the view of the Earth from space and 2) the war converts it into abstract, theoretical space that affords an engagement with the Earth as the background for explanations of war rather than foregrounded description.

In both cases, to the narrator's evident annoyance, Vollmer is exceedingly vocal. Despite this, the narrator cannot help but identify with Vollmer and sympathise with what he voices that the narrator himself cannot: 'Vollmer has never said a stupid thing in my presence. It is just his voice that is stupid, a grave and naked bass, a voice without inflection or breath.'[80] The narrator responds in parentheticals and frequently notes in the subjunctive what he would have liked to vocalise in response. This occurs most interestingly in a monologue by Vollmer about power:

> We study our world-map kits.
> 'Don't you sometimes feel a power in you?' Vollmer says. 'An extreme state of good health, sort of. An arrogant healthiness. That's it. You are feeling so good you begin thinking you're a little superior to other people. A kind of life-strength. An optimism about yourself that you generate almost at the expense of others. Don't you sometimes feel this?'
> (Yes, as a matter of fact.)
> 'There's probably a German word for it. But the point I want to make is that this powerful feeling is so – I don't know – delicate. That's it. One day you feel it, the next day you are suddenly puny and doomed. A single little thing goes wrong, you feel doomed, you feel utterly weak and defeated and unable to act powerfully or even sensibly. Everyone else is lucky, you are unlucky, hapless, sad, ineffectual and doomed.'

(Yes, yes.)
By chance, we are over the Missouri River now, looking toward the Red Lakes of Minnesota. I watch Vollmer go through his map kit, trying to match the two worlds. This is a deep and mysterious happiness, to confirm the accuracy of a map. He seems immensely satisfied. He keeps saying, 'That's it, that's it.'[81]

This ambivalent notion of power is also associated with Vollmer's general authority in the story, subverting the narrator's position – and, literally, his voice, through the disnarrated responses represented in parentheses.

The narrator's focus on change and voice is further exemplified in the only plotted event that occurs in the story: they begin to pick up unidentified voices in their communications system – 'selective noise' – that they realise are World War II radio broadcasts from the United States mysteriously bounced from satellites much higher than their low-Earth orbit, from 22,000-mile geostationary orbit. The disembodied, alien voice is a conventional science fiction trope that is presented dead-on-arrival; it does not advance the plot nor does it become part of the story. Its notability stems from the narrator's obsession with voice and is used to deflect the fact that his own voice is anything but neutral, transparent and omniscient. Vollmer begins to find value in these nostalgic voices: 'Vollmer says he remembers these programs although of course he has never heard them before.'[82] The narrator leaves his own reaction to the broadcasts unnarrated, as if he had heard them before. What is revealed in this gap is the narrator's own differing attitude toward expression in general. The voices are not pleasant and nostalgic but rather 'have the detached and surreal quality of aural hallucination, voices in attic rooms, the complaints of dead relatives'.[83]

Describing the 'Whole Earth'

The narrator describes Vollmer's changing attitudes to the Earth through disnarrating his own reactions, and his annoyance becomes evident through his attitude toward the human voices, his shifting descriptions, and Vollmer's direct dialog. But it is Vollmer's final stage of relationship to the Earth – the negative act of *not describing* – that is most important, the meaning of which is least available from the limited perspective of the narrator. Before Vollmer's 'strange phase' of silence that ends the story, the narrator reports Vollmer's final aerial description, in which he seems to be synthesising his 'board-game' understanding of war space and his former concrete, picturesque descriptions of the Earth. Vollmer says:

> 'It's almost unbelievable when you think of it, how they live there in all that ice and sand and mountainous wilderness. Look at it,' he says. 'Huge barren deserts, huge oceans. How do they endure all those terrible things? The floods alone. The earthquakes alone make it crazy to live there. Look at those fault systems. They're so big, there's so many of them. The volcanic eruptions alone. What could be more frightening than a volcanic eruption? How do they endure avalanches, year after year, with numbing regularity? It's hard to believe people live there. The floods alone. You can see whole huge discolored areas, all flooded out, washed out. How do they survive, where do they go? Look at the cloud buildups. Look at that swirling storm center. What about the people who live in the path of a storm like that? It must be packing incredible winds. The lightning alone. People exposed on beaches, near trees and telephone poles. Look at the cities with their spangled lights spreading in all directions. Try to imagine the crime and violence. Look at the smoke pall hanging low. What does that mean in terms of respiratory disorders? It's crazy. Who would live there? The deserts, how they encroach. Every year they claim more and more arable land. How enormous those snowfields are. Look at the massive storm fronts over the ocean. There are ships down there, small craft, some of them. Try to imagine the waves, the rocking. The hurricanes alone. The tidal waves. Look at those coastal communities exposed to tidal waves. What could be more frightening than a tidal wave? But they live there, they stay there. Where could they go?'[84]

Vollmer's description is a random spatial rush that matches their 'cross-orbit series' which includes 'no repetition from one swing around the Earth to the next'.[85] His aerial description has shifted from the conventional 'globe' before the war that resembles the typical reaction to the *Blue Marble* photography, to the abstraction of theoretical war-space, and finally to a realisation that it is not the war that threatens humans, but the Earth itself – a scale independent of his ways of imagining it. The static images of both his pre-war and early-war aerial descriptions are made dynamic by Vollmer's discovery that it is not really humankind moving around on top of a beautiful 'cosmic eye', but the species is static and enclosed within an Earth that is not singular and is made up of an endless variety of environments that constantly threaten to change.

The narrator does not react to Vollmer's recognition, and afterward when Vollmer falls silent the narrator attempts to construct a similar description as a way of speculating what Vollmer would be saying:

> The view is endlessly fulfilling. It is like the answer to a lifetime of questions and vague cravings. It satisfies every childlike curiosity, every muted desire, whatever there is in him of the scientist, the poet, the primitive seer, the watcher of fire and shooting stars, whatever obsessions eat at the night side of his mind, whatever sweet and dreamy yearning he has ever felt for nameless places faraway, whatever earth sense he possesses, the neural pulse of some wilder awareness, a sympathy for beasts, whatever belief in an immanent vital force, the Lord of Creation, whatever secret harboring of the idea of human oneness, whatever wishfulness and simplehearted hope, whatever of too much and not enough, all at once and little by little, whatever burning urge to escape responsibility and routine, escape his own overspecialization, the circumscribed and inward-spiraling self, whatever remnants of his boyish longing to fly, his dreams of strange spaces and eerie heights, his fantasies of happy death, whatever indolent and sybaritic leanings – lotus-eater, smoker of grasses and herbs, blue-eyed gazer into space – all these are satisfied, all collected and massed in that living body, the sight he sees from the window.[86]

The narrator is doing a kind of virtual reading of the 'whole Earth' through describing what he assumes that Vollmer is seeing as he 'has entered a strange phase' in which 'he spends all his time at the window now, looking down at the earth. He says little or nothing. He simply wants to look, do nothing but look.'[87] The narrator interprets Vollmer's catatonic stare as a regression, and his description here eloquently and persuasively presents a conventional explanation of sublime awe at the view of the 'whole Earth'. This interpretation convinces the previous critics of the short story, described above, who then read the narrator's explanation prescriptively and interpret the story as an existential exploration of Vollmer's status as an alienated soldier. But reducing Vollmer in this way takes for granted what the narrator leaves unnarrated. In these analyses, the image of the 'whole Earth', once again, is used as an icon for the sublime and a revelation of globality and planetarity: as the presentation of a 'scale' that human cognition cannot reckon with and so one must regress or retreat.

But rather than an exemplar of postmodern warfare and alienation, the use of an unreliable narrator and the 'whole-Earth' image as an obstacle for the story's progression becomes a chance to recognise the use of scale as a form that shapes both the encounter with the story and the image of the environment it presents. Vollmer's main recognition is that scale is independent of himself, and he responds through silence.

The reader, in an ironic distance from the unreliable narrator, is able to encounter the 'whole Earth' through Vollmer's explicit negation of the human. A spatial sequence is drawn from the Earth, to Vollmer, to the narrator and finally to the reader. Each presents an instance of viewing that negates the previous. Structurally, each step presents gaps: the Earth is unnarratable, Vollmer's character is unnarrated, and the narrator is disnarrated. This sequence leaves the reader with the opportunity to jump in at any one of these points to interpret the descriptions as well as their sequence in the story. Looking at 'scale effects' is one attempt to remedy the contradictory readings at each of these points of view, reading the Earth, the characters and their environment in low-Earth orbit equally as physical entities that ultimately lead to the stasis of the story.

Another option is to use this opportunity to think about scale as a form constructed from the story as an articulation of the environment that it describes, rather than a concept by which to read it. This is evident in the details of the two contrasting passages quoted above. While both aerial descriptions are indexical, exhaustive and expressive, the narrator's looks much different than Vollmer's. The narrator is fixated on the 'wrong world'. In this case, the 'inner world' of perception and the desires that motivate perception. The narrator is restricted to the naïve scale of 'human moments' and so, naturally, he can only describe desire, the feelings that the 'whole Earth' evokes. Vollmer's silence is an example of a description that cannot be articulated on the level of content, but is only formally communicated as a space of indeterminacy that cannot be accessed from the narrator's scale of interpretation. The story does not present 'distance' as equivalent to the type of screen-warfare of remote pilots. Instead, the scale of the 'whole Earth' entangles these 'soldiers' with the environment; they cannot separate themselves from the aesthetic encounter. This is in opposition to Coker and Martucci: in no way is Vollmer 'dissociated' from the Earth because of war. In fact, he feels intimately tied to a part of war, the environment, that is not recognisable to typical scales of analysis but is present in the silent, unnarrated gaps.

Colors and Forms

The last example of disnarration and aerial description of the 'whole Earth' comes from a split in the final two lines of the story. These lines are the same, but one is direct dialog and the second returns to the narrator's voice:

> 'It is just so interesting,' he says at last. 'The colors and all.'
> The colors and all.[88]

These two utterances function completely differently, not just because of their origin, but because of the forms they evoke. The first is description, the second is narration. It may be controversial to label Vollmer's dialog as 'description', as it is the narrator's report of Vollmer's dialog. But this is precisely the type of analysis that a reorientation toward the image and the form of environment, rather than perception and the form of the text (as apart from the environment), enables. The scale of the environment is not contained by the narrator's massive index of everything related to the anthropocentric conception of it. The entire list summoned by the narrator's response to the meaning of the 'whole Earth' is negated by Vollmer's simple description of its form. The scale as it pertains to the encounter between human and environment is deceptively simple: '"The colors and all."'

There is a radical indeterminacy present in whether the narrator is ironically repeating Vollmer's description as a recognition that it is more elegant than his encyclopaedic description of the meaning of the 'whole Earth', or if he is confounded by another example of Vollmer's apparently 'stupid' regression. Earlier, he wonders: 'Why, then, if I agree with his views on this matter, am I becoming irritated by his complaints? [. . .] Is it the sound of his voice? Is it just his *voice* that is driving me crazy?'[89] This line presents a complex relationship between content and form in the final lines of the story. The narrator has a 'human' conception of form, evident in the above list of human desires as it pertains to the environment; that is, he naively reads Vollmer's voice as a direct expression of his desires. But in this final line, Vollmer is 'voicing' – articulating – the form of environment. As such, Vollmer's 'stupid' voice and the agreeableness of what he says collapses. What he says and how he says it are not separate in this final utterance and so the narrator responds here in a disnarrated line, similar to his parenthetical responses to Vollmer's earlier questions about power. It is not Vollmer speaking in the final lines, but the Earth being articulated, which must end the story: if we recall from Chapter 1, this is the example par excellence of Philippe Hamon's idea that 'description makes all narrative impossible'. Despite the narrator's restriction to the scale of 'human moments', the text becomes a continuous articulation of the environment.

The agency of the Earth scale is further corroborated by the fact that this articulation repeats one of the essential responses to the 'whole Earth'. As noted above, Kelsey points out that the clouds are generally unmentioned in representations of *Earthrise* and *Blue Marble*; everything is reduced to 'colors and forms'. He also notes the historical account that when 'Asked to talk about colors, [Apollo 8 astronaut James] Lovell spends much of his time talking about the bright white clouds that cover most of the earth he can see.'[90] Vollmer's previous image of the Earth that is dominated by destruction, migration and terrestrial power is replaced after his period of silence with this image of the Earth's nonhuman form. The surprise in Vollmer's former description – 'It's almost unbelievable when you think of it' – gives way to *surprise at surprise* that results in silence. What he previously described as an index of everything 'alone' – 'The floods alone. The earthquakes alone [. . .]. The volcanic eruptions alone. [. . .] The lightning alone. [. . .] The hurricanes alone'[91]– becomes impossible to separate discretely. Seeing these terrestrial events and the human reactions 'alone' reproduces the narrator's scale of 'human moments' with an expanded scale to account for the globe. But when finally articulated at the scale of 'the colors and all', the description detaches from human moments and becomes unnarrated. 'Scale effects' are not just the objects of a new mode of critique, but through the story we see how, more directly, scale *affects* human subjects by presenting an encounter with the imaginary form of environment.

This conclusion can be read into this chapter's excursion into historical research relating to the Apollo missions and the reception of the 'whole Earth' images. As I have shown in this chapter, the *Earthrise* and *Blue Marble* photographs are the concretisation of the technological progress and official narrative control naturalised by a determinate system of power and perception in the United States. Aerial description has the unique opportunity to negate these perceptions and assert that this is the wrong world, and 'Human Moments' does so through Vollmer's transition to silence. This can also be seen in the previous two chapters' contexts of first-flight and colonial geographies. Shifting emphasis away from human narratives to the form of environment and the images afforded by aerial description reveal the ways that critical prioritisation of perception and reality neutralise the primary force of fictional worlds. Extent, verticality and scale in the environment affect the ways images can behave, as framed by humans. But their inhuman affordances are always present, and the view from above stretches these three dimensions out of perception and into imagination to reveal the ways that art and the encounter with art necessitate a constant sensitivity to the constraints of naturalised human points of view. In this way, being attuned to the unnatural in art can bring us closer to the natural world.

Notes

1. For an excellent review of historical literature related to the radical cultural influence of NASA in the 1970s see Daniel Sage, *How Outer Space Made America*, Chapter 6, as well as Roger D. Launius, 'Interpreting the Moon Landings'.
2. Matthew D. Tribbe, *No Requiem for the Space Age*, 10.
3. Hugh Kenner, 'Gee!', 391; qtd. in Tribbe, *No Requiem for the Space Age*, 191.
4. Brian McHale, 'Break, Period, Interregnum', 336.
5. Joseph Tabbi, *Postmodern Sublime*, 20.
6. Richard S. Lewis, *The Voyages of Apollo and the Exploration of the Moon*, xi.
7. See Andrew G. Kirk, *Counterculture Green*, 40–41, for an account of this story.
8. Robert Poole, *Earthrise*, 2.
9. United States Senate, *Scientists' Testimony on Space Goals* 88th congress, 1st session 1962, 6; qtd. in James L. Kauffman, *Selling Outer Space*, 106.
10. Poole, *Earthrise*, 3.
11. Don DeLillo, *Ratner's Star*, 49.
12. For an alternative account see Robin Kelsey, who argues that this metaphysical/physical dichotomy may not have been the most accurate way to parse the question posed by the images, as the images more readily present the dichotomy of 'the instrumental ambition of modern science and an ecological understanding of the earth'. See Kelsey, 'Reverse Shot: Earthrise and Blue Marble in the American Imagination', 14.
13. In this way, I recognise that the imagery is not concretely the 'whole Earth' captured from 18,000 miles in the 'Blue Marble' photographs, but the negation of this scale is afforded by the distance and more 'complete' view of these photographs.
14. For example, Bo Pettersson argues that the generic divide between science fiction and realism is exaggerated, as both share the same techniques for mimetic descriptions to satisfy the reader. See Pettersson, *How Literary Worlds are Shaped*, 67–74. An interesting counterpoint is Alex Houen's persuasive arguments that when it comes to literary fiction, the metaphysical distinction that William S. Burroughs, for example, posited between 'science fiction' and 'scientific fact' that is the premise of realist fiction *about* science, trumps the apparently similar descriptive techniques shared by both modes. See Houen, *Powers of Possibility*, 123.

15. Benjamin Lazier, 'Earthrise; or, the Globalization of the World Picture', 608.
16. The Eames animation *Powers of Ten* is a popular target of the critique of modern, global conceptions of scale and power; see Chris Tong, 'Ecology Without Scale;' Derek Woods, 'Scale Variance and the Concept of Matter'.
17. See Timothy Morton, *Humankind*, 186.
18. Sallie A. Marston et. al., 'Human Geography Without Scale', 422.
19. Ibid., 425.
20. See Caroline Levine, *Forms*, 40.
21. Ibid., 420.
22. Michael Tavel Clarke and David Wittenberg, 'Introduction', 12.
23. Kelsey, 'Reverse Shot', 15.
24. Timothy Clark, *Ecocriticism on the Edge*, 31.
25. Ibid., 35.
26. Ibid., 36.
27. Ibid., 22.
28. See ibid., 87–88.
29. See ibid., 99–104.
30. Clark, 'Scale as a Force of Deconstruction', 83.
31. Marston et. al., 'Human Geography Without Scale', 420.
32. Bruno Latour, 'Waiting for Gaia: Composing the Common World through Arts and Politics', 28.
33. Mieke Bal, 'Over-writing as Un-writing', 351.
34. See Daniel Cosgrove, 'Contested Global Visions', 274, for additional photographic details.
35. The *Lunar Orbiter 1* image is actually an 'Earthset'. For detailed astrophysical analysis of the images and their capture, see Lazier, 'Earthrise', 626.
36. See Poole, *Earthrise*, 194–96, for an excellent timeline of NASA space photography.
37. Kelsey, 'Reverse Shot', 12.
38. Cosgrove, 'Contested Global Visions', 274. This is one of my reasons for reprinting these apparently familiar images in colour here.
39. Ibid., 275.
40. Latour, *Facing Gaia*, 136.
41. Kelsey, 'Reverse Shot', 14.
42. Cosgrove, 'Contested Global Visions', 276, points to another misrepresentation of *Earthrise* in which the BBC had flipped the image for use in their logo in 1992.
43. See David Ketterer, *New Worlds for Old*, 35.
44. Poole, *Earthrise*, 192.
45. Joseph McElroy, 'Holding with Apollo 17', 347.
46. As William D. Atwill notes: 'The nature of the space program demanded minute planning – the spatialization of time into discrete tasks – and

the men (there were no women) chosen for this journey were men with high boredom thresholds, men capable of endless rehearsals of routine tasks. They weren't the adventurers of earlier decades, they were "company men" of a corporate government. They were hard to write about in and of themselves; their hardware was more exciting.' See Atwill, *Fire and Power*, 15.
47. Tribbe, *No Requiem for the Space Age*, 51–52.
48. Ibid., 64.
49. Atwill, *Fire and Power*, 16.
50. Kauffman, *Selling Outer Space*, 37; 39; 85.
51. See ibid., 74.
52. See ibid., 110–15.
53. 'NASA itself made the greatest effort at historical quotation by appropriating Greek and Roman mythology. [. . .] But aesthetically, the Manned Space Program was vexing because it came across as rational, calculated, sterile, passionless, routine, and rehearsed.' See Atwill, *Fire and Power*, 14–15.
54. Poole, *Earthrise*, 159.
55. Cosgrove, 'Contested Global Visions', 279.
56. See Joe Luna, 'Space | Poetry', 114.
57. Michael Collins, *Carrying the Fire*, 470.
58. Luna, 'Space | Poetry', 119.
59. Lawrence Ferlinghetti, *Wild Dreams of a New Beginning*, 45.
60. Another striking example is NASA's ambiguous and potentially accidental forms of rhetorical control in the absence of literature in Sagan's *Voyager 1* record – and the commercial book promoting it. As Ronald Weber points out, the famous gold record that attends *Voyager 1* has images and sounds of human life, physical depictions of the Earth, and a variety of spoken world languages, but it avoids literary representation entirely: 'It celebrates a sense of earthly life – and omits from the celebration a literary sensibility at odds, or at least at a remove, from the scientific mind at work in sending a spacecraft to the stars, creating a record to accompany it, and finally making a book about the record.' See Weber, *Seeing Earth*, 15. That this is explainable as perhaps a result of physical limitations related to literary texts, we begin to approach the problem of scale.
61. See Robert Vas Dias, *Inside Outer Space*.
62. Luna, 'Space | Poetry', 138.
63. Gerald Prince, 'The Disnarrated', 2.
64. Ibid., 3.
65. Collins, *Carrying the Fire*, 471.
66. H. Porter Abbott, 'How Do We Read What Isn't There to Be Read?', 104.
67. Clark, 'Scale as a Force of Deconstruction', 86.
68. Christopher Coker, *Men at War*, 66.

69. Ibid., 67.
70. Elise Martucci, 'Place as Active Receptacle in Don DeLillo's *The Angel Esmeralda: Nine Stories*', 85.
71. See Michael J. Shapiro, 'That Obscure Object of Violence', 459.
72. DeLillo, *The Angel Esmerelda*, 26.
73. Fredric Jameson, 'War and Representation', 1547.
74. Brad Congdon, *Leading with the Chin*, 180. The 'men in small rooms' motif starts in *Libra*; see Stacey Olster, *The Cambridge Introduction to Contemporary American Fiction*, 26; Margaret Scanlan, *Plotting Terror*, 138.
75. DeLillo, *The Angel Esmerelda*, 26.
76. Ibid.
77. Ibid.
78. Ibid., 25.
79. Ibid., 29.
80. Ibid., 28.
81. Ibid., 37.
82. Ibid., 38.
83. Ibid.
84. Ibid., 39–40.
85. Ibid., 43.
86. Ibid., 43–44.
87. Ibid., 43.
88. Ibid., 44.
89. Ibid., 42.
90. Kelsey, 'Reverse Shot', 14.
91. DeLillo, *The Angel Esmerelda*, 39.

Conclusion: On Drone and Satellite Images

In conclusion, I want to depart a bit from my method in the rest of this book and focus on mimetic representation of technology that frames images of the view from above. While the form of environment is articulated by aerial description in similar ways as the modernist technique starting from Cather – through the aesthetics of extent, vertical imagination and unnarrated scales – the articulation differs in contemporary literature through explicit reflexive interest in the individual in relation to the view from above. Anxiety following the assertive determinacy of digital technology has motivated this reflexive turn.

The collision of the form of environment and the form of the text, as I have shown, takes place as a negation of the culture of perceptual realities in which the text is embedded. I have shown how this progressed in the twentieth century in the previous three chapters with the grid form and conceptual reductions stemming from first flight, the alienation of Western travellers in an increasingly visible non-Western world, and the sudden omnipresence of 'whole-Earth' images. But the theoretical orientation toward the form of environment in aerial description set out in Chapter 1 shows how my readings of fiction from Cather, Bowles and DeLillo open up new ways of interpreting this technological anxiety. Rather than products of their respective historical perceptual contexts, I have read these texts as primarily engaged with the environment through which the reader can encounter the ways it structures stories and our experiences of them.

The literary work of art is an aesthetic object that always functions as an articulation of the environment it re-implaces. I have shown in both theory and analysis how my redefinition of art and environment is apparent at the edges of criticism and fiction. By using the term 'nonanthropocentric' throughout this book, I have foregrounded how the literary object is constructed as a nonhuman artefact rendered using the tools humans have available. In the face of the technological progress that is the background of this book, I think that this reversal to nonanthropocentric perspectives is a challenge that we must face in order to effect change through the practice of reading and writing.

Hannah Arendt confronted the bleak impossibility of such a project in scientific research. In 1963, she saw the approaching peak manifestation of 'Heisenberg's man', when the construction of more and more complex tools to look at the nonhuman world only produce further detailed images of the human world:

> Every progress in science in the last decades, from the moment it was absorbed into technology and thus introduced into the factual world where we live our everyday lives, has brought with it a veritable avalanche of fabulous instruments and ever more ingenious machinery. All of this makes it more unlikely every day that man will encounter anything in the world around him that is not man-made and hence is not, in the last analysis, he himself in a different disguise. The astronaut, shot into outer space and imprisoned in his instrument-ridden capsule where each actual physical encounter with his surroundings would spell immediate death, might well be taken as the symbolic incarnation of Heisenberg's man – the man who will be the less likely ever to meet anything but himself the more ardently he wishes to eliminate all anthropocentric considerations from his encounter with the nonhuman world around him.[1]

We can ask whether Arendt, writing before any launch of an Apollo mission, would consider the 'whole-Earth' images the ultimate reflection that turns each of us into Heisenberg's man: we can no longer imagine the Earth without reference to the realisation of its perception and its technological mediation. Without access to new tools parallel to Heisenberg's principle of uncertainty, foregrounding the nonhuman becomes farcical and a further hopeless dig into anthropocentrism. This is the meaning of the despair Bruno Latour expresses when he claims: 'What makes the idea of a choice for or against *anthropocentrism* quite implausible is the assumption that there is *a center*, or rather two, man and nature, between which one supposedly has to choose.'[2] This is what my theorisation of extent, verticality and scale – and ultimately, the concept of the form of environment – offers: an updated theory of literary reading and ontology of the literary work of art that renews the relationship between reader and text, rendering it similarly 'indeterminate' to Heisenberg's 'uncertainty'. With Latour, I see the turn toward nonanthropocentrism – or the form of environment in the reading experience – not as a choice, but as a recognition that Earth is an attractor for our behaviour and imagination that cannot be ignored any longer.

And I see an optimistic angle in a romantic idea accidentally constructed in Arendt's lineage that leads to the astronaut. Before the avalanche of fabulous instruments – technological and critical – maybe there was an opportunity to encounter the nonhuman world. I hope to have shown why I think literary art presents this opportunity anew. In the rest of this conclusion, I will turn to the way we can continue this analysis in twenty-first-century literature, way past the timeline of 'Heisenberg's Man'. This is an attempt to show how my method can be applied to texts outside modernism. First, I will outline the situation of commercial drone fiction, move to the precedents for contemporary representations of digitally mediated aerial description, and then turn to instances in contemporary autofiction.

Invisible Drones

It is not surprising that there are essentially no instances of aerial description from the concrete perspective of a drone in American literary fiction. The drone-strike imagery popular in the 2000s on LiveLeak and YouTube (and its censored version on TV news), if it appears in literature, is backgrounded by description of the media situation. Rather than the form of environment in these descriptions, the medium and the attendant affect are foregrounded. The primary experience of aerial views from drones by their operators has not been represented in literary fiction, even though they have been popular in news media.[3]

Criticism and theory on drones and this new visual regime mostly repeat the argument that visual art is the primary aesthetic mode to engage with aerial views afforded by drones. Apparently poetry fails here: 'drones are a historic development which demonstrate the limits of lyric as a technology for imagining and relating to those others whose suppression is part of the general economy in which poetry can be written'.[4] Even the novel form has been broken by this dearth of poetic imagination, as Nathan Hensley suggests:

> However named, our extending present is characterized not just by new forms of warmaking or an expanded capacity for profit extraction and the capture of nature, but by dizzying proliferation

of material technologies and digital genres. These new forms have emerged to mediate and monetize lived experience in late capitalism. One of these forms remains the novel itself, which [...] has stretched and, in some instances, all but fallen apart in an effort to comprehend the coincidence of mediation and death in our contemporary moment.[5]

The drift that has continued the primacy of perception in the view from above mediated by satellites and drones has not reached literary aerial description. The general absence of drone views and digital maps in literature, relative to visual art, is not surprising given the relationship between scale and the unnarrated as outlined in the previous chapter.

After the initiation of the CIA's Predator Drone assassinations in Yemen in 2002, commercial fiction had a brief bump of 'drone thrillers', but these followed the conventional form of popular military techno-thrillers. Regardless, Hensley notes that the failure of these popular novels (and I would also include science fiction focusing on drones) is due to the way drone-perspective 'generates difficulties for the perspectival regime of narrative fiction, a mismatch between message and medium that is legible in these drone thrillers at the level of the sentence itself'.[6] This incongruity goes beyond narrative, as I have argued in this book, and is fundamental to the way the form of environment clashes with human narrative forms through aerial description, even unnarrated aerial description.

By focusing on the form of environment and the imaginary, this book can suggest some further reasons for the reproductive blockage of novel form to contain descriptions of aerial views from drones and other unmanned aerial vehicles. It reaffirms my argument that narrative form cannot manage the unwieldiness of description. While prior studies of aerial views in the twenty-first century focus on the complexity of technological forms of mediation and the unrepresentable networks of global warfare, we can now think about an anti-anthropocentric approach to this scarcity.

The most prevalent structure in drone perception is the reproduction of the *viewing*, not just the view. Civilians viewing these types of images do so as a virtual pilot in the anticipation of a violent climax (given via paratext in the title of a video) with the graphical overlay of obscure targeting and reference systems as well as stylised colour gradation of thermal imaging, all of which further defamiliarise the aerial view. They participate in an effect described by Fredric Jameson: 'there is in fact no view from above insofar as the pilots are expected not to see but rather to determine their movements by map and by mathematical calculation, by radar rather than by "sight."'[7] Even if the drone pilot actually does rely on 'sight' more than the pilot of a manned aircraft, this only further replicates the situation of defamiliarised viewing as mediated by representations on a screen.

In the same way, the viewer of drone images scans what can be seen in order to anticipate what is to come. Commercial fiction, such as Mike Maden's *Drone* series (2013–2016), attempts to naively represent the perceptual situation of disembodied drone vision by supplementing its boredom (relative to piloted air combat) with the conventional excitement of techno-thriller narrative form. Naturally, this also displaces the storyworld from any environment, thus necessarily eliminating the role of the form of environment by reducing it to static clichés in the same way these novels rely on static ideologies in order to portray human violence as heroic.

To contrast, in 'Seven Stories About Drones' (2013), a series of micro-fictions originally posted to Twitter, the novelist Teju Cole reifies these reductions by interpolating existing high-modernist narratives:

> 1. Mrs Dalloway said she would buy the flowers herself. Pity. A signature strike leveled the florist's. [. . .]
> 3. Stately, plump Buck Mulligan came from the stairhead, bearing a bowl of lather. A bomb whistled in. Blood on the walls. Fire from heaven. [. . .]
> 7. Mother died today. The program saves American lives.'[8]

The violence against humans by drone warfare and its representation in media and popular thrillers has been criticised since its outset. But images of violence against the environment and the redeployment of aerial images is harder to represent, and American literary fiction has yet to engage with these issues. Cole's micro-narratives are one example of narrative fiction attempting to innovate beyond the constraints imposed by the new aerial regime of drones, showing how form is the primary battleground in literary engagement with contemporary aerial imagery from drone warfare; Jameson puts it succinctly: 'Abstraction versus sense-datum: these are the two poles of a dialectic of war, incomprehensible in their mutual isolation, which dictate dilemmas of representation navigable only by formal innovation [. . .] and not by any stable narrative convention.'[9]

It is difficult to find formal innovation, or even ambition, in the novels of this already-defunct genre of drone thrillers, but Dan Fesperman's *Unmanned* (2015) attempts a slightly more literary approach that contains some notable aerial description. The narrative follows a drone pilot who is traumatised by the juxtapositions of his 'commuter soldier' life. His environment is structured in a complex weave of virtual and actual space, in which he

> sometimes has to remind himself of what part of the world he's watching. It might be any dry and rocky valley here in Nevada. It could be the vacant lot behind his daughter's school. [. . .] When he departs at the end of the day their images accompany him home, a silent movie unspooling in his head during the long drive to the 'burbs of Vegas – shot after shot of hobbled lives in their slow progress, with Cole as the omnipotent eye above; a kindly uncle with a camera, perhaps, making home movies for the world at large. Until you fired a missile.[10]

The girl in the crosshairs on his screen could also be his daughter; the desert has the same form in the village in Afghanistan as it does in his Nevada neighbourhood.

To remind himself of this distance and the difference between himself and the enemy, he imagines the remote-control signals he inputs flying above familiar places on its way to the drone:

> all his commands tonight have passed above the schools, rivers, farms, houses, malls, and highways of a sleeping America. Each twitch of his hand flings a signal of war across the nation's night owls as they make love, make a sandwich, make a mess of things, or click the remote. The signal then hurdles the Atlantic, Europe, and the Middle East before finally reaching the bright blue afternoon of eastern Afghanistan, nine hours into the future, where at this moment his MQ-1 Predator drone gazes down from ten thousand feet upon the stony valley and mud homes of Sandar Khosh, a remote village of farmers and herdsmen.[11]

The form of environment in this passage functions by contrasting the horizontal distance of the imagined flight with the vertical distance of the drone. The ease with which one can imagine a set of intimate American spaces and the vague place-names representing geographical space from 'here' to 'there' makes the drone's vertical gaze onto remote territory seem more distant than the familiar desert landscape implies. Surveillance and violence are made possible, at least temporarily, by concretising the imaginable flight as traceable horizontal distance that stretches the affective closeness into a distant 'elsewhere', while the vertical aerial view is once again made abstract through digital mediation.

The drone pilot also begins to wonder how this kind of aerial surveillance affects its subjects: 'What must it be like to become an image lodged in the memory of some secret database, your digital signature retrievable by anyone with the proper clearance?'[12] He becomes conscious of all the security cameras that surround him in his daily life, but this pervasive, though mundane, paranoia is supplanted by the traumatic experiences of drone warfare in the novel. The fate of its victims is already sealed by being targets, and the drone pilot becomes caught in this traumatic structure as the virtual perpetrator. He is overwhelmed by the violence he has caused, and the security concerns of surveillance introduced in the first pages of the novel do not enter the structure of images in the novel. This stasis, though an accessible representation of the trauma of virtual war, keeps the novel locked in the 'dilemma of representation' noted by Jameson, above; the images do not articulate the form of environment beyond the dualism of abstraction and affect in explicit representations of human cognition. The historically new ways the protagonist is also structured within his own environment through similar domestic surveillance is supplanted by conventional representations of warfare and trauma.

Aerial description in literary novels by veterans of twenty-first-century US wars exists somewhere between the drone narratives in popular thrillers and the use of mapping in autofiction, described below. Surprisingly, these novels, even at their most aesthetically ambitious, focus very little on drone imagery, personnel or culture. Kevin Powers's *The Yellow Birds* (2012) contains conventional descriptions of coming home from duty on an aeroplane, as well as sentimental descriptions of paper maps:

> I put some tape on the corners and flattened it as best I could against the wall, but the lines of the folds remained. I remember rubbing my finger along one of the creases that ran straight along a very small section of the Tigris. It was the part of the river that ran through Al Tafar. I dug in my bag and found one of my medals and I stuck it in as near as I could figure to the place where we had left him. That map, like every other, would soon be out of date, if it was not already. What it had been indexed to was only an idea of a place, an abstraction formed from memories too brief and passing to account for the small effects of time: wind scouring and lifting the dust of the plains of Nineveh in immeasurable increments, the tuck of a river farther

into its bend, hour by hour, year by year; the map would become less and less a picture of a fact and more a poor translation of memory in two dimensions.[13]

The narrator was a ground soldier, so we see a contrast with the drone pilot in *Unmanned*.[14] Rather than the recurring traumatic image of a drone aerial view, the paper map becomes a space of recovery as the narrator can memorialise the location of a lost friend and be sceptical about the ability of the map as memory to outlive his experience of a place. Notably, the image of the environment is also described apart from human memory or experience, as wind materially changes the river valley beyond what the narrator can imagine or the map can represent.

While *Unmanned* creates cartoon images for a mass-market audience and *The Yellow Birds* sentimentalises images for conventional empathetic climax, they are valuable because they foreground the ways technology short-circuits the relationship between individual memory and environment. Contemporary literary fiction that does not focus on war often presents more self-referential images of the self implaced in digital map-space and so efface the violence of the technologies that now structure the form of environment. Both modes foreground indeterminacy, but by introducing the violent structure of contemporary aerial views, war novels such as *The Yellow Birds* paradoxically present an accessible nonanthropocentric image of the environment.

A World Inside the World

In postmodern and contemporary fiction, the mundane, ambient presence of commercial and government use of military surveillance technology is imagined apart from these traumatic structures. The now-ubiquitous aerial images from satellites used for everyday navigation have become a minor motif, especially in autofiction. Because the medium of satellite imagery and dynamic online mapping platforms emphasise the environment (unlike the emphasis on human targets in drone imagery), the form of environment again comes into play in aerial description. But unlike the fiction examined in previous chapters, these aerial descriptions show how digital images, particularly mediated by commercial services such as Google Maps, do not afford access to the three aspects of form of environment detailed in this book – extent, verticality and scale – but instead emphasise their synthesis in a new dynamic form of aerial description.

An early example of the transition from military to everyday experience of the view from above mediated by surveillance views is presented by descriptions of aerial views from the U-2 aircraft in Don DeLillo's JFK novel, *Libra* (1988). Lee Harvey Oswald is put at the centre of the mystery of these new 'weather planes' that fly at unbelievable heights and produce unprecedented images. The information he learns and the stories – fact and fiction – that he spreads about the U-2 become the central secret that Oswald holds as a sign that he is the privileged node in a network of global revolution. As a figure with indeterminate agency in his own life, Oswald is a transitional figure from the exclusivity of the 'top-down', objective vision of the world represented by surveillance and intelligence operations in the Cold War to the prevalence and general accessibility of surveillance technology in contemporary daily life. These novel images enter into daily life in intimate situations; CIA agent Win Everett tells his wife about the U-2 in bed:

> Spy planes, drone aircraft, satellites with cameras that can see from three hundred miles what you can see from a hundred feet. They see and they hear. Like ancient monks, you know, who recorded knowledge, wrote it painstakingly down. These systems collect and process. All the secret knowledge of the world.[15]

Years after Oswald has left the military and after his defection to Russia, he finds work in Dallas at an office that processes film, some of which happen to be classified U-2 images used for mapmaking. A co-worker confides in him, not knowing Oswald's own history with the U-2: "'I'll tell you what I overheard,' Dale said, 'if you promise not to tell anyone. The maps are made from photographs. The photographs are the really secret things. They come from U-2s.'"[16] Oswald has seen these maps and heard secrets about the photographs, but he has not seen the aerial view for himself.

This aerial view is presented a single time in *Libra*, in a passage typical to DeLillo's mysterious imagist style. Simultaneously an escapist dream from Oswald's perspective, a representation of the captured U-2 pilot introduced later in the novel, and an autonomous image, a pilot imagines what it would be like to eject himself into the open air:

> He comes floating down the endless pale, struck simultaneously by the beauty of the earth and a need to ask forgiveness. He is a stranger, in a mask, falling. People come into view, farm hands, children racing

toward the spot where the wind will set him down. Their rough caps are tilted back. He is near enough to hear them calling, the words bounced and steered and elongated by the contours of the land. The land smells fresh. He is coming down to springtime in the Urals and he finds that this privileged vision of the earth is an inducement to truth. He wants to tell the truth. He wants to live another kind of life, outside secrecy and guilt and the pull of grave events. This is what the pilot thinks, rocking softly down to the tawny fields of a landscape so gentle and welcoming it might almost be home.[17]

Here the form of environment is imagined with the kind of monk-like reverence that makes the environment seem like more than it appears, as an opening beyond objective reality and into secret knowledge. Certainly we can think about extent, verticality and scale as presented in this book as an affordance of the view from above in contemporary images such as this. But this passage opens into a new, dynamic experience of the form of environment unique to drone and surveillance images.

A kind of smooth zoom compresses extent, simulates descent and reduces scale as a new affordance of the form of environment presented by aerial description. That Oswald becomes this transitional figure in *Libra*, entering the 1990s at the birth of the internet (also a military technology), is significant. The refrain in the novel – 'there is a world inside the world' – becomes the primary experience of environment in the twenty-first century, mediated by surveillance technology, digital media and prevalent networked tracking.

William Gibson's *Neuromancer* (1984) introduces another prototype for aerial description mediated by dynamic, computational images:

Program a map to display frequency of data exchange, every thousand megabytes a single pixel on a very large screen. Manhattan and Atlanta burn solid white. Then they start to pulse, the rate of traffic threatening to overload your simulation. Your map is about to go nova. Cool it down. Up your scale. Each pixel a million megabytes. At a hundred million megabytes per second, you begin to make out certain blocks in midtown Manhattan, outlines of hundred-year-old industrial parks ringing the old core of Atlanta [. . .].[18]

Descriptions of screens in fiction go beyond classical formulations of ekphrasis in literature; though they are aestheticised, these descriptions that highlight maps loop back to Edward S. Casey's emphasis of landscape description as 'representation of representation', noted in Chapter 1. In this case, the material environment is animated by a texture that becomes inextricable from nature in the twenty-first century. Data heats the environment figuratively, here through the computer as apparatus, and becomes an image of the literal heat produced at this scale. As the resolution is increased and the scale of data transfer is represented more precisely, cities and human infrastructure become visible once again, making the inhuman world of data transfer invisible.

In *Tropic of Orange* (1997), Karen Tei Yamashita also introduces an early image that is now common in our daily use of GPS-coordinated, live-tracking traffic maps on mobile devices. In the novel, the new satellite TV of a character suddenly intercepts map data presumably collected by cartels tracking drug shipments:

> I picked up the remote and surfed through the channels on the chance I might pick up some news, some CNN. But the thing that caught my attention was a channel that looked like the LA Thomas Guide. Next channel zoomed in for a close-up. I scrutinised the screen and recognised a distorted version of downtown LA. At least that's what the street names indicated, but distances were skewed and the streets weren't parallel. But, it was close enough. A flashing indicator marked X moved around the map. [. . .] I had heard they could implant microchips in pets. Transmitters in dope, or maybe in human organs. Insidious and sophisticated. But who were *they*?[19]

The narrator later calls to ask the person watching the screen where the X is moving, as he follows it back in Los Angeles. Still less than ten years from Google's acquisition of the companies developing what would become Google Maps and Google Earth, '*they*' are an impersonal force. *They* can lead the characters to drive crazily around LA as in *Tropic of Orange* or to travel from Siberia to Dallas in *Libra*, but this paranoid structure of newly imaginable environment does not yet contain a dynamic image of one's own place on the map.

Once it does, the 'world inside the world' transforms from *their* world structuring the world that *I* live in, to a sense of *their* world inside *my* world, through the simple availability of increasingly miniature and readily manipulatable mapping and satellite images. This recursion seems to grant the individual agency to imagine their own environment, but it stems from an illusion generated by the progressive invisibility of the origin of the tools that produce these images. In the early and mid-twentieth century, aerial description could expose this illusion more simply. Cather does so through her focus on the literary image as a built form, and Bowles by displacing narrativisation with imagination. DeLillo is a transitional figure who identifies the 'world inside the world' simply as an image, unable to be transcended, as it produces silence and contemplation. Contemporary literary writers, sensitive to the complete structuring of the world by technology and the attendant illusory sense of agency, produce anxious images of the environment that include an ironic attempt to achieve naïve aerial description, once again.

Dot Perspectives

Today, no longer constrained by physical heat or wired connections, real-time data representations and satellite imagery are now in everyone's pockets. Contemporary autofiction integrates the popular use of GPS tracking in phones mediated by services like Google or Apple Maps in aerial descriptions that formally emphasise human perspective and reflexivity. These descriptions also present the dynamic, smooth zoom form of environment.

10:04 (2014) by Ben Lerner encodes a complex perspectivism where the narrator can simultaneously be 'above' and 'below' as he uses Google Street View to navigate old images of the streets while he sits both writing the present novel and playing with Google Maps:

> the caretaker of the residency houses [. . .] had picked me up at the El Paso airport that afternoon and driven me in amicable silence for three hours through the high desert until we reached the little house at 308 North Plateau Street; I remember the address (you can drag the 'pegman' icon onto the Google map and walk around the neighborhood on Street View, floating above yourself like a ghost; I'm doing that in a separate window now) [. . .].[20]

The aerial description here is now reduced to a street address as the environment is assumed to be readily explorable by the reader at any moment 'you' want to obtain a 'real' image of it. The narrator implies that this is conventionally creepy, ghost-like, but also game-like as a distraction (or research) for writing the novel currently being read. Here, the surveillance connotations are erased, but foregrounding the form of environment as developed in this book, the image opens up. The passage works using mimetic references entirely reliant on signs that are supposedly transparent and materially accessible to the reader. Similarly, it utilises the second-person to signal 'you', the 'real' subject. While this seems to eliminate indeterminacy by giving the precise address of the setting of the fictional story, the recognition of myself as co-constructor of the image and the precise activity of the writer writing generates a simultaneity that multiplies indeterminacy. The reader can imagine the fragmentation of the narrator's experience of the environment, which is not complete or 'inside' his memory, but must be both accessed again while writing – through satellite and surveillance images – and reaffirmed by the reader, who is suggested to do the same. The experience of environment becomes something further outside of daily life, and its form is outsourced to accessible images on the internet.

Similarly, the narrator of Tao Lin's *Taipei* (2013) splits his perspective into himself and a 'dot' version of himself that can be zoomed and expanded. The form of environment here is presented on the opposite extreme as Lerner's precise address; Paul's environment is the entire universe, including his trajectory in a temporal dimension, and finally the explorable territory of his human universe:

> In a taxi to the party, forty minutes later, Paul imagined another him walking toward the library and, for a few seconds, visualizing the position and movement of two red dots through a silhouetted, aerial view of Manhattan, felt as imaginary, as mysterious and transitory and unfindable, as the other dot. He visualized the vibrating, squiggling, looping, arcing line representing the three-dimensional movement, plotted in a cubic grid, of the dot of himself, accounting for the different speed and direction of each vessel of which he was a passenger – taxi, Earth, solar system, Milky Way, etc. Adding a fourth dimension, representing time, he visualized the patterned scribbling shooting off in one direction, with a slight wobble, miles from where it was seconds ago. He imagined his trajectory as a vacuum-sealed tube, into which he'd arrived and through which – traveling alone in the vacuum-sealed tube of his own life – he'd be suctioned and from which he'd exit, as a successful delivery to some unimaginable recipient. Realizing this was only his concrete history, his public movement through space-time from birth to death, he briefly imagined being able to click on his trajectory and access his private experience, enlarging the dot of a coordinate until it could be explored like a planet.[21]

This image is the richest and most innovative use of the new digitally mediated affordances of the self implaced in the total environment. Notably, unlike in *10:04*, it amplifies the abstraction of aerial description, rather than compensating for it by suggesting that the reader 'see for themselves'. Rather, imagination is foregrounded, and the new affordances of surveillance technology obtain a remarkable utilisation of aerial description for existential thought. The passage only suggests brand-name mapping services in a unique, transparent integration of this new smooth zoom form of environment into literary images.

Mobile mapping applications are rarely referenced this transparently, or as purely imaginary, in contemporary literary fiction. They present confusion and distraction in addition to being imaginary tools for the kind of existential reflection found in *Taipei*. In Andrew Durbin's *MacArthur Park* (2017), Google Maps takes the place of memory in a way that makes navigation via smartphone difficult because it is both a materially complex medium and it facilitates flights into memory beyond the present spatial situation:

> In addition to the traffic, LA's crisscrossed with construction, accidents, and often confusing side roads, all of it marked by signs and lights I couldn't interpret in the time needed to follow Google Maps' instructions. When we hit Echo Park (I mistook it for MacArthur Park, telling Simon and Jakob that Donna Summer has a song about it, my favorite song, in fact), my iPhone directed me to turn right on Echo Park Avenue, onto Bellevue Avenue, then left onto Glendale. I fucked up, distracted myself while changing the song to 'MacArthur Park,' Simon said let me do it, and I missed the right turn onto Glendale as I resisted his help.[22]

These three contemporary novels present the ways that daily navigation of the environment is now mediated by images from the same aerial surveillance regime as instantiated by drones. This is given by the dynamic zoom in aerial description, where the ability to manipulate images of the environment provides the paradoxical illusion that it is stable and reliable and so can be handled personally for individual use. Lerner and Durbin do so for aesthetic purposes, in which the autofictional narrator of *10:04* distracts both himself and the reader by reflexively describing this kind of non-writerly play, and, in *MacArthur Park*, it impedes progression long enough to introduce the title and main theme of the novel. *Taipei* utilises these images for philosophical reflection, going beyond Lerner or Durbin's mimetic reflexivity to synthesise 1960s 'Blue Marble' holism of collective consciousness (described in Chapter 4) with twenty-first-century digitally mediated alienation. Paul imagines himself not like the Street View ghost or the driver-navigator-DJ, but as completely sealed off from society. Through the functionality of digital mapping, Paul presents a series of worlds inside worlds that supplant the grid of the satellite view with his own existential grid.

Aerial Contemplation

Like Sylvia from the Sarah Orne Jewett story discussed in my introduction, another young character plays an important role in articulating the form of environment, mediated by a bird, in *A Gate at the Stairs* (2009) by Lorrie Moore. In both stories, indeterminacy is foregrounded both in literary and environmental form. Both deal with contemporaneous aesthetic problems of objectivity through the negation of aerial views. While my analysis of Cather, Bowles and DeLillo also follow this negative form, the analysis is made available by the nonanthropocentric reorientation of critical and readerly practice I have developed in this book. On the other hand, 'A White Heron' and *A Gate at the Stairs* symbolically integrate this nonanthropocentrism.

Late in *A Gate at the Stairs*, the protagonist, Tassie, dresses in a hawk costume to help her father scare away rodents from their farm:

> As the dusk washed over, I galloped up and down the rows of three-season spring mix, and my dreams of flying would return. As ever, in my flying dreams, I never got very far off the ground, and now here if I took a leap I felt my wings supporting me, kitelike, just a split second above the field. I would hover, buoyed, my wings finding a little air, and so when I landed I would instantly leap up again, the ball of one foot pushing off – that split-second feeling of almost being able to set sail was enough of a thrill. Actual sustained flight would have been beside the point, and too scary to boot. This was my modest dream come true: unambitious flight. The kind that never even got high enough for a view.[23]

She realises her modest dream of 'buoyed' groundedness: the pleasure of not transcending and eliminating the possibility of a totalising and transcendent bird's-eye view. Recall Henry David Thoreau's interest in not owning a farm quoted in my introduction. He is ironically the 'monarch of all I survey' by negation. In the same way, Tassie dresses as a bird only to imagine what the aerial view *is not*. There is aerial description elsewhere in the novel, but the multiplication of negative images overwhelms. Human images of the environment from above are not necessary when the imagination is given primacy, and the autonomous form of environment persists beyond the human will to ascend, conquer and own.

A thread that has run throughout this book is the Bachelardian idea that the natural world is already a basically contemplated thing. He also states that humans have a 'will to contemplate' that is shared by nature. His example is still waters; the glassy pool has already seen the world and produced an image of it, which the human figure can then stop and contemplate again, after nature: 'While you were wandering, something here was already looking on. The lake is a large tranquil eye. The lake takes all of light and makes a world out of it. Through it, the world is already contemplated, already represented.'[24] This is the temporal and ontological structure that I hope to have animated in this book by supplementing it with spatial and aesthetic principles. The environment already has a reflexive, contemplated, represented form, and literature grants us access to this despite all anthropocentric distractions. I prefer to translate Bachelard's philosophical arguments into literary ones by calling this structure the form of environment.

Aerial description, like still waters, brings the reader to encounter the eye of nature. Understanding that this eye is not blind, that it produces images that are set apart but accessible through aesthetic experience, is essential as this environment changes above us. The view from above is a sight also seen by the air, reflected in micro-scale by the still waters of the cloud. In this book, I hope to have reoriented the way that we approach these elemental visions from above.

Notes

1. Hannah Arendt, 'Man's Conquest of Space', 537–38.
2. Bruno Latour, *Down to Earth*, 86.
3. See Roger Stahl, 'What the Drone Saw', 669.
4. Andrea Brady, 'Drone Poetics', 125.
5. Nathan K. Hensley, 'Drone Form', 245.
6. Ibid., 241.
7. Fredric Jameson, 'War and Representation', 1546.
8. Teju Cole, 'Seven Short Stories about Drones', n.p.
9. Jameson, 'War and Representation', 1547.
10. Dan Fesperman, *Unmanned*, 5–6.
11. Ibid., 4.
12. Ibid., 8.
13. Kevin Powers, *The Yellow Birds*, 225.
14. A notable text that explores the space in between these two figures is the actual pilot turned drone pilot after an unplanned pregnancy in George Brant's play *Grounded*.
15. Don DeLillo, *Libra*, 77.
16. Ibid., 274.

17. Ibid., 115–16.
18. William Gibson, *Neuromancer*, 43.
19. Karen Tai Yamashita, *Tropic of Orange*, 227–28.
20. Ben Lerner, *10:04*, 163.
21. Tao Lin, *Taipei*, 25.
22. Andrew Durbin, *MacArthur Park*, 135.
23. Lorrie Moore, *A Gate at the Stairs*, 291.
24. Gaston Bachelard, *Water and Dreams*, 28.

Bibliography

Abbott, H. Porter. 'How Do We Read What Isn't There to Be Read? Shadow Stories and Permanent Gaps'. In *The Oxford Handbook for Cognitive Literary Studies*. Ed. Lisa Zunshine. Oxford: Oxford University Press, 2015. 104–19.

Alber, Jan. *Unnatural Narrative: Impossible Worlds in Fiction and Drama*. Lincoln: University of Nebraska Press, 2016.

Arendt, Hannah. 'Man's Conquest of Space'. *The American Scholar* 32.5 (1963): 527–40.

Atwill, William D. *Fire and Power: The American Space Program as Postmodern Narrative*. Athens: University of Georgia Press, 1994.

Azzarello, Robert. *Queer Environmentality: Ecology, Evolution, and Sexuality in American Literature*. Farnham: Ashgate, 2012.

Bachelard, Gaston. *Air and Dreams: An Essay on the Imagination of Movement*. Trans. Edith R. Farrell and C. Frederick Farrell. Dallas: Dallas Institute Publications, 1988.

—. *The Poetics of Reverie: Childhood, Language, and the Cosmos*, Trans. Daniel Russell. Boston: Beacon Press, 1971.

—. *The Poetics of Space*. Trans. Maria Jolas. Boston: Beacon Press, 1994.

—. *Water and Dreams: An Essay on the Imagination of Matter*. Trans. Edith R. Farrell. Dallas: Dallas Institute Publications, 1983.

Baker, Anne. *Heartless Immensity: Literature, Culture, and Geography in Antebellum America*. Ann Arbor: University of Michigan Press, 2006.

Bal, Mieke. 'Over-writing as Un-writing: Descriptions, World-making, and Novelistic Time'. In *Narrative Theory: Critical Concepts in Literary and Cultural Studies*. Ed. Mieke Bal. New York: Routledge, 2004. 341–88.

Barthes, Roland. *A Barthes Reader*. Ed. Susan Sontag. New York: Hill and Wang, 1996.

Benlemlih, Bouchra. *Paul Bowles's Literary Engagement with Morocco: Poetic Space, Liminality, and In-Betweenness*. Lanham: Lexington Books, 2018.

Bennett, Jane. *Vibrant Matter: A Political Ecology of Things*. Durham: Duke University Press, 2010.

Bowles, Paul. *Let It Come Down*. Boston: Black Sparrow Press, 1980.

—. *The Sheltering Sky*. London: Penguin, 2000.

—. *The Spider's House*. Boston: Black Sparrow Press, 1991.
—. *Without Stopping: An Autobiography*. New York: The Ecco Press, 1985.
Brady, Andrea. 'Drone Poetics'. *New Formations* 89/90 (2016): 116–36.
Buell, Lawrence. *The Future of Environmental Criticism: Environmental Crisis in Literary Imagination*. Oxford: Blackwell, 2005.
Butor, Michel. *Inventory: Essays*. New York: Simon and Schuster, 1968.
Caracciolo, Marco. 'Beyond Other Minds: Fictional Characters, Mental Simulation, and "Unnatural" Experiences'. *Narrative* 44.1 (2014): 29–53.
—. 'Leaping into Space: The Two Aesthetics of *To the Lighthouse*'. *Poetics Today* 31.2 (2010): 251–84.
—. *Narrating the Mesh: Form and Story in the Anthropocene*. Charlottesville: University of Virginia Press, 2021.
Caracciolo, Marco and Karin Kukkonen. *With Bodies: Narrative Theory and Embodied Cognition*. Columbus: Ohio State University Press, 2021.
Casey, Edward S. *Representing Place: Landscape Painting and Maps*. Minneapolis: Minnesota University Press, 2002.
Cather, Willa. *Death Comes for the Archbishop*. New York: Vintage, 1990.
—. *My Ántonia*. New York: Vintage, 1994.
—. *Not Under Forty*. Lincoln: University of Nebraska Press, 1988a.
—. *O Pioneers!*. New York: Dover, 1993.
—. *The Professor's House*. New York: Vintage, 1994.
—. *Willa Cather on Writing: Critical Studies on Writing as an Art*. Lincoln: University of Nebraska Press, 1988b.
Clark, Timothy. 'Derangements of Scale'. In *Telemorphosis: Theory in the Era of Climate Change, Volume 1*. Ed. Tom Cohen. Ann Arbor: Open Humanities Press, 2012. 148–66.
—. 'Scale as a Force of Deconstruction'. In *Eco-Deconstruction: Derrida and Environmental Philosophy*. Ed. Matthias Fritsch, Philippe Lynes and David Wood. New York: Fordham University Press, 2018. 81–94.
—. *Ecocriticism on the Edge: The Anthropocene as a Threshold Concept*. London: Bloomsbury, 2015.
Clarke, Michael Tavel and David Wittenberg. 'Introduction'. In *Scale in Literature and Culture*. Ed. Michael Tavel Clarke and David Wittenberg. New York: Palgrave, 2017. 1–32.
Coker, Christopher. *Men at War: What Fiction Tells Us about Conflict, from the* Iliad *to* Catch-22. Oxford: Oxford University Press, 2014.
—. *Warrior Geeks: How 21st Century Technology is Changing the Way We Fight and Think About War*. Oxford: Oxford University Press, 2013.
Cole, Teju. 'Seven Short Stories about Drones'. *The New Inquiry* (2013). https://thenewinquiry.com/blog/seven-short-stories-about-drones/
Collins, Michael. *Carrying the Fire: An Astronaut's Journeys*. New York: Cooper Square Press, 2001.
Congdon, Brad. *Leading with the Chin: Writing American Masculinities in Esquire, 1960–1989*. Toronto: University of Toronto Press, 2018.

Conron, John. *American Picturesque*. University Park: Penn State University Press, 2000.

Cosgrove, Denis. 'Contested Global Visions: One-World, Whole-Earth, and the Apollo Space Photographs'. *Annals of the Association of American Geographers* 84.2 (1994): 270–94.

—. 'The Measures of America'. In *Taking Measures Across the American Landscape*. Ed. James Corner and Alex S. MacLean. New Haven: Yale University Press, 2000. 3–14.

—. *Apollo's Eye: A Cartographic Genealogy of the Earth in the Western Imagination*. Baltimore: The Johns Hopkins University Press, 2001.

de Certeau, Michel. *The Practice of Everyday Life*. Berkeley: University of California Press, 2008.

DeLillo, Don. *Ratner's Star*. New York: Vintage, 1989.

—. *The Angel Esmeralda: Nine Stories*. London: Picador, 2011.

—. *Libra*. New York: Viking, 2001.

Dennerlein, Katrin. *Narratologie des raumes*. Berlin: de Gruyter, 2009.

Dewey, John. *Art as Experience*. New York: Perigee, 1934.

Dias, Robert Vas (Ed.). *Inside Outer Space: New Poems of the Space Age*. New York: Doubleday, 1970.

Dimock, Wai Che. 'Gibraltar and Beyond: James Joyce, Ezra Pound, and Paul Bowles'. In *Moving Modernisms: Motion, Technology, and Modernity*. Ed. David Bradshaw, Laura Marcus, and Rebecca Roach. Oxford University Press, 2016. 59–68.

—. *Through Other Continents: American Literature Across Deep Time*. Princeton: Princeton University Press, 2006.

Durbin, Andrew. *MacArthur Park*. New York: Nightboat Books, 2017.

Edwards, Brian T. *Morocco Bound: Disorienting America's Maghreb, from Casablanca to the Marrakech Express*. Durham: Duke University Press, 2005.

Eggan, Taylor A. 'Landscape Metaphysics: Narrative Architecture and the Focalization of Environment'. *English Studies* 99.4 (2018): 398–411.

Ellis, Patrick. *Aeroscopics: Media of the Bird's-Eye View*. Berkeley: University of California Press, 2021.

Ferlinghetti, Lawrence. *Wild Dreams of a New Beginning*. New York: New Directions, 1988.

Fesperman, Dan. *Unmanned*. New York: Knopf, 2014.

Fiedler, Leslie. 'Style and Anti-Style in the Short Story'. *The Kenyon Review* 13.1 (1951): 155–72.

Fludernik, Monika. 'Description and Perspective: The Representation of Interiors'. *Style* 48.4 (2014): 461–78.

Foltz, Anne. 'Paul Bowles'. *Review of Contemporary Fiction* 20.2 (2000): 82–117.

Fosbutgh, Lacey. 'Why More Top Novelists Don't Go Hollywood'. *New York Times*, 21 November 1976. www.nytimes.com/1976/11/21/archives/why-more-top-novelists-dont-go-hollywood-novelists-who-dont-go.html.

Fox, William L. *Aeriality: Essays on the World from Above*. Berkeley: Counterpoint, 2009.
Friedman, Susan Stanford. *Planetary Modernisms: Provocations on Modernity Across Time*. New York: Columbia University Press, 2015.
Garrard, Greg. *Ecocriticism*. New York: Routledge, 2004.
Gelley, Alexander. 'Premises for a Theory of Description'. In *Fiction, narratologie, texte, genre*. Ed. Jean Bessière. New York: Peter Lang, 1989. 77–88.
Gendlin, Eugene. *Experiencing and the Creation of Meaning: A Philosophical and Psychological Approach to the Subjective*. Evanston: Northwestern University Press, 1962.
Genette, Gérard. 'Boundaries of Narrative'. *New Literary History* 8.1 (1976): 1–13.
Gibson, James J. *The Ecological Approach to Visual Perception*. New York: Psychology Press, 1986.
Gibson, William. *Neuromancer*. New York: Ace Books, 1986.
Goldstein, Bill. *The World Broke in Two: Virginia Woolf, T.S. Eliot, D.H. Lawrence, E.M. Forster, and the Year that Changed Literature*. New York: Picador, 2018.
Goldstein, Lawrence. *The Flying Machine and Modern Literature*. London: MacMillan, 1986.
—. 'The Airplane and American Literature'. In *The Airplane and American Culture*. Ed. Dominick A. Pisano. Ann Arbor: The University of Michigan Press, 2003. 219–49.
Haffner, Jeanne. *The View from Above: The Science of Social Space*. Cambridge: The MIT Press, 2013.
Hamon, Philippe. 'Rhetorical Status of the Descriptive'. *Yale French Studies* 61 (1981): 1–26.
—. 'What is a description?' In *Narrative Theory: Critical Concepts in Literary and Cultural Studies*. Ed. Mieke Bal. New York: Routledge, 2004. 309–40.
Haralson, Eric. 'Modernism'. In *Henry James in Context*. Ed. David McWhirther. Cambridge: Cambridge University Press, 2010. 214–23.
Hawthorne, Nathaniel. *Nathaniel Hawthorne: Tales and Sketches*. New York: Library of America, 1996.
Heise, Ursula. *Sense of Place and Sense of Planet: The Environmental Imagination of the Global*. Oxford: Oxford University Press, 2008.
Hensley, Nathan K. 'Drone Form: Mediation at the End of Empire'. *Novel: A Forum on Fiction* 51.2 (2018): 226–49.
Herman, David. 'Spatial Reference in Narrative Domains'. *Text* 21.4 (2001): 515–41.
—. *Narratology Beyond the Human: Storytelling and Animal Life*. Oxford: Oxford University Press, 2018.
—. *Story Logic: Problems and Possibilities of Narrative*. Lincoln: Nebraska University Press, 2004.

Houen, Alex. *Powers of Possibility: Experimental American Writing Since the 1960s*. Oxford: Oxford University Press, 2011.
Houser, Heather. *Infowhelm: Environmental Art and Literature in the Age of Data*. New York: Columbia University Press, 2020.
Hutchins, Edwin. *Cognition in the Wild*. Cambridge: The MIT Press, 1995.
Ingarden, Roman. 'Aesthetic Experience and Aesthetic Object'. *Philosophy and Phenomenological Research* 21.3 (1961): 289–313.
—. *The Literary Work of Art*. Evanston: Northwestern University Press, 1973.
—. *The Cognition of the Literary Work of Art*. Evanston: Northwestern University Press, 1973.
—. 'On So-Called Truth in Literature'. In *Selected Papers in Aesthetics*. Ed. Peter J. McCormick. Washington D.C.: The Catholic University of America Press, 1985. 133–62.
Ingold, Tim. *The Perception of the Environment: Essays on Livelihood, Dwelling and Skill*. London: Routledge, 2000.
Iser, Wolfgang. *The Act of Reading: A Theory of Aesthetic Response*. Baltimore: The Johns Hopkins University Press, 1978.
—. *The Fictive and the Imaginary: Charting Literary Anthropology*. Baltimore: The Johns Hopkins University Press, 1996.
James, Erin. *The Storyworld Accord: Econarratology and Postcolonial Narratives*. Lincoln: University of Nebraska Press, 2015.
Jameson, Fredric. 'War and Representation'. *PMLA* 124.5 (2009): 1532–47.
Jewett, Sarah Orne. *Sarah Orne Jewett: Novels and Stories*. New York: Library of America, 1996.
Johnson, Rochelle. *Passions for Nature: Nineteenth-Century America's Aesthetics of Alienation*. Athens: University of Georgia Press, 2009.
Kaplan, Caren. *Aerial Aftermaths: Wartime from Above*. Durham: Duke University Press, 2018.
Kauffman, James L. *Selling Outer Space: Kennedy, the Media, and Funding for Project Apollo, 1961–1963*. Tuscaloosa: University of Alabama Press, 1994.
Keck, Michaela. *Walking in the Wilderness: The Peripatetic Tradition in Nineteenth-Century American Literature and Painting*. Heidelberg: Winter, 2006.
Kelsey, Robin. 'Reverse Shot: Earthrise and Blue Marble in the American Imagination'. *New Geographies* 4 (2011): 10–16.
Kenner, Hugh. 'Gee!' *New York Times*, Feb 11, 1973. 391.
Ketterer, David. *New Worlds for Old: The Apocalyptic Imagination, Science Fiction, and American Literature*. Bloomington: Indiana University Press, 1974.
Kirk, Andrew G. *Counterculture Green: The* Whole Earth Catalog *and American Environmentalism*. Lawrence: University Press of Kansas, 2007.
Kohler, Michelle. *Miles of Stare: Transcendentalism and the Problem of Literary Vision in Nineteenth-Century America*. Tuscaloosa: University of Alabama Press, 2014.

Krasner, James. *The Entangled Eye: Visual Perception and the Representation of Nature in Post-Darwinian Narrative*. Oxford: Oxford University Press, 1992.
Kuzmičová, Anežka. 'Presence in the Reading of Literary Narrative: A Case for Bodily Movement'. *Semiotica* 189.1 (2012): 23–48.
Latour, Bruno. 'Waiting for Gaia: Composing the Common World through Arts and Politics'. In *What Is Cosmopolitical Design? Design, Nature and the Built Environment*. Ed. Albena Yaneva and Alejandro Zaera-Polo. Surrey: Ashgate, 2015. 21–32.
—. *Down to Earth: Politics in the New Climatic Regime*. New York: Polity, 2018.
—. *Facing Gaia: Eight Lectures on the New Climatic Regime*. New York: Polity, 2017.
Launius, Roger D. 'Interpreting the Moon Landings: Project Apollo and the Historians'. *History and Technology* 22.3 (2006): 225–55.
Lazier, Benjamin. 'Earthrise; or, the Globalization of the World Picture'. *American Historical Review* 116.3 (2011): 602–30.
Lefebvre, Henri. *Writings on Cities*. Trans. Eleonore Kofman and Elizabeth Lebas. Oxford: Blackwell, 1996.
Lerner, Ben. *10:04*. New York: Picador, 2014.
Levine, Caroline. *Forms: Whole, Rhythm, Hierarchy, Network*. Princeton: Princeton University Press, 2015.
—. 'Three Unresolved Debates'. *PMLA* 132.5 (2017): 1239–43.
Lewis, Richard S. *The Voyages of Apollo and the Exploration of the Moon*. New York: Quadrangle, 1974.
Lin, Tao. *Taipei*. New York: Vintage, 2013.
Lopes, José Manuel. *Foregrounded Description in Prose Fiction: Five Cross-Literary Studies*. Toronto: University of Toronto Press, 1995.
Luna, Joe. 'Space | Poetry'. *Critical Inquiry* 43 (2016): 110–38.
Macready, John A. 'The Non-stop Flight Across America'. *National Geographic* 46.1 (1924): 1–84.
Marcussen, Marlene. 'Reading for Space: An Encounter between Narratology and New Materialism in the Works of Virginia Woolf and Georges Perec'. PhD diss., University of Southern Denmark, 2016.
Marran, Christine L. *Ecology Without Culture: Aesthetics for a Toxic World*. Minneapolis: Minnesota University Press, 2018.
Marston, Sallie A., John Paul Jones III and Keith Woodward. 'Human Geography Without Scale'. *Transactions of the Institute of British Geographers* 30.2 (2005): 416–32.
Martucci, Elise. 'Place as Active Receptacle in Don DeLillo's *The Angel Esmeralda: Nine Stories*'. In *Don DeLillo after the Millennium: Currents and Currencies*. Ed. Jacqueline A. Zubeck. Lanham: Lexington Books, 2017. 83–106.
Mathews, Harry. *The Human Country: New and Collected Stories*. Chicago: Dalkey Archive Press, 2002.

McClintock, Anne. 'Slow Violence and the BP Oil Crisis in the Gulf of Mexico: Militarizing Environmental Catastrophe'. *E-MISFÉRICA* 9 (2012): n.p.

McElroy, James. 'Holding with Apollo 17'. *New York Times*, Jan 28, 1973. 347.

McHale, Brian. 'Break, Period, Interregnum'. *Twentieth-Century Literature* 57.4 (2011): 328–40.

Melville, Herman. *Herman Melville: Pierre, Israel Potter, The Piazza Tales, The Confidence-Man, Billy Budd, Uncollected Prose*. New York: Library of America, 1984.

Miller, Angela. 'Everywhere and Nowhere: The Making of the National Landscape'. *American Literary History* 4.2 (1992): 207–29.

Moore, Lorrie. *A Gate at the Stairs*. London: Faber & Faber, 2009.

Moretti, Franco. *Atlas of the European Novel 1800–1900*. London: Verso, 1998.

Morgan, Benjamin. 'Scale as Form: Thomas Hardy's Rocks and Stars'. In *Anthropocene Reading: Literary History in Geologic Times*. Ed. Tobias Menely and Jesse Oak Taylor. University Park: The Penn State University Press, 2017.

Morton, Timothy. 'Ecology as Text, Text as Ecology'. *The Oxford Literary Review* 32.1 (2010): 1–17.

—. *Dark Ecology: For a Logic of Future Coexistence*. New York: Columbia University Press, 2016.

—. *Ecology Without Nature: Rethinking Environmental Aesthetics*. Cambridge: Harvard University Press, 2007.

—. *Humankind: Solidarity with Non-human People*. London: Verso, 2017.

Mukařovský, Jan. *Aesthetic Function, Norm, and Value as Social Facts*. Ann Arbor: University of Michigan Press, 1979.

Murphy, John J. 'Compromising Realism to Idealize a War: Wharton's "The Marne" and Cather's "One of Ours".' *American Literary Realism* 33.2 (2001): 157–67.

Nersessian, Anahid. 'Two Gardens: An Experiment in Calamity Form'. *Modern Language Quarterly* 74.3 (2013): 307–29.

New, Elisa. 'Beyond the Romance Theory of American Vision: Beauty and the Qualified Will in Edwards, Jefferson, and Audubon'. *American Literary History* 7.3 (1995): 381–414.

Norberg-Schulz, Christian. *Architecture: Presence, Language, and Place*. Milan: Skira, 2000.

—. *Genius Loci: Towards a Phenomenology of Architecture*. New York: Rizzoli, 1976.

Olster, Stacey. *The Cambridge Introduction to Contemporary American Fiction*. Cambridge: Cambridge University Press, 2017.

Ouellet, Pierre. 'The Perception of Fictional Worlds'. In *Fiction Updated: Theories of Fictionality, Narratology, and Poetics*. Ed. Calin-Andrei Mihailescu and Walid Hamarneh. Toronto: University of Toronto Press, 1996. 76–90.

Patteson, Richard F. *A World Outside: The Fiction of Paul Bowles*. Austin: University of Texas Press, 1987.
Pettersson, Bo. *How Literary Worlds are Shaped: A Comparative Poetics of Literary Imagination*. Berlin: De Gruyter, 2016.
Phelan, James. *Living to Tell About It: A Rhetoric and Ethics of Character Narration*. Ithaca: Cornell University Press, 2005.
Plumwood, Val. *Environmental Culture: The Ecological Crisis of Reason*. New York: Routledge, 2002.
Poe, Edgar Allan. *Edgar Allan Poe: Poetry and Tales*. New York: Library of America, 1984.
Poole, Robert. *Earthrise: How Man First Saw the Earth*. New Haven: Yale University Press, 2008.
Pounds, Wayne. *Paul Bowles: The Inner Geography*. New York: Peter Land Press, 1985.
Powers, Kevin. *The Yellow Birds*. New York: Back Bay Books, 2013.
Pratt, Mary Louise. *Imperial Eyes: Travel Writing and Transculturation*. New York: Routledge, 1992.
—. *Toward a Speech Act Theory of Literary Discourse*. Bloomington: Indiana University Press, 1977.
Prince, Gerald. 'Talking French'. *PMLA* 131.5 (2016): 1489–94.
—. 'The Disnarrated'. *Style* 22.1 (1988): 1–8.
Reynolds, Guy. 'Modernist Space: Willa Cather's Environmental Imagination in Context'. In *Willa Cather's Ecological Imagination*. Ed. Susan J. Rosowski. Lincoln: University of Nebraska Press, 2003. 173–89.
—. *Willa Cather in Context: Progress, Race, Empire*. New York: St Martin's, 1996.
Richardson, Brian. *Unnatural Voices: Extreme Narration in Modern and Contemporary Fiction*. Columbus: The Ohio State University Press, 2006.
Rodriguez, David. 'Description in Space: Geography and Narrative Form'. *Frontiers of Narrative Studies* 4.2 (2018): 327–41.
Ronen, Ruth. 'Space in Fiction'. *Poetics Today* 7.3 (1986): 421–38.
Ryan, Marie-Laure, Kenneth Foote and Maoz Azaruahu. *Narrating Space / Spatializing Narrative: Where Narratology and Geography Meet*. Columbus: Ohio State University Press, 2016.
Ryan, Melissa. 'The Enclosure of America: Civilization and Confinement in Willa Cather's *O Pioneers!*'. *American Literature* 75.2 (2003): 275–303.
Sage, Daniel. *How Outer Space Made America: Geography, Organization, and the Cosmic Sublime*. New York: Ashgate, 2014.
Santayana, George. *The Genteel Tradition: Nine Essays*. Ed. Douglas L. Wilson. Lincoln: University of Nebraska Press, 1998.
—. *The Sense of Beauty: Being the Outline of Aesthetic Theory*. New York: Collier Books, 1961.
Sartre, Jean-Paul. *The Psychology of Imagination*. Secaucus: The Citadel Press, 1980.

Scanlan, Margaret. *Plotting Terror: Novelists and Terrorists in Contemporary Fiction*. Charlottesville: University Press of Virginia, 2001.

Shapiro, Michael J. 'That Obscure Object of Violence: Logistics, Desire, War'. *Alternatives* 17 (1992): 453–77.

Skaggs, Merrill Maguire. *After the World Broke in Two: The Later Novels of Willa Cather*. Charlottesville: University Press of Virginia, 1990.

Smith, Mark Lesley. 'Image and Word in the Prints of Robert Rauschenberg, 1951–1981'. PhD Dissertation, The University of Texas at Austin, 1992.

Smith, Zadie. *Changing My Mind: Occasional Essays*. New York: Penguin, 2009.

Soja, Edward W. *Thirdspace: Journeys to Los Angeles and Other Real-and-Imagined Places*. Cambridge: Blackwell, 1996.

Squire, Kelsey. '"Jazz Age" Places: Modern Regionalism in Willa Cather's *The Professor's House*'. *Cather Studies* 9 (2011): 45–66.

Stahl, Roger. *Through the Crosshairs: War, Visual Culture, and the Weaponized Gaze*. New Brunswick: Rutgers University Press, 2018.

—. 'What the Drone Saw: The Cultural Optics of the Unmanned War'. *Australian Journal of International Affairs* 67.5 (2013): 659–74.

Tabbi, Joseph. *Postmodern Sublime: Technology and American Writing from Mailer to Cyberpunk*. Ithaca: Cornell University Press, 1995.

Thoreau, Henry David. *Walden and 'Civil Disobedience'*, New York: Signet Classics, 2012.

Tong, Chris. 'Ecology Without Scale: Unthinking the World Zoom'. *Animation: An Interdisciplinary Journal* 9.2 (2014): 196–211.

Tribbe, Matthew D. *No Requiem for the Space Age: The Apollo Moon Landings and American Culture*. Oxford: Oxford University Press, 2014.

von Mossner, Alexa Weik. *Affective Ecologies: Empathy, Emotion, and Environmental Narrative*. Columbus: Ohio State University Press, 2017.

—. 'Encountering the Sahara: Embodiment, emotion, and material agency in Paul Bowles's *The Sheltering Sky*'. *ISLE* 20.2 (2013): 219–38.

Weber, Ronald. *Seeing Earth: Literary Responses to Space Exploration*. Athens: Ohio University Press, 1985.

Weems, Jason. *Barnstorming the Prairies: How Aerial Vision Shaped the Midwest*. Minneapolis: University of Minnesota Press, 2015.

Wenzel, Jennifer. 'Planet vs Globe'. *English Language Notes* 52.1 (2014): 19–30.

Westphal, Bertrand. *Geocriticism: Real and Fictional Spaces*. Trans. Robert T. Tally Jr. New York: Palgrave, 2011.

Williams, Raymond. *The Country and the City*. New York: Random House, 2013.

Willis, Lloyd. *Environmental Evasion: The Literary, Critical, and Cultural Politics of 'Nature's Nation'*. Albany: State University of New York Press, 2011.

Woods, Derek. 'Scale Variance and the Concept of Matter'. In *The New Politics of Materialism: History, Philosophy, Science*. Ed. Sarah Ellenzweig and John H. Zammito. New York: Routledge, 2017.

Woolf, Virginia. *Mr Bennett and Mrs Brown*. London: Hobart, 1924. www.bl.uk/collection-items/mr-bennett-and-mrs-brown-by-virginia-woolf.

Yamashita, Karen Tei. *Tropic of Orange*. Minneapolis: Coffee House Press, 1997.

Yusoff, Kathryn. 'Indeterminate Subjects, Irreducible Worlds: Two Economies of Indeterminacy'. *Body & Society* 23.3 (2017): 75–101.

Zoran, Gabriel. 'Towards a Theory of Space in Narrative'. *Poetics Today* 5.2 (1984): 309–35.

Index

Abbott, Porter, 146–7
aerial description, 21–31, 40, 45, 62–3, 66, 71–3, 92, 104, 113–15, 129, 144, 153–8, 169, 173–4, 176; *see also* description
aerial photography, 6, 25, 51, 52–6, 66, 76
aeroplane, 11, 51, 53–6
aesthetic experience, 17–18, 31–3, 55, 57–8
affect, 18, 29, 45, 102, 165, 169
affordance, 17–18, 25, 34–6, 44, 58, 65, 102–3, 113, 149, 172; *see also* Gibson, James J,; Levine, Caroline
airplane *see* aeroplane
alienation, 99, 104, 119, 149, 155, 176
anthropocentricism, 18, 37, 41–2, 45, 58, 60–1, 87, 102–3, 115–16, 164–5, 177–8
Apollo 8, 124, 132, 158
Apollo 11, 123, 136–8, 142, 145
Apollo 17, 124, 132, 134
Apollo program, 124–6, 132, 136–43; *see also* NASA
architecture, 20–1, 29–30, 51, 60, 65–7, 78, 86–7, 98–100
Arendt, Hannah, 25–6, 164–5
Atwill, William, 139, 160n46
autofiction, 174–6

Bachelard, Gaston, 8, 11–12, 35–6, 92–4, 96, 98, 101–5, 107, 112, 119, 121n27, 177–8
Bal, Mieke, 131
Barthes, Roland, 20–2, 29, 30, 34, 88n20
Benlemlih, Bouchra, 100–1
Bennet, Jane, 42
bird's-eye view, 18–19, 71–3, 114, 177; *see also* aerial description
Black, James Wallace, 18–19
'Blue Marble', 124, 132–5, 141–3, 145, 158; *see also* 'whole-Earth' photography
Bowles, Paul
 Let It Come Down, 95–7, 106–17
 The Sheltering Sky, 97–8, 107–13, 115
 The Spider's House, 115–20
Brand, Stewart, 124, 141
Buell, Lawrence, 43, 51
built form, 65–8, 75, 76–9, 82–3, 87–8; *see also* Norberg-Schulz, Christian
Butor, Michel, 5

capitalism, 43–4
Casey, Edward S., 4–5, 17, 38, 135, 172–3
Cather, Willa
 Death Comes for the Archbishop, 50, 76–88

My Ántonia, 82–3
O Pioneers!, 62–3, 68–76, 77, 79, 80
One of Ours, 50, 53
The Professor's House, 64–5
Clark, Timothy, 129–32, 143, 146–8
climate change, 11, 26, 127, 128, 130, 143
cognitive science, 38, 91, 114
Cole, Teju, 'Seven Stories About Drones', 167
Collins, Michael, 142, 145–6
colonialism, 24, 25, 27–8, 85, 94–8, 119
Cosgrove, Daniel, 18, 22–4, 132, 142

de Certeau, Michel, 20–1, 29, 30, 34
DeLillo, Don
  'Human Moments in World War III', 125–6, 129, 131–2, 146–59
  Libra, 149, 171–2, 173–4
  Ratner's Star, 125, 146
description, 2, 3–5, 8, 11–12, 17–18, 27–8, 29, 33–8, 40–4, 57–8, 63–8, 71, 81–2, 91–4, 96, 102–3, 106–7, 113–15, 126, 131, 144; *see also* aerial description
Dimock, Wai Che, 105–6, 128
drones, 165–70, 172
Durbin, Andrew, *MacArthur Park*, 176

'Earthrise', 124, 129, 132–5, 141–3, 158; *see also* 'whole-Earth' photography
ecocriticism, 2, 11, 33–4, 44, 51, 65, 105, 129–30
Edwards, Brian, 109–10
Eggan, Taylor, 63–5

encounter (aesthetics), 4–6, 25, 32, 36, 40–1, 51, 102–3, 146–7, 155–6, 164–5
environment, 2–3, 6, 11–12, 17–21, 23, 25, 29, 33, 36–8, 40–4, 46, 51–2, 58–61, 62–5, 67–8, 72–6, 80–2, 87–8, 92, 97–8, 102–5, 113, 115, 118–19, 149, 156–7, 167, 170, 176, 178
environmental imagination, 43, 53, 62
essentialism, 36, 65, 140
experience (phenomenology), 3, 6, 11, 16–18, 31–3, 57, 93–4, 101–4, 126–8
experientiality, 37
extent, 57–61, 64–5, 68–75, 86–8
extinction, 11

Ferlinghetti, Lawrence, 142–3
Fesperman, Dan, *Unmanned*, 167–9
fiction, 3–6, 12, 28, 32–3, 39–41, 42–4, 99, 102–3, 113, 136–7, 143–4, 146, 176
fictionality, 38, 53, 136
flight, 11–12, 87, 96, 140, 168, 177; *see* airplane
Fludernik, Monika, 75, 114–15
focalisation, 62–5, 71, 104, 108–13, 114–15, 116–17
form, 3, 23, 25, 31–5, 44–5, 51, 57, 63–8, 87, 93–4, 127–9, 157–8
form of environment, 2–3, 6, 9, 17, 20–1, 28, 29, 34–5, 36–7, 41, 42–3, 56, 58, 70–2, 76–7, 81–4, 94, 104–5, 115, 119–20, 130–1, 147–8, 157–8
formalism, 3, 33–6, 44–5, 147–8
frame (narratology), 8–9, 28, 36, 39–41, 63–4, 72, 77, 81–2, 111, 143, 163

Frank, Joseph, 31
Friedman, Susan Stanford, 128
frontier, 14, 60–1, 91, 99, 125–6, 140

gaze, 28, 108, 114, 116
Gelley, Alexander, 33
Genette, Gérard, 37, 92
geocriticism, 105, 114–15
geography, 5, 22, 38, 58, 115, 127–9
Gibson, William, *Neuromancer*, 172–3
Gibson, James J., 15n5, 18
globalisation, 16, 22–4, 40, 126, 128
globe, 22, 135, 154, 158
God's-eye view, 24, 26, 126
Google Maps, 127, 170, 173, 174–6
grid, 56, 71–2, 76, 176

Hamon, Philippe, 35–6, 37, 73, 92–4, 105–7, 109, 114, 119, 157
Hawthorne, Nathaniel, 'Sights from a Steeple', 7–8, 10
Heise, Ursula, 128, 143
Hensley, Nathan, 165–6
Herman, David, 33, 38, 93–4
hierarchy, 5, 26, 30
holism, 126, 141, 142, 176
Houser, Heather, 17, 26–7

ideology, 58, 63–5
imaginary, 2–3, 5–6, 8, 11–12, 21, 29–30, 35–7, 39–41, 53, 57, 96–8, 100–1, 102–4, 112–13, 117, 127
imperialism, 24–5, 27–8, 40, 97–8
implied author, 27–8, 44
indeterminacy, 28, 39, 41–4, 72, 114, 130, 144, 164–5
Ingarden, Roman, 31–5, 39–45, 102–3

intentionality (phenomenology), 33, 42–3, 104
Iser, Wolfgang, 39–42

James, Erin, 28
Jameson, Fredric, 149, 166–7, 169
Jewett, Sarah Orne, 'A White Heron', 9–11, 177

Kaplan, Caren, 12, 26, 29, 30
Kauffman, James L., 124, 140
Ketterer, David, 136
Kuzmičová, Anežka, 45

landscape painting, 11, 24–5
landscape, 17, 20, 23, 28, 52–4, 63–5, 76–7, 82–3, 86–7
Latour, Bruno, 3, 24, 46, 131, 135, 164–5
Lazier, Benjamin, 126
Lefebvre, Henri, 25, 29–30
Lerner, Ben, *10:04*, 174, 176
Levine, Caroline, 18, 34–5, 37, 51, 72, 103, 127–8
Lin, Tao, *Taipei*, 175–6
Lopes, José Manuel, 92
Luna, Joe, 141–4, 146

McClintock, Anne, 47n28
McElroy, James, 137
McHale, Brian, 123
Maden, Mike, *Drone*, 167
Mailer, Norman, *Of a Fire on the Moon*, 136, 139
maps, 17, 25, 38, 76, 114, 127, 151–3, 166–7, 169–74, 176
Marcussen, Marlene, 121n27, 122n55
Marran, Christine, 42
Marston, Sallie A., 127–8, 131
materiality, 3, 12, 23–4, 42, 57–8, 60, 82, 86–78, 102–3, 115, 135, 137–8, 151
Mathews, Harry, 'Franz Kafka in Riga', 1–3, 18, 119–20

Miller, Angela, 24–5
modernism, 2, 50, 53, 59, 63, 65–6, 87–8, 105, 123, 163, 167
moon, 123–4, 131–2
Moore, Lorrie, *A Gate at the Stairs*, 177
Moretti, Franco, 58, 63
Morton, Timothy, 3, 127
movement, 12, 97, 101, 106–7, 108–10, 112–13, 175
Mukařovskщ, Jan, 34

narrative discourse, 2, 35–8, 68, 91–3, 100, 113
narratability, 118, 142–3
  unnarratable, 126, 143–7, 156
  unnarrated, 131, 145–7, 151, 153, 156, 158
  disnarration, 144–6, 152, 153, 156, 157
narrativity, 32–3, 36, 37–8
narratology, 8, 34, 48n64, 101, 107, 113–15, 122n55, 146
  classical narratology, 37–8
  postclassical narratology, 91–2
NASA, 124–5, 132–41, 160n36, 161n53, 161n60; *see also* Apollo program
National Geographic, 54–6
nature, 20, 23, 25, 43, 45, 59–61, 65, 76, 86, 178
Nersessian, Anahid, 42
Neubronner, Julius, 18–19
New Formalism, 12, 18, 33–5, 36, 37, 51, 72, 103, 127–8
New Materialism, 42
New, Elisa, 25
nonanthropocentrism, 2–3, 12, 16–17, 41–2, 54, 61, 70, 87, 115, 164–5, 170, 177–8
Norberg-Schulz, Christian, 65–8, 87
novel, 5, 35–6, 42, 50–1, 52, 82, 94, 97, 102, 165–7

objectivity, 5–6, 16, 18, 22–3, 25, 30, 41, 112, 118, 126, 129, 141, 177
Ouellet, Pierre, 3–4, 5

panorama, 7, 11, 21
Patteson, Richard, 97, 98–100, 113, 119
perception, 3–6, 8, 18, 20–2, 24–31, 36–7, 39–41, 54, 57–8, 66, 76, 80, 92–4, 103–4, 127, 129–31, 144, 156, 166–7
perspective, 3–4, 10–11, 27–8, 71–2, 75, 109, 112, 114–18, 141, 166, 174–5
Phelan, James, 33
phenomenology, 5, 16, 18, 40, 42, 101–5, 113–14, 129–31, 145
photography, 5, 6, 18–19, 25, 50–1, 52–6, 68, 76, 80, 87, 124–6, 132–6, 145–6, 171
plot, 8, 12, 31, 32–3, 61, 79, 91–5, 106, 113, 119, 130, 153
Plumwood, Val, 44–6
Poe, Edgar Allan, 'Descent into the Maelström', 8–9
poetry, 2, 12, 104, 136, 141–3, 144, 165–6
point of view, 4–5, 25, 27, 29, 55, 63, 67, 114–15, 132, 144, 146
Poole, Robert, 124, 136
postmodern, 13, 123–4, 146, 155
Pounds, Wayne, 99
'Powers of Ten' (Eames animation), 160n16
Powers, Kevin, *Yellow Birds, The*, 169–70
Pratt, Mary Louise, 4, 22, 27–9, 40, 44, 47n37, 129
Prince, Gerald, 48n64, 144–5

Rauschenberg, Robert, 137–9
reading experience, 8, 21, 33–4, 51, 64, 104, 165

realism, 2, 58, 63, 69, 81, 93–4, 119, 144, 159n14
reality effect, 36
reflexivity, 7, 18, 28, 71, 97, 129, 143, 147, 151, 174, 176
representation, 2, 3, 17–18, 28–9, 63, 91, 103, 115, 123–4, 131, 135–6, 148–9, 169, 172–3
reverie, 103, 107–9
Reynolds, Guy, 63, 65, 71, 77
Richardson, Brian, 75–6
Ricœur, Paul, 31
romanticisation, 10, 24–5, 55, 59, 74, 77–8, 82, 97, 141, 142
Ryan, Melissa, 74–5

Santayana, George, 51–2, 55, 57–61, 67, 76, 87
Sartre, Jean-Paul, 29
satellite imagery, 11, 132, 166, 170–6
scale, 18, 67, 107, 126–32, 143, 144–7, 150–1, 154–6, 158
Soja, Edward, 30

story logic, 33, 91–4, 100, 104, 105, 109, 114, 115, 119
structuralism, 20–1, 30, 33–7
sublime, 24, 39, 124, 131, 155

Tabbi, Joseph, 124
Thoreau, Henry David, 4, 177
Tribbe, Matthew, 123, 139

verticality, 42, 68, 91–2, 96–101, 104–5, 107, 109–11, 116–20
von Mossner, Alexa Weik, 110

Weems, Jason, 53–6
Wenzel, Jennifer, 45
Westphal, Bertrand, 110–11, 114–15, 122n48
'whole-Earth' photography, 126–7, 129, 132–6, 138, 140–6, 149, 151, 155
Williams, Raymond, 58, 63

Yamashita, Karen Tei, *Tropic of Orange*, 173
Yusoff, Kathryn, 43–4

EU representative:
Easy Access System Europe
Mustamäe tee 50, 10621 Tallinn, Estonia
Gpsr.requests@easproject.com

www.ingramcontent.com/pod-product-compliance
Lightning Source LLC
Chambersburg PA
CBHW070356240426
43671CB00013BA/2527